TROPICAL ARCHITECTURE

CRITICAL REGIONALISM IN THE AGE OF GLOBALIZATION

EDITED BY

Alexander Tzonis, Liane Lefaivre
and Bruno Stagno

⊗WILEY-ACADEMY

 C

Fonds

Prince Claus Fund for Culture and Development
The Netherlands

Acknowledgements
Every attempt has been made to contact the copyright owners of each
illustration, but it has not always been possible to do so. However, if
they would like to get in touch with us we will be happy to make
suitable acknowledgement in a future reprint.

First published in Great Britain in 2001 by Wiley-Academy

A division of
JOHN WILEY & SONS
Baffins Lane
Chichester
West Sussex PO19 1UD

ISBN 0-471-49608-1

Other Wiley Editorial Offices
New York, Weinheim, Brisbane, Singapore, Toronto

Cover design: Artmedia Press, London

Typeset in Caslon 224 by Florence Production Ltd, Stoodleigh, Devon

Printed and bound in Italy

CONTENTS

CONTRIBUTORS

Bay Joothra Philip, a practising architect, is an assistant professor at the National University of Singapore and is completing his PhD in the Design Knowledge Systems Center at the Technical University of Delft. He is the author of a book on Singapore, *Contemporary Singapore Architecture* (Singapore, Singapore Institute of Architecture, 1998).

Liane Lefaivre is a historian and critic. A researcher at the Technical University of Delft, she has been nominated Chair of Architectural History and Theory at the University of Applied Arts in Vienna. She has published widely on the period between the Renaissance and the Enlightenment and on architecture since the Second World War. She has written extensively on Dirty Realism in architecture and, with Alexander Tzonis, she has published widely on critical regionalism.

Rahul Mehrotra is a practising architect and author of a book on Bombay. After taking his second Master's at the Harvard Design School he returned to his native Bombay and founded the Urban Design Research Institute and is on the board of governors of the Mumbai Metropolitan Regional Development Authorities Heritage Society. He is the author, with Sharda Dwideri, of a book on *Bombay, Cities Within* (Singapore, 1997).

Gerardo Mosquera is a Cuban art critic and historian who works as a Curator at the Museum of Contemporary Art in New York. He has published extensively, most recently editing *Beyond the Fantastic: Contemporary Art Criticism from Latin America* (Cambridge, MA, MIT Press, 1997).

Severiano Porto is an architect with a prolific practice in Minas Gerais, Brazil. Among his many projects, all environmentally conscious, in the tropical north of the country is his Center for the Environmental Protection at Balbina.

Roberto Segre was educated as an architect in Argentina then moved to Cuba in 1953 where he lived and taught for 30 years. He has been Visiting Professor at Rice University and at Columbia University and is now a Professor at the Architecture School of São Paolo, Brazil and the most prolific and influential author writing today on the subject of Latin American architecture.

Bruno Stagno is an architect from Chile, now living in Costa Rica with an extensive practice. He is the founder of the Institute for Tropical Architecture. In 1997, he won the Dutch Prince Claus Award for his work, with which he organized an international conference bringing together topical architects from all over the world. A monograph has appeared on his designs, *Bruno Stagno. An Architect in the Tropics* (Selangor, Asia Design Forum Publications, 1999).

Tan Hock Beng is principal of MAPS DESIGN STUDIO in Singapore and author of many books on the architecture of South East Asia focusing on the issue of modernity and the development of tropical architecture in the region.

Tay Kheng Soon is a practising architect and author from Singapore. He was a founding member of the SPUR group in the late 1960s. Among his most important projects, carried out with William Lim, are the People's Park Complex and Woh Hup in Singapore in the early 1970s. His project for the Intelligent Tropical City described here is his current ongoing research project. A monograph has appeared on him by Robert Powell, entitled *Line, Edge and Shade. Modern Tropical Architecture, Tay Kheng Soon* (Singapore, Page One, 1997).

Eduardo Tejeira-Davis, a practising architect in Panama City, Panama, studied architecture at the Technische Hochschule in Darmstadt and received his PhD from the University of Heidelberg. His work involves the restoration of the historical architectural and urban fabric of the Panama Zone.

Alex Tzonis is Chair of Architectural Theory and Director of the Design Knowledge Systems Center at the Technical University of Delft. Among his many books are *Towards a non-Oppressive Environment* (1972) and, with Serge Chermayeff, *Shape of Community* (1972). With Liane Lefaivre he introduced the term critical regionalism into architecture and wrote *Architecture in Europe since 1968* (1995) and *Architecture in North America since 1960* (1997) both published by Thames & Hudson. He has also written books on the work of Santiago Calatrava and Le Corbusier.

Ken Yeang is an architect with a broad practice from offices in Kuala Lumpur, Penang and London focusing on a new building type, the bioclimatic skyscraper. He completed his PhD at Cambridge University on ecological factors in the built environment and is the author of many books on sustainable architecture, among them *The Skyscraper, Bioclimatically Considered: A Design Primer* (1997).

FOREWORD

One of the aims of the Prince Claus Fund is to support through international meetings, discussions and publications, a platform for intellectual debate and intercultural exchange of ideas. In this perspective the Fund is pleased to have assisted the production of the present book focusing on tropical architecture.

The book grew out of a conference on the topic of *Tropical Architecture*, organized by the architect and 1997 Prince Claus Award laureate Bruno Stagno in Costa Rica. Its material, ranging from Central America to the Pacific, demonstrates how rich and humane an architecture shaped out of the individual characteristics of a specific region can be. The specific approach to design described in this book is called "critical regionalism". It enlightens design driven by a *critical* reflection on the particularities of the physical environment, the cultural products and the existing bonds of the people of a region. The publication contrasts it to the mindless adoption of difference for differentiation's sake and the imposition of the global for globalism's sake. Thus, as the title of the book implies, "critical regionalism" is not in opposition to globalization and the idea of a worldwide platform based on shared values. On the contrary, it is conceived as a design strategy accentuating the relation between "the global" and "the local", with the aim to sustain diversity while benefiting from universality.

These ideas relate to the broad and dynamic approach to culture adopted by the Fund. It is important that the potential of a region is expressed in all its uniqueness and diversity in different cultural products, such as architecture. In that respect I recommend this book as a worthwhile contribution to the worldwide debate on culture and development.

His Royal Highness
Prince Claus of the Netherlands

PREFACE

In December 1997, the Prince Claus Fund for Culture and Development honoured me with an award. This allowed me to make a long-standing dream come true: to organize a symposium, entitled Tropical Encounter, in Costa Rica, bringing together a number of major architects, academics and critics to come and share with us their particular expertise in tropical architecture: Gabriel Poole from Australia, Severiano Porto from Brazil, Roberto Segre from Brazil, Gerardo Mosquera from Cuba, Rahul Mehrotra from India, Kenneth Yeang from Malaysia, Eduardo Tejeira-Davis from Panama, and Tan Hock Beng from Singapore. I also invited from The Netherlands two scholars who developed the concept of critical regionalism, Liane Lefaivre and Alexander Tzonis.

The event, organized by the Institute for Tropical Architecture in San José, Costa Rica, in November 1998, was of major significance for the architecture of this latitude. It confirmed that our architectures are related and that we have similar problems. It also confirmed that the visions and aspirations we had individually until the symposium are in reality shared.

After the symposium, we became aware of the importance of our regional voices and the planetary significance of tropicality as a way of life and cultural expression as valid as the ones in other latitudes.

Following the symposium the participants decided to put together a book on tropicalism today. Liane Lefaivre and Alexander Tzonis suggested also inviting Philip Bay and Tay Kheng Soon both from Singapore.

I would like to thank the Prince Claus Fund for Culture and Development for their generous support for the publication of this book and make our common voice heard.

Arq. Bruno Stagno
Director, Institute for Tropical Architecture
San José, Costa Rica

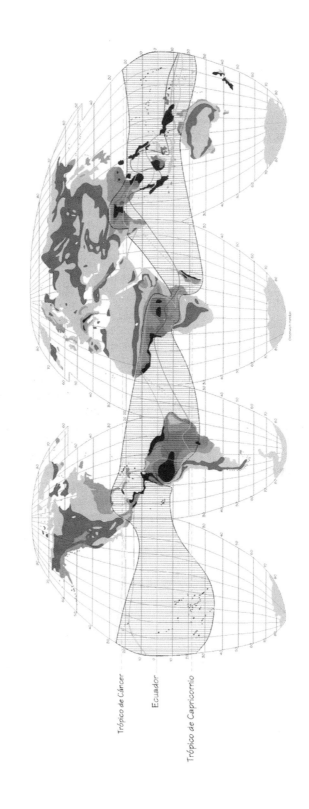

Trópico de Cáncer

Ecuador

Trópico de Capricornio

CHAPTER 1

TROPICAL CRITICAL REGIONALISM: INTRODUCTORY COMMENTS

Liane Lefaivre and Alexander Tzonis

Next to the great ideological struggle between modernism and traditionalism, the conflict between regionalism and globalism has shaped most social, political, economic and cultural debates of the past century. It continues to dominate most discussions today in almost every field. The conflict has also marked architectural and urban planning debates. There is much written in support of global architecture. Most of the architectural press has an implicit agenda in support of global values by giving preference to projects that follow a few major acknowledged trends around the globe, encouraging tacitly the conformity of architectural ideas even when this is expressed in terms of "non-conformist" design. Without doubt discovering, encouraging and applying universal norms in design practice has its benefits. But it also has a serious negative impact when employed uncritically and without consideration of regional scope and regional values. The aim of this book is to make the case for regionalism by presenting a spectrum of ideas and design proposals related to a special case of contemporary regionalist architecture, *tropicalist* architecture.

The present book was assembled with the aim of bringing together representatives as varied as possible from subregions of the overall tropical region. Rather than rushing to impose a consensus among the diverse and a general rule that would have violated the very spirit of regionalism, we wished to present clear, distinct and high contrast views of tropicality. In other words, we opted for difference. If we might cite our collaborator Bruno Stagno, we tried to focus on singular situations, "making it difficult to establish stable parameters of conduct" because "freedom" is "continually adapting and changing". We were brought into the project by Bruno Stagno to introduce the conference he organized in Costa Rica on tropical architecture because of our prior work on regionalism and more specifically on its contemporary problematic which we had framed in previous writings under the term *critical regionalism.*

The opportunity to study the question of tropicalism during the Costa Rica conference of 1998 and subsequent meetings with the original participants and, six months later, to discuss it with Milton Tan, Philip Bay and Tay Kheng Soon during a month's stay at the National University of Singapore in May 2000, enormously enriched our ideas about critical regionalism and its urgent message for contemporary architecture.

As opposed to globalism, which promotes universal values and norms, regionalism stands for the local and the specific to a region, that is to a unique, distinct geographical area occupied homogeneously by similar objects or objects having common characteristics. Such objects, prevailing in the area, can be flora or fauna, people or artefacts, or attributes of these objects, such as shape, size, materials or colour. This makes it appear very simple and straightforward to objectively divide the world into regions. However, the manner in which one can identify an object or an attribute is infinite, and poses a major problem of choice and leads to an infinite number of ways of depicting and dividing the world into regions. It is clear that we "finite" humans construct regions within a finite framework of intentions. We make them through our mind imposing criteria of choice that depend not only on how the real world "out there" is made, but also on how we view the world, a view biased by our prior beliefs as well as our desires.

To discuss tropicalism as a kind of regionalism presupposes that the "tropics" is recognized as a region. At first glance it might not be so easy to see the "tropics" as a region. In fact geographers refer to the Torrid *Zone*, rather than Region, as the part of the earth between the *tropics* of Cancer and Capricorn. Although there are dry areas, the *zone* is characterized mostly by a typically year-round climate that is hot, humid and steamy with high rainfall and has great similarities in vegetation. Geographers talk about the "tropics" more as a *family* of regions lying between and near the boundaries of these parallels. Intuitively, we are accustomed to think about regions as continuous parts of the surface of a body modest in size, uninterrupted, and concentrated. By contrast, the "*zone* of the tropics" is closed but stretched all around the earth, a vast belt that stretches over the entire middle of the globe, from the Pacific Islands, South East Asia and Australia to India, Africa, the Caribbean and large tracts of the Americas. Moreover, regions are usually considered as places with relatively homogeneous cultures. The tropics appear as scattered culturally as they are geographically.

But in spite of these differences, there are many other common attributes present in the tropics so that one might consider it more significant to regard the tropics as a region within a pragmatic framework of architecture. First, throughout the area we call the tropics, people share the problem of having to cope with extreme conditions of a hot and humid climate. As a result of such conditions, to quote the observation of Singapore's long-time prime minister, Li Kuan Yu, high productivity is very difficult to achieve. Second, in spite of the vastness of the area, there is a common historical, political fact: they are all ex-colonies. As a result there is a common need to overcome the post-colonial frame of mind that has its roots in the period of expansion of Europe and the United States during which a common model was applied with small variations from Central Asia to Central America. The vestiges of this long period of domination, political, economic and intellectual, are still there and designers find themselves working as if driven by an automatic pilot inherited from the colonial period. And when such a pilot is not in action, the problem is to fill in the void of social, political, administrative and cultural structures that is left after the departure of the colonial powers with new, up-to-date models. Third, there is a common architectural heritage from the colonial period, individual buildings, building types and urban tissue that serve as a precious precedent. It is a design experience of great value for contemporary practice. The most typical case is the bungalow designed to fit the bio-climatic conditions while at the same time being a cultural construct that responds to the beliefs and desires of the colonialists and remains to be conserved as well as to be reused and redesigned.

The contributions in this volume manifest a set of regionalist values and ways of going about constructing the human environment whose origins go at least as far back as the very beginning of the imperialist expansion of the West during Roman times. Yet, as we will see here, they transform and recast this long tradition rather than being bound to it.

REGIONALISM, HISTORICAL CHAMELEON

The Roman architect/engineer and author, Vitruvius, who extensively discussed the Doric or Ionic temples without referring to the term Classical, does refer by name to *regional* architecture, pointing to the differences in buildings around the world which he explains through climatic conditions and draws a parallel to the variations in the physique of people and concludes that "the arrangement of buildings" should be "guided" by "locality" and "climate". In the very end, however, he did not imply regional pluralism and respect for difference. On the contrary, his what we would call today "environmental determinism" conveys ideas of hierarchy and value, and leads to the legitimation of Roman hegemony. According to him, northern people are "like snakes in wintry and rainy seasons" who display a marked "slowness of mind". Similarly, the people of the south, approaching what we would consider today tropical, have a kind of wild thinking. By contrast, Romans, living in a region that is the "true mean within the space of the world" have a temperate, strong and "divine" mind. And as a consequence they are fit to rule the world. By extension we may infer that Vitruvius, after recognizing regional differences, legitimizes the Classical cannon as fit to rule the world of architecture.

But history is cruel and full of surprising turns. A millennium after Vitruvius wrote about regional architecture, the Romans are under a formal rule and

Classical architecture has gone "underground". And it is the "Gothic" that reigns in the world. Nicolaus Crescenzii, a Roman citizen aligned with the local Republican party, leads a fight against the papacy which is perceived by the Romans as an illegitimate foreign force occupying their region. His party enjoyed a short victory which Nicolaus wanted to commemorate. For that he employed architecture. He designed for himself the small *palazzo* that is still standing in Rome next to the Temple of Minerva and today is known as the Casa dei Crescenzi. Interestingly, he incorporated into his tower-like building, almost like badges of *romanità*, a row of half columns to one side of his building recalling a roman colonnade, and onto the façade the message "in order to restore the ancient glory of Rome", a verbal counterpoint to the architectural manifesto of regional identity and political emancipation. What we have here is the embedding of the regional concept inside a cultural/political movement, the regionalist movement.

PICTURESQUE REGIONALISM

What is interesting is that regionalism in architecture was never by definition anything but variant and changing. Chameleonic in character, it always adapted to situation and environment, physical, cultural and political. If the Classical universal in the Roman times becomes the regional in the time of Crescenzi, by the seventeenth century it takes yet another turn and becomes, for reasons whose description go beyond this chapter, associated with the new universal absolutist order. By reverse symmetry, regionalism, formerly the architectural expression of agonistic anti-absolutism, recruits characteristics diametrically opposed to those of the universalist Classical order. William Temple (1628–1718), perhaps the earliest theoretician of this new phase of emancipatory regionalism – a member of the Whig party, a precursor of liberal parliamentarism – urged for an architecture which drew from the natural topography of the specific location, rejecting the illegitimate, alien and rigid rule enforced by arbitrary and unjust princely authority. Along the same lines, the influential writer Shaftesbury encapsulated the new values of topographic regionalism, which eventually came to be called the Picturesque Movement. "Your Genius, the Genius of the Place", he wrote about the English, will be "more engaging and appear with a Magnificence beyond the formal Mocquery of Princely Gardens".

ROMANTIC REGIONALISM

The ideas of regionalism linked to ethnic emancipation and expressed in design by the English found their most passionate exponent in Goethe's *Sturm und Drang* text, *"Von deutscher Baukunst"* of 1772 written when he was 19 years old. The text contrasts the Gothic cathedral of Strasbourg with "classical" or "French" architecture. The cathedral has an almost "divinatory" power in its "barbaric" "mass" of details. It appeals to the people of the region. In contrast to the "paternalist" classical cannon imposed from "another region of the world", producing a "uniformity" of buildings "which presses upon the soul", it has the capability to transmit a message "without the need of an interpreter" from the "region of truth" reuniting the members of an ethnic group – past, present and future.

Following the writings of Goethe about architecture, and the proliferation of the nationalist movements around the world, the political role of buildings and design products in support of emancipation of ethnic groups becomes central. They are used to prove but also to impose the identity and the right to autonomy of a region, throughout the nineteenth century. Special studies were carried out targeted to document the uniformity and originality of the architecture of an area in order to use that as an argument for legitimizing the political independence of its inhabitants. When the area under consideration was disputed by more than one ethnic group, the arguments became much more passionate and less rational. Despite that, the discipline of history of architecture as we know it today, although after different targets and functioning within a very different framework, owes much to this phase of nationalist activity.

OVER-FAMILIARIZING REGIONALISM

As the decline of nationalist movements turned sour, becoming jingoistic and even racist during the twentieth century, a highly debased regionalist architectural movement, transforming itself once more, became a political instrument deprived of a genuine emancipatory function and served instead as a tool of totalitarian repression and intolerant chauvinism. It massively employed typified folkloristic motifs, leading to over-familiarizing, "as if" settings in the second quarter of the twentieth century. The universalist doctrines of modern architecture are interpreted as "cosmopolitan" and therefore as subversive to national unity. A neo-tribal, true to the race, the blood and land architecture is called forth. It came to be known in Germany as Volkisch or Heimatsarchitektur, but similar trends occur in the late 1930s parallel to the takeovers of large parts of the world by totalitarian regimes.

At the same time a new version of regionalist architecture grows in support of the new "lifestyle", commercial activity: tourism. This is a regionalism aimed at those "strangers, visitors, curious restless travellers", words that Goethe, in a novel of his mature period the *Elective Affinities*, puts in the mouth of an alienated wondering Englishman. It is the professional architecture of the *genius commercialii*, of travelling and entertainment. In other words, commercial regionalist environmental settings, simulacra of places, and façades permitted – for a good price – effortless access to and possession of a make-believe region. They offered the illusion of participation in a distant, bygone group for the vicarious visitor promising to alleviate the pain of atopy and anomy of contemporary life. Like other kitsch works or mass media products and not unlike the chauvinist version of regionalist architecture it fed the most simple emotions and starved rationality. Commercial regionalism became an architectural pornography of sorts.

LEWIS MUMFORD AND CRITICAL REGIONALISM

It is at this time of crisis that Lewis Mumford, the American writer, cultural historian and critic, entered the debate on regionalism. Mumford gave to regionalism a new life, reviving its emancipatory programme and giving a new significance to the idea of community and a new reason why an area should be considered independent. In doing so he eliminated from the argument aspects of nationalism and gave to human bonding a more deep but also broader and more flexible meaning relevant to the new realities of what he called the new neotechnic era. Mumford reinvented regionalism by reframing it. It was a critical act which removed regionalism from its nationalist bias and reintroduced it to the new conditions of an unavoidably global world.

Mumford first became involved with the question of regionalism as a young man when he was writing for the Journal *Menorah* in reference to the architecture desirable for Palestine. Even in these very early pieces his conception of regionalism excludes any chauvinistic references focusing on rational and universal reasons why an architecture of a specific location ought to emerge bottom up, out of the specifics of the area rather than arbitrarily and automatically imposed top down by some external authority. The specifics of a region Mumford had in mind were economic as well as what we today call ecological and social.

Mumford had come to regionalism through his association with the Scottish biologist and botanist Patrick Geddes. Geddes had pioneered in the analysis of ecological systems. The concept of region was fundamental to these studies applied to natural objects and attributes and to natural territories. At the time Mumford met him, Geddes was busy expanding his experiences and model from biology to the study and also planning of the human man-made environment. Because he was a Scot, one might suspect that Geddes had a personal interest in regionalism. Careful examination of his writings, however, reveals that his ideas were not inspired by nationalist desires for independence. His thinking in fact comes more from humanist, universalist and rationalist ideas of the physiocrats and the Enlightenment. These origins are also evident in Mumford despite the fact that frequently he expressed admiration for certain aspects of the Romantics and even Surrealists as expressions of protest against antihumanist and deeper irrationality of contemporary culture.

It is because of this background, to a large degree, that Mumford was able to reframe regionalism, identifying in relation to it technocracy and bureaucracy as the new "imperial" forces and defining the emancipated state for independence as one governed by economic rationality, ecological sustainability and community. His first regionalist work, *Sticks and Stones: American Architecture and Civilization* was published in 1924 and was the first history of American architecture. Here he attacks the grandiose École des Beaux-Arts educated "wedding cake" designers who, during the decade between 1890 and 1900, "placed a premium upon the mask" of buildings. Mumford calls this phase of American architectural development that of the "Imperial Façade" because, in addition to a preoccupation with the façade, the approach expressed the "imperialist" policies of the "holders of privilege in the 'capital city'", to exploit to their own benefit "the life and resources of separate regions". Like the Romans, the contemporary "new nobility of finance" applies architecture not only as means of concealing contemporary misery, of "putting a pleasing front upon a scrappy building, upon the monotonous streets and the mean houses", but also as a means of expressing economic domination.

At the beginning of the Second World War, in a series of lectures entitled *The South in Architecture* (New York, Harcourt, Brace, 1941) addressed to a young audience many of whom were soon to leave for the battlefront, Mumford attacks the "deification of *Heimatsarchitektur*" and defends instead the idea of a "humane" regionalist architecture. He is anxious that his critique of the mystical regionalist *Heimatsarchitektur* in the name of "human" regionalism not be taken as a suggestion to return to traditional picturesque or romantic regionalism in search of the "rough", the "primitive", the "purely local", the "aboriginal", "the self-contained". For this reason he rushes to stress that human regionalism is not a matter of using the most available local material ... or "construction". Neither is it in conflict with the "universal". He argues in fact that regionalist architecture has to overcome the "deep unbridgeable gulf between the peoples of the earth", which *Heimatsarchitektur* is deepening. At the same time regionalism has to help people come to grips with "the actual conditions of life", make them "feel at home". "Regional insight" has to be used to defend us from the "international style", the "absurdities" of present technology and the "despotism" of "the mechanical order".

As in every allegory where the personae are chosen because of deep structural analogies, so in Mumford's lectures the term "regionalism" is chosen because of the analogies between the old "despotic" order of the Roman Empire and the imperialist "colonization and conquest of Asia, Africa, the Americas" and a new "mechanical order" of the "no less ruthless control of the new kings" of industry with the old academic tradition and the new international style". In his view the inhumanness of the pseudo-regionalism of *Heimat* is the equivalent of formalism and mechanistic functionalism. They all fail to create a better social condition that gives "form and order to a democratic civilization". "The brotherhood of the machine", he argues, alluding to the international, technocratic bureaucratic order, "is not a substitute for the brotherhood" of people. The problem lies not with science or technology but with society, institutions and moral failures. Lacking the will to create a better social order, "half of our scientific knowledge and technological innovations are either not used at all, or are extravagantly misused", he warns.

"Critical" in this sense originates in the serene essays of Kant and is developed in the agitated writings of the Frankfurt School. Critical works challenge not only the established actual world but the legitimacy of the possible world views in the mind of people. From an architectural design point of view critical function is achieved by bringing about the special cognitive aesthetic effect on the viewer which is known as defamiliarization. Defamiliarization, a concept closely related to Brecht's *Verfremdung* but also to Aristotle's *xenikon* was coined, as we mentioned in the beginning of this chapter, by the Russian critic Victor Shklovsky. It was initially applied to literature. But it can easily be applied in architecture and help it to carry out its critical function. Defamiliarization is at the heart of what distinguishes critical regionalism from other forms of regionalism and its capability to create a renewed, versus an atavistic, sense of place in our time.

Romantic regionalism, as we have seen, despite its adversarial stance, employed familiarization. It selected regional elements linked in memory and inserted them in new buildings constructing sentimental scenes which aroused "affinity" and "sympathy" in the viewer, scenes which contrasted with the actual despotic architecture but rendered consciousness insensible. The proliferation of commercialism and propaganda regionalism in our time with its over-familiarizing immediate, easy, titillating, as if narcissistic, *Heimat* settings, had an even more narcotic – if not hallucinatory – effect on consciousness.

The critical approach of contemporary regionalist architecture reacts against this explosion of regionalist counterfeit settings by employing defamiliarization. Critical regionalism is interested in specific elements from the region, those that have acted as agents of contact and community, the place-defining elements, and incorporates them "strangely", rather than familiarly, it makes them appear strange, distant, difficult even disturbing. It disrupts the sentimental "embracing" between buildings and their consumers and instead makes an attempt at "pricking the conscience". To put it in more traditional terms the critical approach reintroduces "meaning" in addition to "feeling" in people's view of the world.

We hope we have made clear that critical regionalism tries to solve global problems, those of anomy and atony, which are most apparent in super-developed parts of the world and are becoming so in developing countries also. It does not aim at supplying a regionalist architecture for peripheral "regions" of the world which express a need to be fortified against advanced technology and bureaucracy just because they are imported innovations.

An alternative kind of regionalism, good old romantic regionalism, might be more fit in this case for those who believe the trend towards higher levels of technology, multinational economy and culture ought and can be arrested. Critical regionalism should be seen as complementary rather than contradictory to trends towards higher technology and a more global economy and culture. It opposes only their undesirable, contingent by-products due to private interests and public mindlessness.

THE CONTRIBUTIONS TO THIS BOOK

The first contribution to the present book, by Gerardo Mosquera, develops a much more theoretical theme that touches upon the core of the tropicalist and regionalist debate today. The new global order consists of "an effective interconnection of the whole planet by means of a reticular network of communication and exchange". It threatens individual variety and difference through universalization of practices, but also accentuates the worst of a world of differences. It polarizes further a hierarchical dependence of regional differences rather than encouraging the diversity necessary for creativity. Mosquera paraphrases George Orwell when he writes that "globalization is more global for some than for others". We hope that the present book is a step towards reversing this process, enhancing a world to come about within which preserving, exploring and mining regional differences brings about a world more genuinely global.

The picture of critical regionalism that emerges from these contributions is in great contrast to the simplistic ideas that the local is good by definition, that sustaining community and nature means both blind conservation and resistance to change and that understanding the context is a simple process that requires no special effort or analysis. Accordingly, Tan Hock Beng in his "Modernizing Appropriations/Appropriating Modernity" stresses that traditions are always contested, transformed, resisted and invented. For Severiano Porto, working in Manaos, in the Amazon of northern Brazil, this prevents an architect being seduced by already existing practices of architecture and applying them without consideration in a situation alien from the one they have originated in. His regionalism originates not from hostility towards the outside world of his region but from respect of needs and opportunities at hand. Regionalist architecture is defined by the appreciation of the identity and uniqueness of the problem rather than the solution.

Roberto Segre's article surveys the long overlooked traditions of Caribbean architecture and urban planning from the eighteenth century to today from the French, Spanish and Dutch colonial possessions of Cuba, Puerto Rico, Martinique and Guadeloupe. He emphasizes the sensual aspects of what he terms this paradise: the particular sociability of its streets, parks and coastlines, the beauty of its botanical lushness, the coolness of its interiors shaded by the sun and caressed by breezes. These are features that are invariants that run through the changing architectural styles that mark the history of the region across the historical periods and the broad national traditions. Will these aspects of life survive the kitschifying process of Miamiization, however? In spite of his optimistic concluding statement, the question, we believe, still remains.

Eduardo Tejeira-Davis, writing on the architectural legacy of the Canal Zone in Panama, points out the many valuable features of the architecture of the colonialist outsiders. In his extensive history of this regional architecture, the French and subsequently the Americans created an architecture of Tropicality. Despite the fact that many cannot "forget that Zonian society was based on inequality and segregation", Tejeira-Davis argues that "it is in the end irrational and goes against the regionalist logic to reject its structures by definition". Many figures like Frederick Law Olmsted Jr worked hard to produce an environment which today provides "a paradise of order, ampleness and tranquility not to be found among the recent post-colonial structures".

Bruno Stagno, in presenting his own work in Costa Rica, shows that developing places through buildings which promote to its maximum the potentials of the tropical region does not require sticking dogmatically to traditional construction materials. Local materials might prove eventually to be superior to imported ones. In the end, however, what is superior is what maximizes the possibilities that the tropical environment can provide for an alternative way of living and unique human aesthetic experiences. Stagno, originally from Chile, arrived in Costa Rica via Paris and Le Corbusier's office ran at that time, after Corbusier's death, by José Oubrerie. His regionalist findings were the result of intensive study of precedents well adapted to the tropical region: the adobe houses of the Spanish colonialists providing through their long corridor excellent ventilation, the pre-Colombian buildings and their palm leaf and wood walls filtering and modulating light and air. And the domestic architecture of the company towns exploiting Costa Rica's *fincas bananieras* founded by the United Fruit Company. This latter example proved to be most successful environmentally. Designed by outsiders, European and American engineers, this architecture like that of the Spanish colonialists adapted foreign principles to the tropical climate admirably in a way with which contemporary endogenous commercial architecture cannot compete. The *finca bananiera* buildings especially, thanks to the light weight and economical frame structures, open walls and multiple parallel rows of long overhanging eaves made up of zinc sheets, protected structures from sun and rain in the most immediate, rational manner. The message of this approach is that instead of trying to invent a new architecture appropriate to a region from scratch one should rely rather on syncretic recombination of solutions accumulated over time. The heuristics of Stagno lead to a "hybrid" or rather *mestiza* architecture (*mestiza* means mixed blood).

One of the most significant aspects of the quality of the built environment which has been systematically ignored and violated by superficial thinking, biased judgment and seductive illusions is the skin of buildings. The impact of bad choices of materials on the skin of a building is not immediate. It is here that deep knowledge of the materials and the climatic attributes of a particular area is needed that cannot be substituted by reductive technical descriptions and even more by photographic media reproductions. The thoughtless transfer of glass as well as concrete to the tropical region led to indifferent if not hostile environments. Rahul Mehrotra makes this point about such an invasion to the tropical region of India. In particular he focuses on the issue of weathering, which until very recently has frequently been overlooked. For ordinary people, however, it might have much more significant value not only in terms of comfort but also symbolism than the geometrical, spatial aspects of a structure.

Ken Yeang's approach is in a similar vein to that of Bruno Stagno. He mobilizes cutting edge technologies of construction and climatic control for the design of tall buildings. His explorations involve a combination of visionary intuitive thinking together with rigorous micro-climatic analysis. In addition, Yeang combines the potentials of such technologies with explorations of the new typology of high-rise buildings. His tropical structures stress further that contemporary three-dimensional conceptions of space combined with new mechanical devices and building materials can lead to new experiences of the environment within the tropical region.

Philip Bay, in his concise study of tropicalism in Singapore, points to the different interpretations that tropicalism is taking there today against the background of the major tropical building experiments of the late 1960s and 1970s such as Lim Chong Keat Singapore Conference Hall and Trade Union House (1962–65), and Tay Kheng Soon and William Lim's People's Park

(1967–70) and Woh Hup (1973). He isolates three paradigms of current practice, and ends with comments on some recent projects. He singles out the Institute of South East Asian Studies (1998) by Cheah Kok Ming and The Market Place (1995) by Tang Guan Bee as expressing a "symbiosis of both scientific form/space and poetic place all at once".

Tay Kheng Soon's "Tropical City Concept" was written as direct response to the Singapore government's proposed plan to develop Kampong Bugis, an extensive central area of the city measuring 76 hectares, a site that is still vacant. Tay is one of the most important architectural thinkers of our time and this article is the most complete statement of his credo. The concept he presents here is the logical extension of his writings for *SPUR*, the magazine of the Singapore Planning and Urban Research Group which he co-founded in 1965 (1965–71). It is also the outgrowth of his first tropicalist projects carried out in the 1960s and 1970s – the People's Park Complex of 1967–70 and Woh Hup of 1973 – with William Lim and their architectural firm, Design Partnership. Like People's Park and Woh Hup, this project addresses the problem of climate control and comes up with two ideas as novel as they are clearly formulated, both in opposition to the "northern" models: the vertical garden, use of vegetation on buildings to cool down the external wall temperature, and the idea of an unenclosed porous architecture, what he calls "Line, Edge & Shadow", rather than of a clearly demarkated box typical of northern architecture. Of particular significance is the megastructural scale on which Tay Kheng Soon thinks. This he applies as alternatives to current large-scale, urban high-rise building, again as in People's Park and Woh Hup. He also addresses the issue of city life. He proposes high density, mass transit intensive, mixed use programmes as a means of rationalizing urban life and keeping the destruction of tropical natural context to a minimum. In addition, Tay Kheng Soon also addresses the issue of sustainability.

Our own paper tries to draw some parallels between tropicalism and regionalism in the post-Second World War, post-colonial period.

CONCLUSION

What emerges from the contributions to this book is a manifesto for difference. This is not simply an adversarial stance, difference for the sake of difference. It is rather a declaration for reflection and respect of the individual contexts in the framework of interconnections and dialogue that leads to a more diverse and thus richer world. It is no surprise that this message emerges out of a "zone" or region of rainforests characterized by the richest variety of forms of life, the most complex patterns of sustained

interdependencies between organic and inorganic matter. It is the region that
gave the inspiration for the concept of biodiversity to be born. Perhaps an
equivalent concept of cultural and design biodiversity is the most significant
contribution of the present volume.

CHAPTER 2

THE SUPPRESSION AND RETHINKING OF REGIONALISM AND TROPICALISM AFTER 1945

Liane Lefaivre and Alexander Tzonis

CRITICAL TROPICALISM

Tropical architecture has traditionally been taken to mean an architecture adapted to the tropical climate. This has been the case since the late eighteenth century, when the British transformed the peasant Bengali *banggolo* into the colonial bungalow and diffused it all over the British Empire (Figures 2.1a, b).[1] It is also true about the more recent, post-colonial work of Otto Koenigsberger,[2] Olgyay and Olgyay,[3] and Maxwell Fry and Jane Drew.[4] However, after the Second World War, some architects building in the tropics started to view this definition in a critical manner and rethink its limited and narrow scope. They began to conceive of architecture not only in terms of sun shading and ventilation devices, but also as an extension of the mind, a cognitive tool, that expresses the values of a particular people and time in the way that film, art and music do. This critical rethinking is what distinguishes, we believe, a mere tropical architecture from a tropicalist one.

Tropicalist architecture has emerged in great part as a response to two major challenges that have arisen since Second World War. The first is postcolonialism. Indeed, if there is a common feature unifying the highly diverse countries of the tropics – besides their climate – it is that they are, without exception, former colonies. Postcolonialism involves the issue of identity and otherness in a cultural world predetermined by a once hegemonic power.[5] But the end of traditional colonialism has also meant that major architects are either local or commissioned by local clients and that, instead of being imposed top-down from a dominating outside power, architecture has, in principle, been allowed to evolve out of specific local cultural and economic conditions and meet the specific cultural and economic needs.

The second and more recent challenge is globalization. Since Marshall McLuhan wrote with relative optimism about the "global village" in 1964,[6] most authors have shrunk from extolling the benefits of globalization. They have tended to find more risks than benefits in the new fiercely competitive, super-libertarian, unregulated, super-connected, transnational corporation-driven world order.[7] These risks have been seen as affecting every aspect of life, from the kitsch commodification of local culture to the Disneyfication of tradition, McDonaldization of food,[8] the rape of the environment, the dissolution of traditional roots, the end of history. There is nothing unique about this attitude in the tropics. The threat of globalization is felt all over the world, including the country seen as its epicentre, the United States.[9] For architects the problem is especially pressing. Sassen first spoke of the consequences of the flexible corporate investment strategies for cities, forced

(a)

(b)

Figure 2.1 (a) The "banggolo"; (b) the bungalow adapted by Europeans (source: Grant, Anglo-Indian Domestic Life, London, 1849)

to compete in a world market in order to attract capital.[10] In this context, tropicalist architects have been faced with the task of trying to avoid the pitfalls of globalization, to sustain a sense of place, and of halting the slide of architecture, cities and the environment into humanly, socially, environmentally devastated examples of what may be called "glarchitecture" "glurbanism" and "glandscape" without falling back on a nostalgic retreat into extinct definitions of "tradition".

Confronted with these challenges, of post-colonialism and globalization, tropical architecture has undergone a radical rethinking of its strategies. It has come to encompass, besides issues of climate, broader problems of place, tradition, memory, community, new hard and soft technologies, and sustainability. In other words, its concerns have come to resemble those of the critical regionalists in other parts of the world. We will look at the work of a number of architects who have given different form to this strategic rethinking: Minette da Silva in Sri Lanka, Tay Kheng Soon and William Lim in Singapore, Mick Pearce in Zimbabwe, Lina Bo Bardi in Brazil, Oluwole Olumuyiwa in Nigeria, Ricardo Porro in Cuba, Richard Neutra in Puerto Rico, Paul Rudolph in Florida, Oscar Niemeyer and Affonso Reidy and Burle Marx in Brazil, Renzo Piano in New Caledonia and, last but not least , Lewis Mumford himself in Honolulu. Although this list is in no way exhaustive – a more exhaustive list would embrace the architects included in the present book, among others – it does present what we believe are important moments in the emergence of a tropical critical regionalist architecture in the post-war period.

New thinking never comes easy, especially if it is big. The bigger it is the more frameworks it breaks and reconstructs, and these are institutional as well as cognitive. This is why, as we shall see, the emergence of a new critical regionalism was not without friction.

THE POST-WAR SUPPRESSION OF REGIONALISM

In the period immediately following the Second World War, there was an almost automatic, knee-jerk reaction against regionalism on the part of the architectural establishment. The writers who were to become the main figures of international post-war architectural criticism over the next two or three decades all came out concertedly in opposition to it. Englishman John Summerson, one of the most widely read architectural critics and historians of the period, who was associated with the prestigious *Architectural Review*, was the first to take it on. It was 1945, the very year the war ended. "One often hears people talk of a 'national tradition'", he declared but "just what does this mean? Can there really be any such thing?" "I am sure that there cannot", was his answer, dismissing what he called the "atrocious fog of humbug that hangs about this question".[11]

It was in the United States, however, that the strongest, most concerted opposition came. Moreover, it came from establishment figures like Henry-Russell Hitchcock, Alfred Barr, Philip Johnson, Sigfried Giedion and Walter Gropius. Together they set up the most high-powered and richly endowed opinion-making machine of the time with global ambitions in the world: the Museum of Modern Art.[12] And they all had vested interests in perpetuating the formalist values of the pre-war International Style for which they had turned the MoMA into a show case thanks to the famous exhibition with the same name in 1932 by Johnson and Hitchcock.

Ironically, American regionalism had got off to a good start at the post-war MoMA. Nothing could be explicitly farther in spirit from a show entitled *International Style* than one called *America Builds*, and this was the title of the major exhibition mounted there in 1944. Its purpose was to project home grown, patriotic American values during wartime. Historian and critic Talbot Hamlin was its General Director. It consisted of four sections:

1. The Pioneers: Richardson, Sullivan and Wright
2. Outstanding Buildings of the Past Ten Years
3. Housing in War and Peace (where public housing was emphasized)
4. Planning in the USA (typified by Chicago and the Tennessee Valley)

The one section of the show that caught on was the one devoted to the *Buildings of the Past Ten Years*. Curated by a young architect, Elizabeth Mock, it enjoyed such popular success that it became a separate travelling exhibition on its own. Renamed *Built in USA since 1932,* it was accompanied by a special catalogue of its own in 1947, the only publication that was to come out of the original exhibition.[13] The only other trace of that original exhibition is the text of the panels of the original exhibition in the archives of the MoMA.[14] A largely forgotten figure, as opposed to her more famous sister Harvard and Berkeley Professor Catherine Bauer,[15] Mock had trained as an architect under Frank Lloyd Wright at Taliesen in Wisconsin and then studied architecture in Switzerland at the Gewerbeschule in Zurich, the equivalent of a regionalist Arts and Crafts School. She started as a temporary employee in the Department of Architecture and Industrial Design at the MoMA in 1937, and became Acting Curator of the Department of Architecture and Design between 1942 and 1946.[16]

Mock's section of the MoMA exhibition was not merely regionalist, it was polemically so. She did not mince her words. She was direct in her criticism of the International Style exhibition of 1932 organized by her seniors, Philip Johnson and Henry-Russell Hitchcock, calling it an example of "badly assimilated European modernism". As one of the panels of her section of *America Builds* reads, "ten years ago the few modern designers in the United States were following, literally and belatedly, the forms and theories

of revolutionary European work of the 20s." The trouble with this approach is
that it saw itself, in its own words, as "irreconcilable" with Wrightean regionalist tradition.[17]

This last statement of Mock's is remarkable. It springs from a highly uncon-
ventional and novel conception of regionalism. First, instead of seeing
modernism and regionalism the way Johnson and Hitchcock had, that is as
"irreconcilable", she saw them as complementary. Both had their place in
the picture of American architecture that she drew. She saw modern
American architecture, on one hand, as embracing, naturally, Frank Lloyd
Wright. But, on the other, more unexpectedly, highly technical buildings like
Albert Kahn's factories and the Great Lakes Naval Training Section. "The
modern architect has a view of the scope and social responsibility of his
profession. He realizes that architecture deals with mechanical equipment,
furniture, textiles and utensils, the space around buildings and the relationships of one building to another." "The architectural process of rational
analysis and creative synthesis goes over without break into design for crafts
and for industry, into regional and city planning", she explained. "Since
that time", she argued, however, "the same movement toward humanization
in architecture which has taken place in other countries has occurred here
to an extraordinary degree."[18] In this she was voicing a position that Mumford
had already formulated and amply developed. We will come back to this
point in the next section. Second, she drew parallels between the regionalism of Frank Lloyd Wright and that of European regionalists like Alvar Aalto
and Sven Markelius. More remarkably, perhaps, she was not beyond including that symbol of pre-war Modernism, Le Corbusier, some of whose work
she correctly saw as incorporating a regionalist dimension. She was, in other
words, including matters of pure architectural formal language within the
definition of regionalism, and expanding to include architects Mumford
refused to deal with as regionalists.

1947 started off as an auspicious year for regionalism. First Mock's *Built
in USA* exhibition. Then Lewis Mumford made waves by writing what became
the most sensational article of his career, defending regionalism in the *New
Yorker*.[19] These were followed by yet another exhibition about American
architecture, which was also positive about regionalism, organized by the
American Institute of Architects, held in Havana, Cuba and curated by Mary
Mix. The exhibition catalogue was published in English, then mounted for a
tour of post-war Germany extolling American values and accompanied by a
German catalogue.[20]

But by the end of year the tables had turned. The momentum that had
been gathering suddenly slammed to a halt. Mock's position at the MoMA did
not outlast the show she had helped curate. In spite of the popular success
of her exhibition, she vanished from the MoMA Staff List in 1947.[21] Philip
Johnson took her place in 1948 as acting director and then, from 1949 to

1954, as director. Mix too disappears from the scene. Mumford, a major cultural figure of the time, was more difficult to sweep under the carpet. Instead, he became the target of a smear campaign at the MoMA, carried out with the utmost sense of etiquette.

At first glance it is hard to see why the MoMA's response to Mumford was so tough. In retrospect there is nothing sensationalistic about the tone of his *New Yorker* article. The article, in fact, seems perfectly innocuous. It simply criticized both Henry-Russell Hitchcock and Sigfried Giedion, one for his embrace of Frank Lloyd Wright personalism and the other for his promotion of monumentalism. And it identified for the first time a group of regionalist architects – the San Franciscan Bay Region School of architecture extending from Bernard Maybeck to William Wurster – which Mumford called a "native and humane form of modernism".[22]

But Mumford had hit a nerve and the MoMA lost no time reacting. It took barely three months for Alfred Barr, the director, and his mentor Hitchcock, to take the unprecedented step of organizing a public round table to respond to him on 11 February 1948. The title, "What is happening to Modern Architecture?", echoes their alarm. The alarm was not limited to the MoMA. In spite of the short notice, much of the east coast architectural establishment responded en masse to the invitation to be part of the panel. It was a "who is who" of post-war architecture: Marcel Breuer, Walter Gropius, Henry-Russell Hitchcock, Philip Johnson, Edgar J. Kaufmann, George Nelson, Matthew Nowicki, Eero Saarinen, Peter Blake, Vincent Scully, Edward Durrell Stone. Among the people who attended as part of the audience and commented from the floor were Serge Chermayeff, Talbot Hamlin, Gerhard Kallmann and Isamu Noguchi.

Alfred Barr's opening remarks were an exercise in mud-slinging. He referred to the Bay Region style as kitsch, "a Cottage Style redolent of *Neue Gemütlichkeit*", his use of the German term insinuating that there might even be a tinge of Nazi *Heimat* sympathy to Mumford's position.[23] Hitchcock spoke next and in the same vein. His talk, aimed mostly at praising Frank Lloyd Wright and criticizing the present Corbusian solutions for the United Nations Headquarters, dismissed regionalism as a "Cottage style" embodying a backward looking "reaction" to Modern architecture which was "synonymous" with the phrase International Style. A number of participants from the profession, schools of architecture and architectural magazines stepped in to defend the heritage of pre-war Modernism and CIAM. Gropius took the floor next. As the ex-director of the Bauhaus it was perhaps natural for him to get up and defend the functionalism of the Bauhaus as open-ended and non-dogmatic, but it was totally beside the subject. Then, just as irrelevantly, he remarked that the International Style had been "regional in character, developing out of the surrounding conditions". His next *non-sequitur* leap was to the suggestion that the kind of regionalism Mumford was advocating was based on "chauvinistic sentimental national prejudice". In the wake of these damning statements several participants took the floor. Marcel Breuer did not attack anyone, but in case anyone had any doubts about whose side he was on, he defended the Modernism of Le Corbusier. George Nelson condemned the regionalist character of contemporary English new empiricism as "an ostrich-like and historically insignificant reaction to the impact of modern architecture". Peter Blake took an almost patriotic stance. The current regionalism was, he declared, an attempt to "delay" the "industrial revolution in building" that was finally taking place in America.

The MoMA organizers were probably right to be worried. Mumford's regionalist proposals had not fallen on deaf ears. They struck a deep chord in some of the younger generation in attendance. In fact this generation was closer to Mumford's sensitivity than to that of the older generation. Gerhardt Kallmann, the recently immigrated young German architect who was teaching at the Harvard Graduate School of Design, for example, distinguished the post-war regionalism from "folkloristic revivalism" and saw it as an attempt to overcome the "over schematic and blatant solutions in earlier phases of modern architecture". He went so far as to declare that architects had "more to learn from the work of Frank Lloyd Wright and Alvar Aalto", two regionalists, than from what he saw as the empty, formalist "form world" of Le Corbusier.[24]

Another young member of the audience was American architect Ralph T. Walker. Like Mumford, he was highly critical of the older, CIAM generation. He spoke out at length, and his comments deserve to be reproduced:

> I have been around South America recently and I have just come back from Europe, and I find everywhere that modern architecture means a slab on pillars. It means the same thing in the United States because you pick up the architectural magazines and practically every issue has as its leading number a slab on pillars . . . Functionalism of materials has blazed our thinking around the world because you will find that the building in Rio for the Education Ministry looks exactly like a building that was designed for a giraffe in the London Zoo, and it looks exactly like the building that has been designed for the United Nations. In other words, you have a cover of unthinking uncritical acceptance of things.

He went on to argue that what was needed was "humanism" because it is the "basis of all art . . ." and "what we are trying to do first of all is to develop surroundings for people to live in, that will give them the greatest amount of the happiness and warmth of life".[25]

Christopher Tunnard, a young assistant professor of city planning at Yale, was also present. He was the most pointedly critical of all with regard to the generation of the old boys who were in charge at the MoMA. Indeed, he launched into an *ad hominem* attack on Johnson and Hitchcock. He declared that

> we were brought up in the school of modern architecture, we were bred on the *Architectural Review*, and Mr Johnson's and Mr Hitchcock's book, and we have

gone through a period of modern building, and it seems there are limitations. One of the limitations I think can be laid at the door of M. Le Corbusier, who, perhaps fortunately, does not practice what he preaches, but one of his slogans is "The plan is the generator"; and another is "The styles are a lie." Now, when you are very young and interested in new things, you tend to swallow these statements whole, and I think it is only now that those of us in my generation are able to see beyond and through such statements, which are rather glib and probably not at all important.[26]

It might seem strange that there was no statement by Mumford that day. But the organizers had given him the responsibility of chairing the meeting, and so he was kept from actively defending his own view. In his concluding remarks he claimed never to have written an article "that was worse understood".[27] As for Elizabeth Mock, she was conspicuous by her absence.

Harvard Professor Sigfried Giedion, who had left one of the greatest architects of Europe at the time, Alvar Aalto, out of the first edition of his *Space, Time and Architecture* (1941) because he was considered too much of a regionalist, now castigated the current regionalist trends in the introduction to his *A Decade of New Architecture* (1951).

> Architecture has been shifted back to a lifeless eclecticism and its development has been slowed down and even twisted backwards. For example, the retrogressive movement which occurred in Holland . . . Most of its rebuilding projects . . . exhibit unscientific or pseudo-romantic tendencies . . . [Sweden is] endangered by sentimental trends such as the "new empiricism" which under the cover of "humanizing" architecture leads only into another cul-de-sac. Switzerland, supreme in the detailed finish and technique of its architecture, is moving under a similar cloud of "cosiness" for its housing schemes . . . [28]

The MoMA meant business. In 1951, Hitchcock took advantage of the 25th anniversary of his and Johnson's exhibition on the International Style entitled *The International Style Twenty Years Later* once again to attack Mumford's *New Yorker* article of 1947.[29]

> It is an old story now, . . . that Wright came very close indeed to the International Style in certain projects of the late 1920 . . . and that many of his most famous later works, such as Falling Water, seem to include definitely "international" ideas. The architects of the San Francisco Bay Region whom some critics have wished to build up as the protagonists of a more humanistic school opposed to the International Style, have also frequently followed its principles almost down to the point of parody – although admittedly not in their best and most characteristic country house work.[30]

And in 1952, highjacking the title that Mock had used six years earlier, *Built in USA: Post-War Architecture*, Hitchcock and Arthur Drexler, the director of architectural exhibits, organized a new exhibition at the MoMA. They also wrote the catalogue that was prefaced by Philip Johnson. The book was distributed on an international scale and translated into many languages thanks to a Rockefeller Brothers Fund that made possible a five-year project, the International Circulating Exhibition Program. Porter A. McCray was appointed director of program, and 22 of the first 25 exhibitions prepared under him travelled outside the United States.[31]

It was as if Mock's exhibition had never existed. In a triumphant paean to himself and Hitchcock, Johnson boasted that

> the battle of modern architecture has long been won. Twenty years ago the Museum of Modern Art was in the thick of the fight, but now our exhibitions and catalogues take part in that unending campaign described as simply the continuous, conscientious, resolute distinction of quality from mediocrity – the discovery and proclamation of excellence. To make this proclamation from time to time is the prime function of the Department of Architecture and Design . . . [as a judge] we chose Professor Henry-Russell Hitchcock of Smith College, the leading historian of modern architecture in this country. With me, Mr. Hitchcock was responsible for our first international exhibition of modern architecture exactly twenty years ago . . .[32]

There was nothing but the International Style in American architecture according to him. He declared:

> If we should think back twenty years to the 1932 exhibition, the change is . . . striking. The International Style . . . [has] spread and [has] been absorbed by the wide stream of historical progress. Every building in this book would look different if it had not been for the International Style. With the mid-century modern architecture has come of age.[33]

Hitchcock was as straightforward in his anti-regionalism as Mock had been in her regionalism. "Today there is no further need to underline the obvious fact that what used to be called 'traditional' architecture is dead if not buried", he declared. An interesting indication of just how well coordinated the anti-regionalist campaign was run, Hitchcock's text was a word-for-word repetition of a whole phrase of Giedion's. He too decried "a reaction, notably before and during the war, in Switzerland and the Scandinavian countries: a new 'Empiricism' or a new 'cosiness'".[34]

This kind of self-congratulatory, mutual backslapping at the MoMA resounded in schools and magazines, almost drowning out the issue of Mumfordian regionalism throughout the 1940s and mid-1950s, at least in the United States.

THE CRITICAL RETHINKING OF REGIONALISM: LEWIS MUMFORD

The MoMA establishment could not have been more wrong about the kind of regionalism Mumford stood for. Of course Barr, Johnson and Hitchcock had a vested interest in being wrong. They were, naturally, guarding the post-war success of their pre-war International Style exhibition. The last thing that interested them at this point was regionalism. It was, at best, irrelevant to their concerns. It was perceived as an obstacle that had to be removed.

Mumford himself, on the other hand, did not make things easy for anyone wishing to get a clear overview of his regionalist paradigm. He never put forth a systematic manifesto or exposition of it, although, arguably, it informs his every position. Mumford's paradigm of regionalism must be put together piecemeal, on the basis of his many writings. One must consult his entire *oeuvre*, as early as his *Sticks and Stones* (1924) down to later works such as *The City in History* (1961) and *The Urban Prospect* (1968) as well as others such as his masterpiece *Technics and Civilization* (1934), and his *The South in Architecture* (1941) and *Report on Honolulu* (1945).[35]

Mumford's lack of systematic exposition is partly understandable. His views are extremely novel. His writings break with regionalism as it developed out of the Renaissance and was different from anything that had been formulated before. He departed from a rejection of Nazi *Heimat* regionalism, of course, but also of Romantic regionalism before it, and Picturesque regionalism even earlier.[36] To use his own expression in relation to Emerson, Thoreau, Whitman, Melville and Hawthorne, he represented "an imaginative New World", a "new hemisphere in the geography of the mind". Mumford's originality stems from his radically critical rethinking of traditional definitions of regionalism. His approach ultimately goes back to the origins of critical philosophy in the works by Emmanuel Kant, *Critique of Judgment* and *Critique of Pure Reason*. These books of Kant's departed from a critique of the limitations of current philosophical theories. Instead of a rejection of these theories, they were attempts to redefine their foundations. It is in this sense that we use the term "critical regionalism", a regionalism evolved from an internal criticism, directed at regionalism itself. Mumford was the first to systematically rethink regionalism from within.

We now examine the five poles of that rethinking: strangemaking versus historicism, advanced technology versus nostalgic craftsmanship, sustainability versus Picturesqueness, multicultural community versus traditional community, and the fusion of local and global.

1. The first point on which Mumford broke with older forms of regionalism was in his approach to tradition. Although he did advocate the preservation of actual historical buildings, notably those built in the vernacular brick tradition of the South, which "deserves to be regarded with a far more appreciative eye than people usually apply to it",[37] he was opposed to their imitation in new buildings.

Let us be clear about this, the forms that people used in other civilizations or in other periods of our own country's history were intimately part of the whole structure of their life. There is no method of mechanically reproducing these forms or bringing them back to life; it is a piece of rank materialism to attempt to duplicate some earlier form, because of its delight for the eye, without realizing how empty a form is without the life that once supported it. There is no such thing as a modern colonial house any more than there is such a thing as a modern Tudor house.[38]

Mumford's strongest worded statement is the following:

If one seeks to reproduce such a building in our own day, every mark on it will betray the fact that it is fake, and the harder the architect works to conceal that fact, the more patent the fact will be . . . The great lesson of history – and this applies to all the arts – is that the past cannot be recaptured except in spirit. We cannot live another person's life; we cannot, except in the spirit of a costume ball . . .[39]

Mumford's idea that tradition is not timeless but constructed is echoed in Eric Hobsbawm's and Terence Ranger's *The Invention of Tradition*, a study of the creation of Welsh and Scottish national culture.[40] In that book, Hugh Trevor-Roper pointed out how the kilt, the symbol of Scottish identity, was to a great extent an invention of nineteenth century England.[41] For Mumford the fact that tradition is not timeless did not mean it was relegated to the status of kitsch, to be abandoned. Between the extreme of mimicking traditional forms and their absolute rejection, he saw the possibility of a more complex approach. His position is close to that more recently taken up by the philosopher Edward Shils, who noted that traditions which survive are the ones that evolve constantly, and become subject to reinterpretation and renewed adaptation to the present,[42] and, more recently, of Anthony Giddens who has also taken up the argument that traditions are not merely invented, but also "reinvented".[43] The inexorable fate of all architectural practices that remain rigidly attached to bygone forms is to become the stuff of theme parks, and Shelly Errington has pointed out several examples of this process in her study of theme parks in South East Asia.[44] Perhaps, the reason regionalism has survived for centuries and is still alive in so many parts of the world today is because it has been able to redefine itself and adapt in response to new historical realities.[45] Mumford summed up this approach when he writes that "our task is not to imitate the past," but "to understand it, so that we may face the opportunity of our own day and deal with it in a creative spirit."[46] Indeed, for Mumford the persistance of a need for a constantly rejuvenated sense of tradition was an inseparable part of modernity.

With Mumford's rejection of historicism as the architectural equivalent of a masked ball was his rejection of local materials when they were not adapted to the function of the building. "Regionalism is not a matter of using the most available local material, or of copying some simple form of construction that our ancestors used, for want of anything better, a century or two ago".[47] In fact he was for the total abandonment of historicist precedents because they were not adapted to the evolving needs of the region.

> People often talk about regional characters as if they were the same thing as the aboriginal characters: the regional is identified with the rough, the primitive, the purely local. That is a serious mistake. Since the adaptation of a culture to a particular environment is a long, complicated process, a full-blown regional character is the last to emerge. We are only beginning to know enough about ourselves and about our environment to create a regional architecture.[48]

This is why he disapproved of some of the details of Thomas Jefferson's designs for the University of Virginia: Jefferson had made the mistake of using the local schist for the capitals of the columns just because it was a local stone. As it was brittle, there was much damage to the ornaments carried out in it. Mumford praised instead Richardson because he was much more interested in adapting the local to new building techniques, new materials. In this he was a rigorist in the tradition of the nineteenth century sculptor and writer Horatio Greenhough and rejected Jefferson as overly indulgent in decoration.[49] He was more inclined to Richardson's more functionalist, radically antidecorative, rigorist, functional design that made references to local traditions through a process we have earlier called "strangemaking".[50]

2. As concerns the return to nature, another mainstay of regionalism, Mumford also broke with tradition. He rejected picturesqueness, the purely aesthetic or spiritual enjoyment of landscape for its own sake.[51] For him "regional" meant something else besides "a place for the personal touch, for the cherished accident", although he did love the land in these terms. This is only natural as his roots are to be found in the tradition of Rousseauist love of nature. He wrote that "there was in the romantic movement from its beginning in Rousseau, an element of energy and vitality that could not be denied: the belief in nature, as a resource of the human spirit." But he did not limit his attachment to the land to a form of pastoral nostalgia or bucolic sentimentality. He was for redefining the meaning of the adaptation of the landscape in order to deal with the new realities. "Regional forms", he believed, "are those which most closely meet the actual conditions of life and which fully succeed in making a people feel at home in their environment: they do not merely utilize the soil but they reflect the current conditions of culture in the region."[52] This is what made him a disciple of the Garden City movement, and of the regional planning of Patrick Geddes who saw the garden city not just as a technique for designing green residential areas but as a policy guiding economic and social planning based on decentralized neighbourhood planning.[53] But, in the end, questions of regional planning are subsumed in Mumford's thinking within the larger questions of

what has come since to be called ecology and sustainability, what he himself referred to in *Technics and Civilization* as the "biotechnic" age that he believed was the next order, following the present neo-technic order, "over the edge of the horizon".[54,55] Among the aims of bio-technic regionalism were the restoration of the balance between man and nature, the conservation and restoration of soils, of the forest cover to provide shelter for wildlife.

This ecological or sustainable aspect of Mumford's approach is apparent in his "Report on Honolulu" prepared during a consulting trip to Honolulu in 1938 published in 1945.[56] The text contains his master plan for the city, the only proposal he ever carried out as a designer, and the first tropical city planned along the lines of a garden city. As a garden city, Mumford saw Honolulu as a "great park", accordingly, made up of "tropic foliage, with the pepper red of the Poinciana, the brilliant yellow of the golden shower, the feathery greens of the palms, the dark tones of the banyan trees".[57] He suggested widening and planting the major thoroughfare, Bishop Street, the provision of a parking area and the wiping away of the collection of miscellaneous buildings marring the view of the mountains. But he was also critical of the fact the present parks were restricted to "recreation zones",[58] and proposed that they be used in a more integrated way in urban life, first as a potential cooling device capable of "renewing the air, tempering the heat of the sun, reducing glare and strain, providing visual delight for play and relaxation and supplying one of the most sanative of all modes of work – the care of plants itself."[59] As an extension of the garden city idea and regional planning idea, he also suggested the provision of greenbelts or park girdles, as little as a hundred feet wide, which could give as much coherence to a modern neighbourhood superblocks "as the ancient wall used to for the medieval city".[60] "The spurs of the mountains that lead into the city form natural open areas that can only be developed for urban building at an extravagant cost. Where these areas have not been sacrificed to the subdivider, they should be retained and connected together as a greenbelt", he specified. Canals too should be bordered by parks.

3. On the other hand, for all his ecological concerns, he was also for the use of the most advanced technology of the day. Again, this was not in line with traditional regionalists. As is evident from his Honolulu text, he was for the air conditioner. Although scientific research had shown that the lowering of temperature was not so important as the direct air in cooling the body, still Mumford allowed that "mechanical air conditioning might be a useful auxiliary to nature under special conditions" such as the workplace, preceding Singapore's founding premier Lee Kuan Yew's famous statement that the air conditioner was the best invention of the twentieth century.[61] In most circumstances, natural modes of ventilation are best Mumford believed.[62] Thirty years before Reyner Banham's *Theory and Design of the First Machine Age*

of 1960,[63] in Mumford's *Technics and Civilization* of 1934 we have a celebration of technical inventions such as the modern steamship. He had great
admiration for Buckminster Fuller's streamline Dymaxion car, the Union
Pacific train, and the Soviet "Rail Zeppelin spherotrain", Brooklyn Bridge and
the Galerie des Machines in Paris. Finally, he admired Neutra's image of the
modern city put forth in his largely forgotten Rush City Reformed scheme
published in his early *Wie baut Amerika* of 1927, where the emphasis was
placed on movement, with ubiquitous freeways, local and express elevated
train systems, railroads, airports all interlinked.[64] An interesting feature were
landing strips for helicopters at the railway station and on the roofs of
elevated stations. Mumford wrote in 1949 that that "kind of thinking should
now be resumed and perhaps public competitions should be held to enlist
the imagination of the younger generation of architects and planners . . ."
(see Figure 2.2).[65]

4. Another radically new departure of Mumford's regionalism was his definition of "community". He was uneasy with the traditional regionalist idea of
community as monocultural, based on tribal associations, blood ties and an
attachment to a soil that was purely native. Mumford espoused the view that

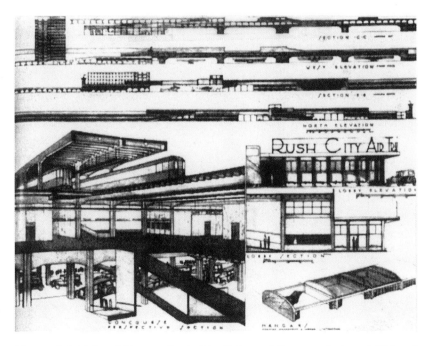

Figure 2.2 *Richard Neutra: Rush City Reformed (by permission of Richard
Neutra Archives, Pomona, CA)*

community could be something multicultural. In this he was an heir of two different schools of thought. The first was that formed by the mid-nineteenth century so-called American Renaissance figures of Emerson and Whitman in America.[66] And second, was the work of Martin Buber in Germany who was the first philosopher to propose an alternative to the "Blood and Soil" theory of community that had dominated German thought since the theme had been introduced by Simmel. Mumford's *South in Architecture*, written in 1941, during the Second World War, makes the point most forcefully of all his writings. His "Report on Honolulu", written in 1938 is typical of his approach. He described it as a multicultural city, made up of original Polynesians, Japanese and Chinese, and various *Haole* groups (Western) which makes it "a significant experiment in the hybridization of cultures which perhaps will mark the future development of human society; it is a miniature experimental station".[67]

5. Finally, Mumford did not see an opposition between what he called the "local" and the "universal", between what we would call today the "regional" versus the "global". He saw regionalism not as a way of resisting globalization, or rather, not completely. Mumford struck a balance between regionalism and globalism. He introduced the notion in *The South in Architecture*.

> The philosophic problem of the general and the particular has its counterpart in architecture; and during the last century that problem has shaped itself more and more into the question of what weight should be given to the universal imprint of the machine and the local imprint of the region and the community.[68,69]

This was another way of saying that

> . . . every regional culture necessarily has a universal side to it. It is steadily open to influences that come from other parts of the world, and from other cultures, separated from the local region in space or time or both together. It would be useful if we formed the habit of never using the word regional without mentally adding to it the idea of universal – remembering the constant contact and interchange between local scene and the wide world that lies beyond it. To make the best use of local resources, we must often seek help from people or ideas or technical methods that originate elsewhere. . . . As with a human being, every culture must both be itself and transcend itself; it must make the most of its limitations and must pass beyond them; it must be open to fresh experience and yet it must maintain its integrity. In no other art is that process more sharply focused than in architecture.[70]

The originality of this last position cannot be overestimated. For the first time a regionalist steered a middle course between the particular and the universal, and asserted that there was nothing mutually exclusive between one region and another, or between one region and the globe, that there was the possibility of mutually beneficial negotiating to be carried out within a wider, in principle collaborative so to speak, scheme of things. This marked a major cognitive swing away from a centuries-old mental pattern of regionalist thinking based on an adversarial stance – against an authoritarian imperialist domination – to one based on what we may call Fusionism. In his *New Yorker* article of 1947 he had praised the Bay Region Style as a "product of the meeting of Oriental and Occidental architectural traditions" which he believed was a "far more universal style than the so-called International Style of the nineteen thirties, since it permits regional adaptations and modifications".[71] It runs through the other regionalist positions he took – his antihistoricism, his ecological consciousness, his belief in technological progress, his redefinition of community.

CRITICAL REGIONALISM/CRITICAL TROPICALISM

In spite of all the time, energy and money poured into MoMA's campaign, regionalism slipped in through the back door. When one flips through the *Built in USA* catalogue of 1953, one cannot help but be struck by the ironically high regionalist content of the selection, which includes Neutra's Tremaine House, Paul Rudolph's Healy House, Harwell Hamilton Harris's Johnson House, Lloyd Wright's Wayfarer's Chapel, Frank Lloyd Wright's House for Herbert Jacobs, Eliel and Eero Saarinen's Opera Shed for Berkshire Music Center, and Paolo Soleri's Desert House.

Indeed, the winds of change were blowing. That is an image Mumford had used in his *New Yorker* article of 1947. A thoroughly new, critical regionalism was slowly taking shape. Although it is to be found piecemeal in the work of many architects since the Second World War, taken as a whole, it forms a way of thinking, a spirit of the time, a Hegelian *Zeitgeist*.

Indeed other architects began writing in the same vein as Mumford. Among them was Ernesto Rogers. In an article of 1954,[72] he attacks the dogmatism of the modernists who "fail to realize that the modern style contrasts with the old precisely because it laid the ground for a dynamic approach to problems as well as 'neo-Arcadian populism'," which was "anachronistic if not hypocritical or downright demagogic lying", both tendencies being in fact antimodern in their lack of a realistic, socially responsible approach to the actual architectural problems of the day. A later article[73] of his attacks the "autonomous visions" of the "frozen", "a priori thinking" of the "so-called modern" architecture. He urged for an "extension of the Modern Movement" true to the original spirit of functionalism and for an architecture which, while innovative, considered the "environment". This "environment", as in Mumford's case, is the natural context inside which a new project had to be inserted, but it also means the "cultural" one, the "historical setting".

"To consider the environment means to consider history." He refers further-more to his own efforts the Torre Velasca as a project "seen through a language which more *closely adheres to reality*" (our emphasis). To point out the regionalist, cultural environmental qualities of the project, Rogers cites Alvar Aalto who exclaimed upon seeing it, "It is very Milanese." In fact, Aalto's work is cited frequently at that time as a most successful example of an architecture which continued but also superseded the adver-sarial stance of romantic regionalism interpreting modernity as including within it a protesting attitude to power, to bureaucratic and technocratic imperialism, rallying in support of this view on the idea of regionalism. Kenzo Tange's work in the second part of the 1950s, particularly his Kagawa Prefectural Office of 1956, the project with which Japan definitively enters the international architectural forum, contributes significantly to the specific post-war debate on regionalism and the need to redefine modern architec-ture. Indicative are the comments after its presentation in the CIAM 1959 meeting in Otterlo. Ernesto Rogers greets the building as "a very good example of what we have to do", "a step forward" which, while affirming the latest technology and the most contemporary institution, democracy, manages to avoid the pitfalls of an inhuman and anonymous technophilia by giving "roots" to these new ideas. Tange's response is guarded. He is opposed to any misinterpretation of his use of regional elements. "I cannot accept the concept of total regionalism", he asserts, adding that "tradition" can be devel-oped through challenging its own shortcomings, implying the same for regionalism.[74] This last statement by Tange encapsulates the thinking typical of what we have called critical, that is self-examining and self-questioning, regionalism that is self-examining and self-questioning. "Critical" in this case does not simply mean adversarial. After all, as we have seen, the picturesque and romantic phases of regionalism were adversarial with respect to a ruling universalist order. This does not make them critical in the more restrained sense we apply.

The debate about regionalism became one of the main themes of the post-war architectural debate and architectural practice. It is too long to include here. We will limit this overview to some of the major architects working in the tropics.

The earliest, clearest, most critical reformulation of tropical architecture was by the Sri Lankan architect Minnette da Silva. She is one of the two most important women architects with a practice of their own of the post-war period, along with Lina Bo Bardi of Brazil. Like Lina Bo Bardi's, her work was unknown outside her local circles until she took it upon herself to write and publish a monograph at her own expense. In da Silva's case, she only completed Volume 1 before her death (Figures 2.3 a–c).[75]

Da Silva returned to Sri Lanka from the Architectural Association in London where she had studied architecture in 1949. She had started her

architecture career working for one of the three persons who would become the most important tropical architects of the post-war period, Otto
Koenigsberger, and she remained on intimate terms with the two others, Jane
Drew and Maxwell Fry. Yet she broke with their approach to tropical architecture. For her, an architecture of the tropics had to be more than just a
form of microclimatic control, although it was that too. For her, practice in
Sri Lanka was necessarily linked to broader questions of regionalism and
national identity. This is hardly surprising. Da Silva's father was a leading
figure in the anticolonial movement of the then Ceylon and in the post-
colonial government which gained independence in 1948. Her mother, an
early Ceylonese suffragette, campaigned actively for the preservation of the
traditional Sinhalese arts and crafts. And her sister, Anil, founded the most
important Bombay-based, post-colonial Indian cultural magazine, *Marg*.

As early as 1950, da Silva was conscious of her highly original position.
She coined a phrase to describe it: "modern regional architecture in the
tropics".

> Ceylon, like much of the East, emerged after the Second World War from a
> feudal-cum-Victorian past and was exposed to new technological influences from
> the West. A veneer of modernism was acquired second hand, ill digested and
> bearing no relationship to Ceylon's traditions or to the region. No attempt was
> made to synthesize the modern and the traditional . . . It is essential for us to
> absorb what we absolutely need from the modern West, and to learn to keep
> the best of our own traditional forms. We have to *think* understandably in order
> to develop an indigenous contemporary architecture, and not to lose the best
> of the old that has meaning and value.[76]

She went on to say that "accepting the need to synthesize our past with
present technology, we need to examine our own roots and understand them
before achieving a creative life – in literature, music, painting, education,
society, and architecture". Like Lewis Mumford, da Silva rejected the idea of
using traditional building materials, methods and ornament just for the sake
of continuity when these were disfunctional. Her second project, the Red
Cross Hall of 1950, had none of the trappings of traditional Sri Lankan architecture. This is how she defended her position:

> As an architect I believe in and so cannot subscribe to copying the architec-
> ture of an era that is long past. As an architect I believe in building to suit our
> living needs in a living way, utilizing the most suitable modern and progressive
> means at our disposal, and on adopting these sound and fundamental princi-
> ples of building of the past, which are as authentic today as before. It is from
> this that a beautiful and satisfying modern architecture can result. The era of
> the Kandyan style roof is dead. It was achieved in a feudal era with feudal
> means.[77]

This is not to say she rejected traditional materials and ventilation techniques in principle. For example, she suggested using the traditional rammed

earth for low cost housing, as long as it was combined with modern construction techniques.[78] Among the elements she retained in her otherwise historicist-free designs was the veranda, that Asian tropical invention, a shaded area both separating inside and outside, a bit like an immaterial, virtual non-wall. This is a remarkable aspect of her design thinking. Her "Modern Tropical Architecture" went beyond programmatic post-colonial cultural positions and into concrete building details. She was a remarkably free and inventive thinker, and did not fall under the sway of dominant Western ideas about tropical architecture although she was on intimate terms with the most influential figures: Jane Drew, Maxwell Fry, Otto Koenigsberger, and last but not least, Le Corbusier. They had all tended to stress the screen, brises-soleil and louvers as the main devices of tropical architecture – all, in fact borrowed from Le Corbusier and his experience with Mediterranean architecture. In all her designs, which aimed explicitly at the fusion of local and global, in her words the "synthesis of the modern and the traditional", but "without eclecticism", we find other, originally tropical ventilation and

TOP-ROW 1. (Left to right)
1. Milton (England).
2. Browne (England).
3. Rogers (Italy).
4. Cedercreutz (Finland).
5. Grannasztoi (Hungary).
6. Hruskai (Czechoslovakia).
7. Neumann (Czechoslovakia).
8. Marshall (England).
9. Kadleigh (England).
10. van Bodegraven (Holland).
11. Entwistle (England).
12. Richards (England) Jim
13. Elle (Holland).
14. Samuel (England).
15. Roth (Switzerland).
16. Emery (Algeria).
17. Bijhouwer (Holland).
18. de Vries (Holland) Rouke
19. van den Broek.
20. Kloos (Holland).

21. Kleykamp (Holland).
22. Michel (Belgium).

ROW 2.
23. Cadbury-Brown (England).
24. Shepheard (England).
25. De Syllas (England).
26. Cox (England).
27. Moffett (Ireland).
28. Batista (Cuba).
29. Arroyo (Cuba).
30. Fuchs (Czechoslovakia).
31. Honnegger (Switzerland).
32. Fisher (Hungary).
33. Steiger (Switzerland).
34. Mrs. Stam Beese (Holland).
35. Katona (England).
36. Pritchard (England).
37. Bakema (Holland).
38. Hogan (England).
39. Singer (Czechoslovakia).

ROW 3.
40. Papadaki (U.S.A.).
41. Morton Shand (England).
42. Rosenberg (England).
43. Martin (England).
44. Goldfinger (England).
45. Jensen (England).
46. Ling (England).
47. Ferrari Hardoy (Argentina).
48. Mrs. Wiener (U.S.A.).
50. Maxwell Fry (England).
51. Wells Coates (England).
52. Townsend (England).
53. Krejcar (Czechoslovakia).
54. Oberlander (Canada).
55. Schütte (Austria).
56. Merkelbach (Holland).

ROW 4. (Front row).
57. Le Corbusier (France).
58. Vivanro (Argentina).

59. Sadie Speight (England).
60. Susan Cox (England).
61. Malnai (Hungary).
62. Mrs Malnai (Hungary).
63. Barbara Randell (England).
64. Monica Pidgeon (England).
65. Sert (U.S.A.).
66. Girdion (Switzerland).
67. Jane Drew (England).
68. van Eesteren (Holland).
69. M. da Silva (India).
70. Gropius (U.S.A.).
71. Mrs. Fischer (Hungary).
72. Blauche Limco (Canada).
73. Kalivada (Czechoslovakia).
74. Mrs. Sert (U.S.A.).
75. Mrs Schütte (Austria).
76. van Tregan (Holland).

Figure 2.3 (a) *Minnette da Silva, seated between Cor van Eesteren and Walter Gropius at the CIAM Bridgewater meeting, 1947. She is seated first row, eighth to the right.*

(b)

(c)

Figure 2.3 (cont.) (b) Minnette da Silva. Conceptual drawing. Red Cross Hall, Kandy, 1950. Her first dismissal of the traditional Kandian style in favour of "tropical modernism". (c) Senanayake Flats, Gregory's Road, Colombo, 1954–57. Two identical blocks of flats built around an interior courtyard to ensure cross-ventilation both vertically and horizontally

shading devices. In one of her early projects she writes that "with the features of site I had to think about the life of the Sinhalese Buddhist family who were to live in the house, to consider climate, regional influences and amalgamate these with the knowledge I had acquired both in the West and from the wonderful building traditions of India and Ceylon". She even mixed different Asian building elements. For example, in her first project, the Karunaratne House of 1949–51, in an open-plan interior living area she articulated movable Japanese screens, "an ancient Japanese feature now taken over into Modern Architecture", with the traditional Sri Lankan veranda.[79]

Besides the veranda she retained the midula. In her Cost Effective Housing Studies (1954–55), she wrote that "we must re-orient our ideas for living confortably in congested towns like Colombo, where we no longer have expansive acres of garden and spacious pillared halls of the pre-Second World War days. How can we create this comfortable atmosphere in small restricted sites of 15 or 20 perches of ground?" "I considered the movement of air within the house as one of the primary concerns and was to achieve this with the utilization of split-levels, midulas and stairwells situated in the center of the plan." In other words she was applying the Venturi principle, allowing drafts to be "able to move horizontally and vertically through the house – a feature not normally accommodated in small town houses". Another priority was "the provision of privacy within a townscape – I had various ideas as the sketches show of walled gardens and screens". Her Senanayake Flats (1954–57) in Colombo are interesting in this connection. It can be seen as an attempt to adapt Le Corbusier's Unité d'Habitation to the tropics. It borrows Le Corbusier's idea of the pilotis and the roof garden – but in order to allow for the greatest ventilation and circulation of breezes, it turns the façade into a row of immaterial verandas and uses the midula.

For da Silva, again like Mumford, tropical architecture was explicitly linked to questions of community.

> Our community and social needs should find regional expression in town plans, housing schemes and public buildings. What so often happens is that we copy the closed-in types of western building quite unsuited to our region, or adapt traditional architecture in an equally unsuitable way, forgetting that carved stone and wooden pillars belong to a social age of the past, and that it is merely ludicrous to make them concrete now.

And in her plan for the Karunaratne House again, she created special spaces for extended family rituals.[80]

Although the work of Jane Drew and Maxwell Fry was not as wide ranging and complex, even technically speaking, as that of Minette da Silva, it would be wrong to underestimate the beneficial importance of their influence on post-war tropicalism. It is to them that Africa owes the introduction of the design vocabulary of the brise-soleil or louver – originally created by Stamo

Papadaki and subsequently popularized by Le Corbusier and Antonin Raymond – through their own design practice and through the publication of their now classic book on *Tropical Architecture*[81] (see Figures 2.4 a–d). It freed tropical architecture of the region from narrow constraints of the bungalow, suitable for small-scale buildings only, and allowed it to adapt to larger scale urban projects such as extensive housing projects, banks, schools and commercial buildings. Their own designs for Somanya College, Ghana, and their school in Lagos, Nigeria deserve a mention in this perspective as do some of the work of their contemporaries, such as Godwin & Hopwood Offices and Showrooms for Lagos and James Cubitt & Partners Bank Buildings in Accra, Ghana. But an indication of their lack of concern for some of the deeper design issues involved in post-colonial African architecture is that their book does not mention any native-born, black African architects. The work in particular of Oluwole Olumuyiwa, in particular his project for a cultural centre in Lagos of the early 1960s, is absent from the 1964 edition of their *Tropical Architecture*. It is to be found in two books by Udo Kultermann, however, along with the work of other Africans.

Olumuyiwa's design thinking is not restricted to factors of climate, which is not to say that he is oblivious to them. But his schemes deal with different issues. They are typical of the younger generation of the post-CIAM 1960s, mixed use, more complex, based on concerns of how to enhance community through mobility. He was trained in England in the 1950s under the influence of the Smithsons and he worked for Jacob Bakema in Rotterdam. His design for his cultural centre – a combined technical institute, teachers' college, and community centre – was conceived, like Bakema and van den Broek's Lijnbaan, as a combination of low rises and high rises linked through a network of pedestrian paths. At the heart of the complex stands an elevated entrance area with offices, assembly hall, two storey foyer and music rooms; it leads to an area with workshops around a rectangular court. The gymnasium with a glass barrel vault and a lower level includes a kitchen and dining rooms that are set off. He also planned an outdoor theatre between the entrance and dining areas and a sculpture garden. In a way typical of Team Ten's explicitly community-enhancing designs, the circulation pattern linking the different activities is reminiscent of the Smithsons' early sketches for circulation routes in their projects, or of Shadrach Woods's idea of the Stem or Web.[82] Here, however, it is adapted to the tropical climate, through the use of covered walkways and of pilotis opening the ground level to the flow of users and enhancing shaded and ventilated areas for encounters (Figures 2.5a–b).

The Viennese architect Richard Neutra was another major post-war critical tropicalist architect. Although labelled an International Style architect in the 1937 MoMA exhibition, he must be seen as a regionalist in order to be fully understood. The influence on him of Wright's regionalist theory of

(a)

(b)

Figure 2.4 (a) Stamo Papadaki: View of the southern façade of Christopher Columbus Memorial Lighthouse. Designed for a competition in 1928. Horizontal layers of reinforced concrete cantilevered from the main structural columns protect the north, east, and south façades of the chapel, which were to be entirely glazed. (b) Ministry of National Education and Public Health, Rio de Janeiro. Le Corbusier, Lucio Costa, Oscar Niemeyer, Affonso Reidy, Carlos Leao, Jorge Moreira, Ernani Vasconcelos, Architects. The first louvered Modernist building in South America, 1936

(c)

(d)

Figure 2.4 (cont.) (c) Example of the influence in Africa of Maxwell Fry and Jane Drew's now classic book Tropical Architecture. *Godwin and Hopwood, Office Block, Lagos Nigeria, 1958. (d) Another example of Drew's and Fry's influence. Henry Chomette, Bank, Brazzaville, 1959*

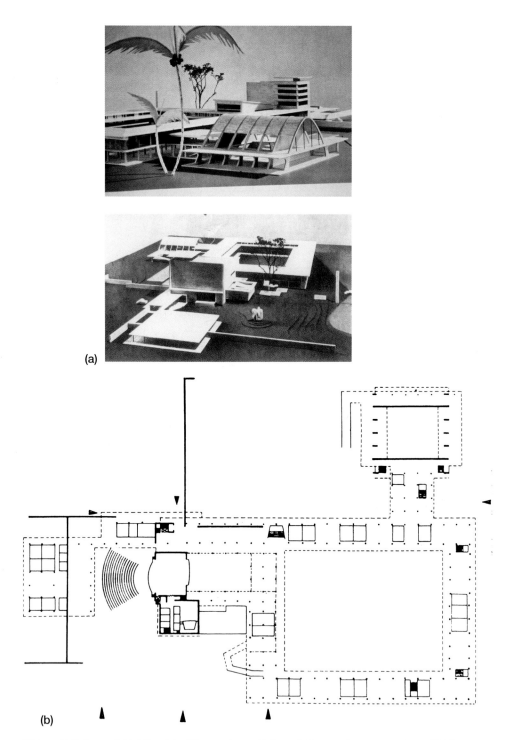

(a)

(b)

Figure 2.5 *(a and b) Oluwole Olumuyiwa, Cultural Center, Lagos, project, 1960*

"site", that is of the harmonious relationship between building and topography, is clear in Neutra's *Mystery and Realities of the Site*[83] and not
surprisingly influenced the masterful manner in which his one built tropical
house, the Schultess House designed in Cuba in 1954, is integrated with landscaping by the Brazilian landscape architect Roberto Burle Marx. But Neutra's
even earlier and ignored post-war tropicalist designs for the Committee on
the Design of Public Works set up by the Roosevelt administration and local
Puerto Rican politicians in 1943–44 are also significant. The programme was
aimed at village school rooms, hundreds of health centres in town and
country, four large district hospitals, an island home for girls and university
buildings. These designs are remarkable for a couple of reasons. First, as
Sigfried Giedion noted, they were a turning point. From Neutra's experience
of adapting his designs to the tropical climate in Puerto Rico will come,
according to Giedion, the increased lightness of his subsequent designs
produced by the use of shading and rain-protecting overhangs for continuous
soffit air change over lowered spandrels creating cross-ventilation and the
diffusion of light right under the ceiling, and by the use of slim beams set
on edge together with their thin roof slabs.[84]

But what makes these designs equally remarkable is how close they come
to the regionalist thinking of Lewis Mumford, in particular regarding community. Neutra spent much time studying the psychological aspect of medical
facilities. One of the most important ideas in his plan is, accordingly, his
grouping together of school, health centre, cistern, fountain, dance floor and
a social hall to provide some real focus for social life. His rural health sub-
centres, for instance, were places for entertainment and lectures, but also,
given the propensities of Latin Americans, for music and dance.[85] At a time
when he was preparing his book on *Architecture of Social Concern*,[86] the
plans of these buildings not surprisingly always clearly indicate the importance of spaces devoted to community.

Neutra's master plan for the Island of Guam in the late 1940s and early
1950s is another instance of a regionalist approach. Here he explicitly adopted
"regional thinking",[87] a concern for creating a kind of tropical garden city
environment reminiscent of Lewis Mumford's plan for Honolulu. The Guam
Master Plan begs comparison with Neutra's earlier project for Rush City
Reformed which, we would argue, must also be seen as regionalist. This would
explain why Mumford was so positive about it.[88] What Esther McCoy wrote
about Rush City Reformed also holds for Guam. The emphasis was on "reform-
ing" cities that were dominated by the private car – he had Los Angeles
in mind – by creating places for human contact and for contact with nature.
By mixing public transportation to the car, creating in addition to freeways,
local and express elevated train systems, railroads, airports and docks,
all forms of transportation were interlinked, and the city was kept fluid.
While charting the movement of transportation vehicles he also planned for

community, providing neighbourhoods with traffic-free plazas and parks for "face-to-face" encounters, which in spite of their small size were of greater importance to him than extensive parks. All houses, for example, whether row, double or single, always faced on to green, landscaped roads, and children at play were thus safely separated from automobile traffic.[89] The plan also included provisions for neighbourhood and community planning, a hierarchy of roads into primary and secondary systems, and with a strong, typically Neutra-like emphasis on "wholesome" relation to nature and landscaping.

The only other important post-war North American critical tropicalist architect was the young Paul Rudolph, the first Southerner to leave his mark on American architecture (he was raised and schooled in Kentucky, Alabama) since Richardson and Jefferson. Rather than a socially conscious architecture, what he was interested in was a regionalist architecture that was in tune with the latest technological advances. Eager to put the cutting-edge technical experience that he had gained as a marine in the Second World War to use in his chosen, architectural profession, he came up with what he termed the "Cocoon" house, built between 1948 and 1952, in partnership with Paul Twitchell, in Sarasota, Florida. The word "cocoon" itself originated from the expression "wrapped in cocoon", used by the US Government to refer to the durable sprayed-on liquid vinyl chloride acetate copolymer plastic spray sheeting – the immediate predecessor of Saran Wrap – used for packaging industrial equipment, as large as entire airplanes, for outdoor storage.[90] What was hailed as the revolutionary aspect of this new material was that it was a jointless "skin" not affected by movements of structure, and that it was adaptable to any shape regardless of scale, at great savings. What Rudolph appreciated about the new material most was its potential for "light and graceful" structures, for strong and flexible sheet material stronger than steel alloys, and for the possibility it offered of building with a spray gun rather than a crane. His design for the light timber structure of the Cocoon House, a single rectangle with a wooden platform jutting out into the surrounding lagoon, although extremely diminutive in scale, created a sensation when it was built because of the new materials it experimentally incorporated into its design in order to create a building well adapted to the local tropical climate conditions of the Florida Keys – simultaneously with the two other famous glazed houses of the period, the Eames House and the Philip Johnson House, both of 1949 (Figures 2.6 a–g).

It was in South America that post-war tropicalist architecture reached the greatest heights of formal expression. The visual thinking is far superior to anything designed in North America at the time. Here, tropicalism became synonymous with the formal vitality and creativity of the 1940s and 1950s, all based on the art of making strange the Baroque architectural tradition of the region, its sensual curves, its lightness, its transparencies. The formal

(a)

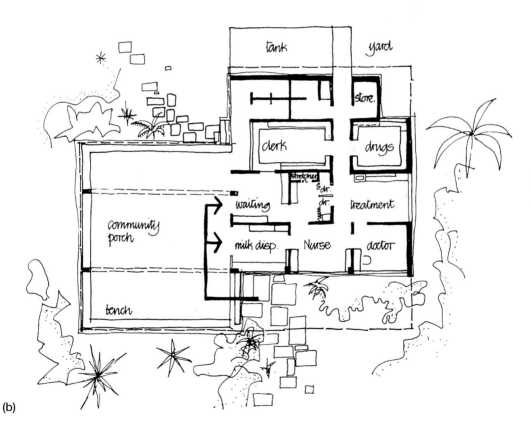

(b)

Figure 2.6 *(a and b) Richard Neutra, Rural Health Center, Puerto Rico, 1944: elevation and ground plan (by permission of Richard Neutra Archives, Pomona, CA)*

(c)

(d)

*Figure 2.6 (cont.) (c) 500-bed District Hospital, Mayaguez, Puerto Rico, 1944
(d) Richard Neutra, Master Plan for Guam: aerial view of a neighbourhood. Through
traffic within the residential area is minimized, an idea that goes back to his Rush City
Reformed of 1927 (by permission of Richard Neutra Archives, Pomona, CA)*

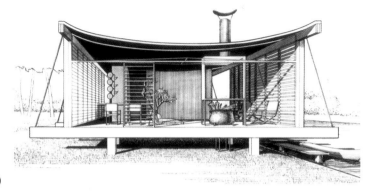

(e)

(f)

(g)

Figure 2.6 (cont.) (e, f and g) Paul Rudolph, the so-called Cocoon House, Sarasota, 1948–50. (Copyright © Ezra Stoller)

richness and variety of the different approaches are remarkable. It was Le Corbusier himself who had introduced the brise soleil. In 1936, he had gone to Rio de Janeiro, Brazil, where he designed the Offices of the Ministry of National Education and Public Health in 1938 with Lucio Costa, Oscar Niemeyer, Affonso Reidy, Carlos Leao Moreira and Ernani Vasconcelos. The brise-soleil, along with the blockwork screen, was used with renewed inventiveness and became the mainstay of 1940s and 1950s tropicalist architecture. Among the many examples are Affonso Reidy's Pedregulho (1950–52) and his Unidade residencial de Gavea (1952), Lucio Costa's Edifcio Caledonia (1954) and Edificio Bristol e Nove Cintra (1948–52), Rino Levi and Roberto Cerqueira Cesar's Edificio Seguradora Brasileira (1946–56). Oscar Niemeyer redefines "Brazilianness" in terms of the sensuous curves of his early projects in Pampúlha (1942–44) Sao Francisco Chapel with its parabolic shells, the circular restaurant and its sun roof, the Yacht Club with its inverted double slope roof Predio of apartment houses in Belo Horizonte (1945) and the Casa de Bailes de Pampúlha (1942). Ricardo Porro's School of Modern Dance and the Plastic Arts (1961–63)[91] represents, carrying over to architecture overt references to the flowing forms of a the female body, and was extremely novel from the formal point of view for the time. Lina Bo Bardi's designs for the Chame Chame House (1958) is also daring, integrating as it does the foliage of the Brazilian rainforest into the walls of her buildings[92] (Figures 2.7 a–c).

Singapore's People's Park Complex (1967–70) and Woh Hup (1973)[93] designed by Design Partnership by Tay Kheng Soon and William Lim are the most ambitious of all the post-war tropicalist projects. In both cases the aim was to recreate traditional forms of urban community in conditions of extreme density that characterize modern, post-independence Singapore. Both projects are highly original. They are mixed-use housing and commercial centres – in fact among the first built in the world. The site of the People's Park Complex had previously been occupied by an open-air night-market in Chinatown, known as People's Park. Woh Hup was especially adventurous as a concept. Compared to Mumford's plan for Honolulu it is more detailed about the issue of circulation. From this point of view it is an heir of theories put forward in Louis Kahn's Philadelphia Plan of 1953, and so is influential on the circulation and movement studies of members of Team Ten, such as the Smithsons and Shadrach Woods, and on the Metabolists.[94] As opposed to Mumford's plan, rather than the low-density blocks, it favours megastructures. As in Neutra's Rush City Reformed, the emphasis was on movement and flow, of consumers, residents, office workers, consumer goods, by light rail, car and forms of public transportation on several levels. It was a city where flow was maximized. Here the architects explored the idea, inspired by the Japanese Metabolists, of how the multiplication of blocks along the urban streets could serve as connectors throughout the tropical city. That in

(a)

(b)

(c)

Figure 2.7 (a) Oscar Niemeyer: The Dance Hall at Pampúlhia (1942–44) (by permission of Oscar Niemeyer); (b) Affonso Reidy, Pedregulho Residential Neighborhood, Rio de Janeiro (1947–52). The winding contour of the building hugs the surrounding landscape. The project includes a clinic, laundry, shops and school; (c) Lina Bo Bardi, the Chame Chame House, Salvador, Bahia, Brazil, 1958 (both by permission of the Institute Lino Bo Bardi)

theory formed the basis for a future cityscape of interconnected internal cool spaces as well as the external sheltered urban and communal spaces, serving as platforms for mass rapid transit stations, bus stops and activity nodes. "Two dimensional planning on the horizontal should give way to planning in four dimensions, introducing the element of the vertical (buildings in height) and the element of time (in transportation and programming of areas for building)", Tay Kheng Soon insisted.[95]

The purpose was not just efficient transportation but, once again, community. Tay Kheng Soon was critical of low-density solutions such as the "bungalow semi-detached dwelling" because it is "self sufficient self-contained, creating no sense of community". Anyone with an appreciation, he continued

> ... for the sense of a city will agree that a true city is a congested city – congestion not of cars but of people drawn close together by a multitude of related activities. We must reject out-dated planning principles that seek to segregate man's activities into arbitrary zones. No matter how attractive it may look in ordered squares on a land use map ... Rather there should be in cities many areas that are of multiple land use where all the advantages of city living – shops, schools, recreation and even work, if not for the main breadwinner, for those who seek a supplementary income – are never far away.[96]

Quoting Lewis Mumford, he wrote that the ideal he had in mind was a city where "work and leisure, theory and practice, private life and public life were in rhythmic interplay ... [where] one part of life flowed into another. No phase was segregated, monopolized, set apart."[97]

Part of the reasoning for this high density solution was also ecological. It helped guarantee the "protection of the agriculture plain", a priority in land-scarce Singapore. At Woh Hup, the ecological concern was responsible for the design of the residential tower block so that each apartment unit would have cross-ventilation, efficiently catching the sea breeze and eliminating the need for air-conditioning.

The People's Park Complex has been the most successful of the two projects. A million people visited it within its first month, and although it was planned as a single building, it has become the epicentre of a network of similar buildings in its vicinity, with pedestrian links across the super highway separating it from Chinatown. As for Woh Hup, although it was planned as the first of four blocks, only one was built. The massive economic development initially planned for the street it is located on moved to another, Orchard Road, thus stranding the one building off from other commercial buildings. Planned as a one of a series, it remained isolated. However, it remains one of the most inventive design concepts not just of the tropics but globally since the Second World War (Figures 2.8 a–c).

Since Tay Kheng Soon and William Lim's projects of the early 1970s, the tropical cities have tended to be subject to unprecedented speculation and

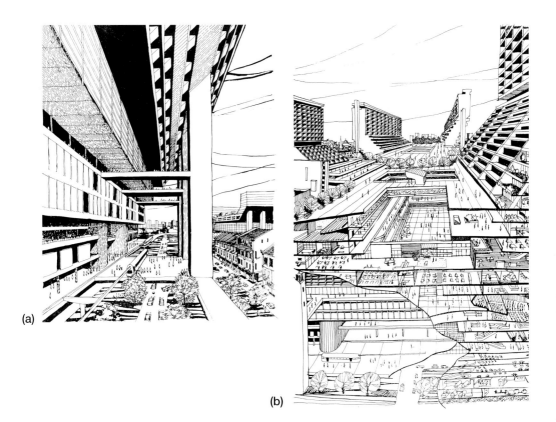

(a)

(b)

(c)

Figure 2.8 (a–c) Design
Partnership, run by
William Lim and Tay
Kheng Soon. These are
three section views of
the initial proposal for
Woh Hup, Singapore,
1972 (by permission of
Tay Kheng Soon and
William Lim)

insensitive development. Tropical cities have become a mass of high-rise buildings unsuited to the climate and the tropical lifestyle. It is only recently that tropical architects have once again begun to rethink their roles, with the work of Kenneth Yeang in Malaysia, Bruno Stagno in Costa Rica, Renzo Piano in New Caledonia, Severiano Porto in Brazil, Gabriel Poole in Australia and Rahul Mehrotra in India, many of whose works are to be found in the present book (Figures 2.9 a–d).

Among the recent projects, Mick Pearce's Eastgate, a mixed-use office and retailing high-rise built in Harare, Zimbabwe, in 1995, is particularly innovative in the way it responds to issues of sustainability. It is a biomorphic project modelled on a bioclimatic control of a typical termite mound that is to be found in the savannah of the countryside. Bernard Rudofsky's *Architecture without Architects* in the early 1960s was an important influence. "It marked my whole evolution as an architect because it opened a whole new world of possibilities. That's when I saw that a bio-climatically efficient architecture could be derived organically rather than mechanistically."[98] But he did not come across the sophisticated insect architects before he watched a television film made by English wildlife film director David Attenborough one day in the early 1990s. It presented the termite mound as an engineering feat. Indeed, termites must live in a constant temperature of exactly 87°C to survive. The difficulty is that the temperature outside fluctuates greatly, from between 35°C at night to 104°C during the day. The solution they have devised is to dig a kind of breeze-catcher at the base of the structure that cools the air by means of chambers carved out of the wet mud below and sends the hot air up through a flue to the top according to a Baroque circuitous Venturi principle. They constantly alter the construction, opening up new tunnels and blocking others to regulate the heat and humidity. The film was a revelation. Since then he has become an avid reader of *New Scientist* from which he gleans architectural ideas. "Buildings are living systems and we have a lot to learn from biologists", he says.

Succinctly put, the principle he has discovered in termite architecture is the use of the thermal mass of a building and the changing environmental conditions to cool it. It is at the heart of Eastgate. The outside is made of four massive masonry and concrete walls inspired by the stone walls to be found in Great Zimbabwe, a city 200 miles southeast of Harare and over 900 years old which was the capital until colonial times (*zimbabwe* means "stone house" in the Shona language). Inside, there is a seven-storey high, naturally lit atrium full of delicately detailed steel lattice girders, suspended walkways on tendons, bridges and filigreed tiaras atop the main entrances to the complex. The hot air is pulled out through 48 brick funnels on the roof, modelled according to Pearce on the wind scoops from Hyderabad that he came across in Rudofsky's book. The building takes advantage of the diurnal temperature swings outside. Normally the high volume fans run at night to give ten air changes per hour and low volume fans run during the day giving two air changes per hour.

For all his organicist claims, Mick Pearce has not rejected mechanics at all. He is simply bending the machine to suit his purposes. His buildings would be impossible, he freely admits, without the help of the mechanical engineers at Ove Arup Associates, with whom he has always worked. "Ove Arup were the only people who could possibly have done it. They were able to build computer models that simulated the temperature and air circulation conditions, and only in the London office. These designs are very much a joint effort." As a result, ventilation running costs for Eastgate are a tenth of those for a comparable air-conditioned building. It uses 35 per cent less energy than the average consumption of six other conventional buildings in Harare and the client has saved 3.5 million dollars on a 36 million dollars building due to the fact that no air conditioning plant had to be imported. This is what makes him say that his architecture is "a regionalized style that responds to the biosphere, to the ancient traditional stone architecture of Great Zimbabwe and to local human resources" (Figure 2.10 a–j).

To Conclude

The kind of critical rethinking Mumford outlined in his many writings on regionalism seems more relevant today than ever before as the forces of globalization come ever more frequently face to face with regional realities – cultural, social, technical, economic and, last but not least, ecological. Nowhere is this more true than in the tropics.

(a)

(b)

Figure 2.9 Gabriel Poole: (a) Closter House; (b) Schubert House; (c); (d) Paradise Drive (by permission of Gabriel Poole)

(c)

(d)

Figure 2.9 (cont.)

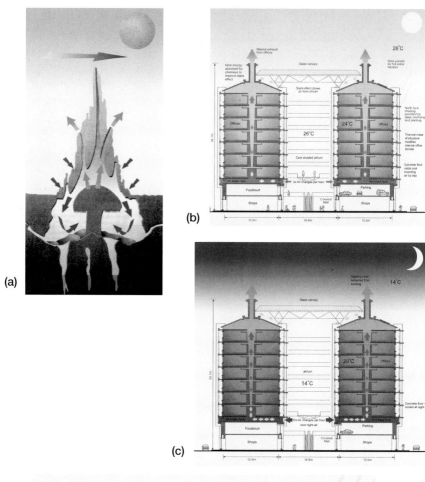

(a)

(b)

(c)

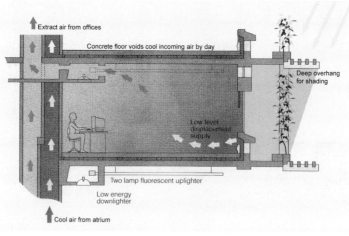

(d)

Figure 2.10 *(a–j) Mick Pearce, Eastgate, Harare, Zimbabwe (1993–1995) (by permission of Mick Pearce)*

L   Offices
M   Suspended concourse
N   Information point
O   Bridges and circulation cores

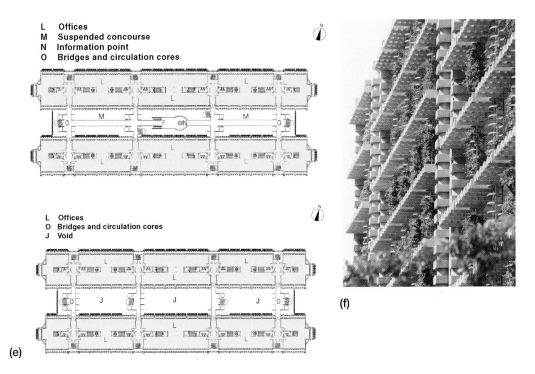

(e)

L   Offices
O   Bridges and circulation cores
J   Void

(f)

(g)

Figure 2.10 (cont.)

(h)

(i)

(j)

Figure 2.10 (cont.)

REFERENCES

1. See Anthony D. King, *The Bungalow. The Production of a Global Culture*. Routledge & Kegan Paul, London, 1985.
2. See Otto Koenigsberger *et al.* (eds) *Manual of Tropical Housing and Building: Pt. 1, Climatic Design*. Longman, London, 1974.
3. See Aladar Olgyay and Victor Olgyay, *Solar Control and Shading Devices*. Princeton University Press, Princeton, 1957 and *Design with Climate; Bioclimatic Approach to Architectural Regionalism*. Princeton University Press, Princeton, 1963.
4. See Jane Drew and Maxwell Fry, *Tropical Architecture in the Humid Zone*. BT, London, 1956; *Tropical Architecture in the Dry and Humid Zones* (2nd edn). R.E. Krieger, Malabar, FL., 1964; *Tropical Architecture in the Humid Zone*, Reinhold, New York, 1956.
5. Frantz Fanon, *The Wretched of the Earth*, 3rd edn, trans. Constance Farrington, Penguin, Harmondsworth, 1990; Edward Said, *Culture and Imperialism*, London, Chatto & Windus, 1993; Gayatri Spivak, *The Postcolonial Critic: Interviews Strategies, Dialogues*, ed. Sarah Harasym, Routledge, New York, 1993; Homi Bhabha, *Nation and Narration*, Routledge, London, 1990; P. Chatterjee, *The Nation and its Fragments: Colonial and Postcolonial Histories*, Princeton University Press, Princeton, 1993; Gulsum Baydar Nalbantoglu and Wong Chong Thai (eds), *Postcolonial Space(s)*, Princeton Architectural Press, Princeton, 1997.
6. Marshall McLuhan, *Understanding Media*, New York, 1964; *The Gutenberg Galaxy*, University of Toronto Press, Toronto, 1965.
7. Saskia Sassen, *Globalization and its Discontents. Selected Essays*, New Press, New York, 1998; Frederick Jameson and Masao Muyoshi (eds), *Cultures of Globalization*; Anthony King, *Culture,Globalization and the World System: Contemporary Conditions for the Representation of Identity*, Basil Blackwell, Oxford; Edward Luttwak, *Turbocapitalism Winners and Losers in the Global Economy*, Harper Perennial, New York, 1999; Anthony Giddens (ed.), *Global Capitalism*, New Press, New York, 2000; and *Runaway World: How Globalization Is Reshaping Our Lives*, Routledge, London, 2000; Ulrich Beck, *What is Globalization*, Blackwell, Oxford, 2000; Richard Falk, *Predatory Globalization: A Critique*, Polity, London, 1999.
8. See José Bové, *Le Monde n'est pas une Marchandise. Des paysans contre la malbouffe*, La Découverte, Paris, 2000.
9. Kevin Dahaner (ed.), *Corporations Are Gonna Get Your Mama: Globalization and the Downsizing of the American Dream*, Common Courage, Boston, 1997, with contributions by Noam Chomsky and Ralph Nader among many others.
10. Saskia Sassen, *The Global City*, Princeton University Press, Princeton, 1992.
11. John Summerson, "Russian Architecture: The Historic Background", *The Architect and Building News*, 23 November 1945. pp. 128–130.
12. For the role of the MoMA in the Cold War international cultural politics see Frances Stonor Saunders, *The Cultural Cold War. The CIA and the World of Arts and Letters*, The New Press, New York, 2000 (first published London, 1999).
13. Elizabeth Mock, *Built in USA since 1932*, New York, Simon & Schuster, 1945. It was translated into German as *In Amerika Erbaut*, Gatje, Wiesbaden, 1948.
14. *America Builds*, Museum of Modern Art Archive, New York, 1944. The complete archive of the captions for the exhibition is to be found in Box 34.
15. Catherine Bauer mentions that Elizabeth Mock is her sister in "Bauer speaks her mind", *Forum*, March 1946, p. 116.

16. See MoMA Staff List, under Kassler, Elizabeth Bauer (Elizabeth Bauer Mock).
17. *Guide to the Records of the Department of Circulating Exhibitions*, Museum of Modern Art Archives, p.v, Box 34 (1).
18. Ibid., Box 34 (1).
19. The first place we mentioned this article in relation to critical regionalism is in Tzonis and Lefaivre and Alofsin, "Die Frage des Regionalismus", in M. Andritsky *et al.* (eds), *Fur eine andere Architektur*, Band 1, Frankfurt, Fischer, 1981, pp. 121–134.
20. Mary Mix, *Americanische Architektur seit 1947*, Allgemeiner Verlag, St. Gallen, 1951.
21. See list of directors of the Architecture Section of the MoMA, compiled by Peter Papademitriou, MoMA.
22. Lewis Mumford, "Skyline", *The New Yorker*, 11 October 1947.
23. "What is Happening to Modern Architecture?", *The Museum of Modern Art Bulletin*, Spring 1948, XV, 3, pp. 8–21, p. 8.
24. Ibid., p. 15.
25. Ibid., p. 13.
26. Ibid.
27. Ibid., p. 18.
28. Sigfried Giedion, "A Decade of New Architecture" in *A Decade of New Architecture*, Girsberger, Zurich, 1951, pp. 1–3.
29. Henry-Russell Hitchcock, "The International Style, Twenty Years Later", *Architectural Record*, August 1951, pp. 89–97.
30. Ibid., p. 92.
31. *Guide to the Records of the Department of Circulating Exhibitions*, Museum of Modern Art Archives., p. v. Box 34.
32. *Built in the USA*, New York, Museum of Modern Art, 1952, p. 8.
33. Ibid., p.9.
34. Ibid. p. 14.
35. See Liane Lefaivre and Alexander Tzonis "Lewis Mumford's Regionalism", in *Design Book Review*, 19, Winter 1991, pp. 20–25 for an overview of Mumford's paradigm of regionalism as culled from his many writings.
36. For an overview of the *longue durée* history of regionalism from the early Renaissance, its successive phases, from Picturesque regionalism to romantic regionalism to nationalistic regionalism see our "Critical Regionalism," in Arie Graafland (ed.) *The Critical Landscape*, 010, Rotterdam, 1996, pp. 126–148.
37. Lewis Mumford, *The South in Architecture*, New York, 1941, p. 13.
38. Ibid., p. 14
39. *The South in Architecture*, pp. 15–16
40. Eric Hobsbawm and Terence Ranger, *The Invention of Tradition*, Canto/Cambridge University Press, Cambridge, 1983.
41. Hugh Trevor-Roper, "The Highland Tradition of Scotland", in ibid., pp. 15–42.
42. Edward Shils, *Tradition*, London, Faber, 1981.
43. Anthony Giddens, *Runaway World: How Globalization is Reshaping our Lives*, Routledge, London, 2000.
44. Shelly Errington, *The Death of Authentic Primitive Art and Other Tales of Progress*, University of California Press, Berkeley, 1998. See in particular her chapter on "The Cosmic Theme Park of the Javanese", pp. 188–227.
45. Alex Tzonis and Liane Lefaivre, "Critical Regionalism", in Spiros Amourgis (ed.) *Critical Regionalism, The Pomona Meeting Proceedings*, California State Polytechnic University, Pomona, 1991, pp. 3–28.

46. Ibid. p.18
47. Ibid., p. 30.
48. Ibid.
49. Edward R. de Zurko, *Origins of Functionalist Theory*, Columbia University Press, New York, 1957.
50. Tzonis and Lefaivre, in Graafland, *Critical Landscapes*.
51. Ibid., p. 32.
52. Ibid., p. 30.
53. The book that impressed him here was Patrick Geddes, *City Development: a Study of Parks, Gardens and Culture Institutes* published in 1904.
54. Lewis Mumford, *Technics and Civilization*, Harcourt, Brace, Jovanovitch, New York, 1934, p. 353.
55. Ibid., pp. 431–433.
56. Lewis Mumford, "Report on Honolulu," in *City Development*, A Wartime Book, New York, 1945, pp. 84–154.
57. Ibid., p.77.
58. Ibid., p. 95.
59. Ibid., pp. 89–90.
60. Ibid., p. 98.
61. See Chapter 12 by Philip Bay in the present book for a reference to this statement of Lee Kuan Yu.
62. *The South in Architecture*, p.95.
63. Reyner Banham, *Theory and Design of the First Machine Age*, Architectural Press, London, 1960.
64. Richard Neutra, *Wie baut Amerika?* Hoffmann, Stuttgart, 1927.
65. See Mumford's *New Yorker* article of 8 January 1949, p. 60.
66. See F.O. Matthiessen, *American Renaissance*, Oxford University Press, London, 1941, and David Reynolds, *Beneath the American Renaissance. The Subversive Imagination in the Age of Emerson and Melville*, Harvard University Press, Cambridge, Mass. 1988.
67. "Report on Honolulu", p. 90.
68. *The South in Architecture*, p. 32.
69. See Udo Kulterman, *New Architecture in Africa*, Thames and Hudson, London, 1963, and *New Directions in African Architecture*, Studio Vista, London, 1969.
70. *The South in Architecture*, p. 32.
71. Lewis Mumford, *New Yorker*, 11 October 1947.
72. Ernesto Rogers, "Our Responsibility Towards Tradition", *Casabella*, August 1954.
73. Ernesto Rogers, "The Existing Environment and the Practical Content of Contemporary Architecture", *Casabella*, February 1955.
74. Kenzo Tange, in *New Frontiers in Architecture*, CIAM'59 in Otterlo, Oscar Newman, (ed.), Universe, New York, 1961, pp. 170–182.
75. Minnette da Silva, *Minnette da Silva, The Life and Work of an Asian Woman Architect*, Minnette da Silva Ltd, Kandy, 1998. Vol. 1. All quotes and illustrations here are taken from that book. See also Lina Bo Bardi, *Lina Bo Bardi*, Edizioni Charta, Milan, 1994.
76. *Minnette da Silva*, pp. 116–117.
77. Ibid.
78. Ibid., p. 190.
79. Ibid., p.126.
80. Ibid., p. 126.
81. Jane Drew and Maxwell Fry, *Tropical Architecture*.

82. See Liane Lefaivre and Alexander Tzonis, Shadrach Woods, "Beyond Monuments". In *Shadrach Woods*, Architectural Press, London, 1989.

83. Richard Neutra, *Mystery and Realities of the Site*, New York, Morgan & Morgan, 1951.

84. Sigfried Giedion, "R.J. Neutra. European and American" in W. Boesiger (ed.) *Richard Neutra Buildings and Projects*, Zurich, Girsberger, 1951, introduction by S. Giedion.

85. Ibid., pp. 168–183.

86. Richard Neutra, *Architecture of Social Concern*, São Paolo, Gerth Todtman, 1948.

87. Richard Neutra in W. Boesiger (ed.) *Richard Neutra, 1950–60*, Girsberger, Zurich, 1959, pp. 228–229.

88. See, once again, Mumford's *New Yorker* article of 8 January 1949, p. 60. He wrote that "that kind of thinking should now be resumed and perhaps public competitions should be held to enlist the imagination of the younger generation of architects and planners . . .".

89. Esther McCoy, *Richard Neutra*, George Braziller, New York, 1960, p. 25. "The common use space for the community gathering area of our towns has shrunk disastrously, although pavement may amount to as much as a deplorable 35 per cent of the total urban ground."

90. See "Rudolph and the Roof; How to make a Revolution on a Small Budget", *House and Home*, June 1953, pp. 140–141.See also: Guy Rothenstein, "Sprayed-on Vinyl-Plastic Sheeting", *Progressive Architecture*, July 1953, pp. 98–99.

91. John Loomis, *Revolution of Forms, Cuba's Forgotten Art Schools*, Princeton Architectural Press, New York, 1999.

92. Lina Bo Bardi, *Lina Bo Bardi*, Edizioni Charta, Milan, 1994.

93. See Rem Koolhaas's "Singapore Songlines", *S,M,L, XL*, pp. 1011–1087. He does not deal with them as tropicalist buildings, however.

94. See Lefaivre and Tzonis, "Beyond Monuments" in *Shadrach Woods*.

95. Tay Kheng Soon, "Environment and Nation Building", September 1967, 65–67 *SPUR*, Singapore, pp.43–48, p. 46.

96. Ibid.

97. Ibid., p. 43.

98. Mick Pearce, interview with Liane Lefaivre, August 2000.

CHAPTER 3

GLOBALIZATION:
SOME CULTURAL DILEMMAS

Gerardo Mosquera

THE GLOBAL WORLD

What we call globalization does not consist of an effective interconnection of the whole planet by means of a reticular network of communication and exchange. In reality, our global world's structure is rather an atlas of radial nuclei and "unplugged" areas that keeps large zones of silence. These zones are disconnected among them, or just connected indirectly via self-decentralized centres. From them circuits that articulate an *urbi et orbi* dynamic are structured.

There has been little progress in south–south linking, other than economic recessions. It is true that globalization has activated and pluralized cultural circulation, but it has done so following the same channels designed by the economy, largely reproducing the power structures. The lack of horizontal interaction is a post-colonial legacy barely modified. The economic, cultural and communicational pivots are still headed towards the old – and some new – metropolis. This situation urges the peripheries to undertake stronger efforts to establish and develop horizontal circuits that act as cultural life spaces. Such circuits will contribute to pluralize culture, internationalizing it in the real sense, legitimizing it in their own terms, constructing new epistemes, unfolding alternative actions. The Institute of Tropical Architecture represents an example in that direction.

In a sense, globalization is perhaps more about enclosing than opening. The world gets increasingly urban as a human flood displaces constantly from the countryside to the overcrowded megalopolis. These are permanently extending, swallowing towns and nearby landscapes, and even uniting with one another, as is going to happen with São Paulo and Rio de Janeiro. Or spring out of the blue, as occurs in China. Globalization bears a massive and infinite process of concentration from the peripheries to the centres. Almost one half of the world's population lives today in urban environments. This situation creates multiple physical and mental displacements.

The border is one of the major themes of our time. Globalization, migrations, falling of walls, strengthening of others and the erection of new ones, changes in maps and transterritorializations of every type have problematized the very notion of "border". We speak of border culture in terms of osmosis. Crossing physical and mental borders is today the rule.

The great paradigm of global opening is the Internet. Paradoxically, it depends on the screen, the most captivating cloister of our time, the contemporary monastic cell. It is interesting that science fiction and other discourses have always imagined the future in terms of cities, inner spaces and urban technology. Space epics' narratives are more about the extremely constricted hi-tech environment of a spacecraft than about infinity.

THE GLOBALIZATION OF DIFFERENCE

Globalization has marked two opposing cultural processes. Their interaction constitutes a critical point in the rearticulations of symbolic power, and a paradox that signals the epoch. On the one hand, it constitutes the *de post* moment of expansion of industrial capitalism, which is part of the extension of Europe and its culture since the Renaissance. This expansion has been narrated as a story of the expansion of the world. The acquisition of worldwide power was seen as a globalization: the local-Western became universal through the conquest of planetary power, colonialism and the construction of a totalizing rationality from that power. The idea of expansion culminated in an inverse notion, that of contraction: "the world becomes smaller day by day", and even a global village.

Western culture was imposed as an operating metaculture of the contemporary world. This was done with the purpose of conversion and domination, but implicitly meant generalized access. If imposition seeks to convert the Other, access facilitated using this metaculture for the "Other's" own, different ends, transforming the metaculture from within. Western metaculture has become a paradoxical means for the affirmation of difference, and for the rearticulating subaltern camp's interest in post-colonial times.

Hence globalization times are simultaneously those of the difference. This is the other contradictory process to which I referred at the beginning. The existence of an operative metaculture has allowed the globalization of difference beyond the local environments. This cultural globalization implies an interaction between the extended Western metaculture and the cultural plurality of the world. If the first maintains its hegemonic character, the others have taken advantage of its capacity for international broadcasting to supersede local frameworks.

There has always been a pressure from power to assimilate and use alien elements for its own benefit. Western metaculture has procured elements of other cultures, absorbing them for its own use, while globalizing fragments of the rest of the world's cultures from a hegemonic point of view. But employed from the other side, this metaculture has permitted the diffusion of different perspectives, and has undergone modifications in accordance with these perspectives. Imposed by colonialism and in spite of it, globalization has become an instrument for decolonization and the international activity of the new countries of Africa, Asia and the Caribbean.

Besides, any vast expansion, such as Buddhism in Asia or the Latin language in the Roman Empire, carries a high degree of tension that opens pores and cracks. This globalization–differentiation process is an intricate conflictive articulation of forces more than dual dialectics. It implies contaminations,[1] mixtures and contradictions in many directions. Although it directs current processes of culture, it cannot be taken passively, as a necessary inclination that occurs without any pressure exerted by the subaltern sectors. Among other problems, there is the metacultural tendency to generalize practices from many diverse environments – from yoga to karate – in a consumer-driven, culturally "aseptic" method as isolated elements of a cosmopolitan mosaic. Nevertheless, some of the most successful experiences in non-occidental regions have consisted, as in the case of Japan, in managing Westernization to their benefit, empowering it from their own different background.

It is in this labyrinth of displacements and ambiguities where the current cultural power lies. It becomes more evident that at this point there is no viable return to pre-colonial traditions, because that would consist precisely of regression to the myth of an unpolluted past with a small margin of action in the contemporary world. The issue is to build the contemporary from a plurality of experiences that are able to transform the metaculture. I am not referring only to processes of hybridization, resignification and syncretism, but to orientations and inventions of the global metaculture from subaltern positions. The key point is who exerts the cultural decision,[2] and for whose benefit it is taken. A utopian agenda would envision a metaculture rebuilt on a much broader plurality of perspectives. The post-colonial structure makes this extremely difficult due to the distribution of power and the limited possibilities for action that vast sectors have today.

THE CULTURAL DEBATE

Even when imposed by a dominant culture over a dominated one, cultural appropriation is not a passive phenomenon. Receivers always transform, resignify and use according to their visions and interests. Appropriation, and especially the "incorrect" one, is usually a process of originality, understood as a new creation of meaning. Peripheries, due to their location in the maps of economic, political, cultural and symbolic power, have developed a "culture of resignification" of the repertoires imposed by the centres. It is a transgressing strategy from positions of dependency. Besides confiscating for their own use, appropriation functions by questioning the canons and authority of the central paradigms. As stated by Nelly Richard, authoritarian and colonizing premises are thus disarranged, meanings re-elaborated, "deforming the original (and in the end questioning the dogma of its perfection), trading reproductions and de-generating versions in the parodic trance of the copy".[3] It does not mean only a disassembling of totalizations in the Postmodern spirit, since it also involves the anti-Eurocentric deconstruction of self-reference in the dominant models, and, further, of every cultural model.

Conscious and selective cultural "antropophagy" (a critical appropriation of the dominant culture), proclaimed by Brazilian Modernists in the 1920s, has been a constant in Latin American modernisms, curiously pre-Postmodern. The tensions of the double prefix underscore the intricacy of this cultural yarn in an already heterogeneous and fragmentary environment. "Anthropophagy" is not a seemingly fluid programme, because it is not carried forward in a neutral but in a submitted terrain, with a praxis that tacitly assumes the contradictions of dependency and post-colonial "deformities". Who eats whom?

Another problem is that the flow cannot be always in the same north–south direction, driven by the power structure, its diffusion circuits, and accommodation to them. No matter how plausible the appropriating and transculturing strategy might be, it implies a rebound action that reproduces the hegemonic structure. The problem remains although the strategy confronts domination, and even takes advantage of it in the form of those martial arts that combat without weapons, using the force of a more powerful adversary. It is also necessary to invert the flow. Not only to turn a binary transference scheme, challenging its power, but also to contribute to an enriching pluralization in a truly global sense.

Today culture constitutes a post-cold-war tension field, where hegemonic and subaltern social forces struggle. Beyond that, cultural factors are gaining more importance in the social fabric, in reconfigurations of power and international politics. As analysed by Samuel P. Huntington, the alignments defined by ideology are giving way to those defined by culture.[4]

Cultural debate has become a political arena for power struggle, both in the symbolic and the social aspects. The debate takes place on assimilation, tokenism, rearticulation of hegemonies, affirmation of difference, critique of power, and appropriations and redefinition in all directions, among other tensions. If stimulating pluralism is a basic feature of Postmodernism, the implied decentring remains under the control of centres that "self-decentre" in a Lampedusan strategy of changing so that everything remains the same. Today hegemonic forces do not seek to repress or homogenize diversity, but to control it. However, the strategy itself responds to a different distribution of power, and the disadvantaged groups exert increasingly active pressure and infiltration.

It is seen both in the cultural adjustments that the subaltern and peripheral sectors are making, as well as in the heterogenization that immigrants are causing in the contemporary megalopolis. Every large city today is a dynamic crossroads of cultures. There are many and diverse people "incorrectly"[5] and unabashedly reworking Western metaculture in their own way, de-Eurocentralizing it in plural form. What we call Postmodernity is, in good measure, the result of the overlapping of all of these contradictory processes. They also determine an extraordinary dynamic of identities, with complex adjustments: multiple identities, identities in the form of Chinese boxes, neo-identities, mixture of identities, displacement among them, "ethnic games". . . . All borders mutate and turn into the critical spaces of our age.

The border and its culture have become paradigms of contemporary cultural processes. But these and other paradigms are at risk of developing into a narrative of harmonization of diversity, levelling contradictions and masking confrontations of interests. There is a certain Postmodern optimism in this sense, which is observed, for example, in recent anthropology. It can be a tonic, but also an accommodation. Key categories such as "appropriation", "post-national", "decentring", "syncretism", "rearticulation", "negotiation", "community", "deterritorialization" and "transculturation" have a tendency to be used in a very affirmative way, without criticism. There is also a naive tendency to think of globalization in terms of a world of transterritorial contacts in all directions. All of this can lead towards a complacency in subordination that inhibits response to change. It can jag the critical edge of culture, believing all are participating – deceptively – in the global pie. To paraphrase George Orwell, globalization is more global for some than for others, the majority.

REFERENCES

1. Jean Fisher, "Editorial: Some Thoughts on 'Contamination'", *Third Text* (London) Fall 1995, 32, pp. 3–7.
2. Guillermo Bonfil Batalla, "Lo Propio y lo Ajeno: Una Aproximación al Problema del Control Cultural". In Adolfo Colombres (ed.), *La Cultura Popular*, 1987, México City, pp. 79–86, and "La Teoría del Control Cultural en el Estudio de Procesos Étnicos", *Anuario Antropológico*, University of Brasilia, No. 86, 1988, pp. 13–53. See also Ticio Escobar, "Issues in Popular Art". In Gerardo Mosquera (ed.), *Beyond the Fantastic: Contemporary Art Criticism from Latin America,* INIVA and MIT Press, London, 1995, pp. 91–113.
3. Nelly Richard, "Latinoamérica y la Postmodernidad: la Crisis de los Originales y la Revancha de la Copia". In her *La Estratificación de los Márgenes*, Francisco Zegers, Santiago, 1989, p. 55.

4. Samuel P. Huntington, *The Clash of Civilizations and the Remaking of World Order*, Touchstone, New York, 1996.
5. Boris Bernstein, "Algunas Consideraciones en Relación con el Problema 'Arte y Etnos'", *Criterios*, Havan, 5–12, January 1983–December 1984, p. 267.

CHAPTER 4

TROPICALITY*

Bruno Stagno

"I have discovered what the Greeks ignored: uncertainty"

Jorge Luis Borges

PROLOGUE

In 1973 I went to live in Costa Rica, a tropical country engaged in conservation and the protection of the environment. I had previously studied architecture in Chile and in France; in schools strongly influenced by the Modern Movement, and most particularly by Le Corbusier. My participation on one of his many projects in France was not only the logical continuation of that education but also its culmination.

Moving to the tropics meant for me an immersion in a new world that I discovered little by little. It was a world that I had to adapt to in order to understand it. I was accustomed to Cartesian thought and forming conclusions accordingly but, very soon, my everyday experiences led me to doubt the universal application of this method and the presumed infallibility of its rational logic. I began to realize that there were other forms of thought that could enrich understanding and that regional literature had commented on this fact.

In this style of thinking I found an explanation for the way that people behave. It also gave me a personal incentive to consider the realities of tropical life and form theories on it. I soon came to understand that an attitude, which privileged humanist values in relationships, predominated, as a definite approach in the decision-making process, and so outweighed the reasoned approach. A life that alternated between rigorous reason and pliant interconnectivity, and in which both competed for dominance, presented me with a fresh intellectual environment. Here the precision of reason coexisted in perfect harmony with the wisdom of imagination.

The sensuality that pervades the atmosphere infiltrates the intellect of the tropics and influences reasoning. The natural environment of the tropics, already at variance with that of other latitudes, is a colonized territory in which there has been a cultural invasion. That has produced an amazing consequence, because the existing culture has been only partially transformed by the incoming mode of thought. In the tropics, philosophy did not develop any interest in the essence of being, as has been said by Edouard Glissant, who confirms this by quoting the Cuban writer Alejo Carpentier; who referred to this characteristic of tropicality by stating: "This is what distinguishes tropicality from Occidental cultures; especially those derived from European cultures where the absolute equals the essence of being and where the self cannot exist unless it is conceived of as the absolute."[1]

Due to this preoccupation with the essence of being, tropical cultures have been perceived as ingenuous or even primitive. However, I am convinced that this appearance of ingenuousness and innocence is only an insignificant façade of tropicality conjured up by a comparison with more metropolitan philosophies. Such rational and systematic philosophies, centred on the consideration of the essence of being, tend towards idealization and are fundamentally abstract. This is why it becomes so hard to understand a tropicality that is rich in relationships and multiple subjectivities. In this

Figure 4.1 *Wild forest, French Guyana, drawn by Laroche, in accordance with M.E. Viaud, Gravure de Best, Hotelin et Cie, in* L'Illustration, La France au Dela des Mers, *1843*

tropical culture, humanity submerges itself in a storm of disparate sensa-   *67*
tions, which permanently engulf humanity and induce an emotional state in
which sensuality is vital. This state is characterized by a regenerative optimism which, at worst, leads to anguish; in contrast with that pessimism and
metaphysical depression typical of a philosophy, whose central theme is a
reflection on the essence of being.

This is why, in order to understand tropicality, it is more appropriate to
think, as Glissant says: "In a poetics of relationships, more than in a poetics
of being."[2] This allows us to claim that (in the tropics): man exists in proportion to his integration with a place (I am here, therefore I am); that challenges the principle of "I think therefore I am". This contradicts, or at least
questions, the concept of "*cogito ergo sum*", which is more engaged with the

Figure 4.2 Amazon waiting for the Indian in her hammock, according to
the ritual depicted by Cristobal de Acuña, published in Voyages Autour du
Monde, Woodes Rogers, Amsterdam 1717

Figure 4.3 *Most of the Caledonian houses are dressed in white in response to the climate: the heat.* Maisons Calédonnienes, *Editions Solaris, Nouméa, 1989, p. 34*

Figure 4.4 *"La forêt vierge", Henri J.-F. Rousseau*

essence of being. This quality is presented as one of the most defining char-
acteristics of tropicality, since it perceives life in relation to its environment.
Salman Rushdie, the Indian writer, comments on one of the characters in
Midnight's Children whose tropicality had been lost: ". . . had succumbed
to abstraction, had embraced the cause of truth and made illusions flee"[3]
(Figure 4.4).

INTRODUCTION

Since the Enlightenment a belief that privileges the sole dominance of a single
system of reasoning has become widespread. Within the circles where modern
thought originated, this has become the only universally accepted way of
thinking. However, René Descartes warned about its limitations, in stating

Figure 4.5 Colegio panamericano – detail of roof
(architect and photo Bruno Stagno)

that: "It is good to know something about the customs of other peoples, in order to judge our own more accurately and avoid thinking that everything which is the opposite of ours is ridiculous or unreasonable, as is said by those who have never seen anything."[4]

The Enlightenment was characterized, above all, by its belief in the power of reason as a system of thought and in the possibility of reorganizing society down to the roots on rational principles. It is a well-known fact that European philosophers, from the seventeenth century onwards, searched for a fully rational interpretation of reality. This was an attempt to reduce reality to an idealization more susceptible to rational configuration. The Cartesian method, which was erected as a universal model, despite what we have said about the author, is a good example of such an attitude.

This situation led to the dismissal of a variant system of thought, which was more subjective than objective. This system had been scorned or, at the least, perceived as primitive and, more specifically, ingenuous. Thus, it was disregarded as a system of thought. Its methodology of reflection was also discounted and, therefore, its results were not considered as intelligent by those accustomed to "think according to the Enlightenment way of thinking".

Cartesian thought, as expressed in the *Discourse of Method*, arose from the desire of the author to establish absolute truth; on which to build a

Figure 4.6 Colegio panamericano – façade
(architect and photo Bruno Stagno)

system of thought, founded on certainties, primarily applicable to sciences such as geometry, physics and algebra. This method, which examines each part in order to understand the whole, leads, step by step, to a conclusion. It begins with an analysis, which selects elements or variables, concentrating on those which are relevant. The fewer variables that are in play the more effective and rapid is the process and the more coherent the conclusion becomes. Each conclusion arrives as an unsuspected development and, paradoxically, becomes a law, which acts as a norm for the subsequent stages of the process. If obeyed, these norms will condition an important part of human behaviour.

However, it is necessary to understand that rational Cartesian thought is not the only way to think coherently. Despite its abstraction and simplicity and its having been applied for some centuries, its hegemony has not been truly established globally. One cannot help but be concerned about the fact that during scientific procedures (in which analysis and experimentation are the basis for progress) intuition, subjectivity, and even fortuitous coincidence play an important role. This leads us to presume that these must form part of a way of thought that has as much validity as rational Cartesian thought.

In those social sciences that study human behaviour there is, at least, an acknowledgement of the existence of mental developments possessing another rationality. These are the cause of behaviours as explicable and valid as those that are guided by Cartesian thought. For Claude Levi-Strauss this form of thought exists alongside others, which he refers to as "domesticated" and which are, essentially, specialized ways of thought oriented towards productivity. This becomes even more evident and unquestionable in relation to creativity in the visual arts. In this respect, Zimbabwean novelist and curator Yvonne Vera points out (after visiting an extraordinary exhibition of African art in Zurich) that: ". . . it was possible to see the vast universe of ritual, play and the potential life that these figures embodied. I envy an African world, which has engendered, with innate and flourishing ability, such an unmatched confluence of reason and aesthetics . . . and to experience this vividly, rather than theoretically, is liberating."[5]

This other way of thought is not as pure or linear and therefore is less single minded. From the beginning, it has been affected by an impossibility or unwillingness to prioritize variables. The stages are not in sequence and it is frequently difficult to recognize any stages. Therefore, the conclusions cannot be considered as norms because they are relative, transient and consequently fluid. We are looking at a way of thought that is centred more on doubt than on any search for absolute certainty. This is the kind of thought that predominates in the tropics.

One of the consequences of such a way of thought is that this tropical latitude has been subjected, for centuries, to a racial and cultural hybridization. This has become distilled into unique modalities of reflection that widen the vision of existence. We have learned to finely blend various extremes, resulting in the creation of new realities, which differ from the original components. Such a hybrid culture enhances the autochthonous, by incorporating new contributions and thereby becoming an alternative.

The spirit of relativity that pervades and surrounds this style of thinking, together with the countless variables in play, create a complex and diverse way of thinking with multiple certainties. These certainties are not only relative, but they also vary in their nature in accordance to the balance between the variables. This happens, likewise, with the deductive process, for it is neither a method nor a succession of postulates, for these are not absolute truths in the minds of those engaged in tropical thinking. However, there is a form of deduction that seeks resolution. These resolutions are short lived because their validity is determined by the hierarchy and the number of variables, which are generally numerous and diverse. Therefore, the conclusions do not have the normative rigour of Cartesian conclusions. This is

Figure 4.7 *Colegio panamericano – façade (architect and photo Bruno Stagno)*

explained by Alejo Carpentier when he claims that: "In refusing to acknowledge the '*cogito ergo sum*', (which has been debarred from any relevance,
in an ethos where what matters is the 'We feel therefore we exist') we do
not comprehend any reason or philosophy other than the sense of the sense-
less in our confused anatomies."

Tropical thought not only represents an alternative to the mode of
thought imposed by the Enlightenment, but is also utilized by most of the
planet, being for its denizens a beacon in the decision-making process.
Psychological, sentimental and sensual aspects play an equal part with
rational aspects in the deductive process that practises this thought. Such
aspects enable reason to recognize that rationality itself can surpass the
narrow confines within which it has been imprisoned by those who practise
Cartesian thought. In fact, these aspects expand the boundaries of rationality
and enrich thought.

The multiplicity of these aspects is, perhaps, the cause of the abundance,
novelty, surprise and astonishment produced by both the results and
the manifestations that arise from tropical thinking. The abundance is the

Figure 4.8 *Colegio panamericano – rear view*
(architect and photo Bruno Stagno)

Figure 4.9 Restored
shophouse, Bangkok,
Thailand. Ping
Amranand and William
Warren, Heritage
Homes of Thailand,
The Siam Society
Under the Royal
Patronage, Thailand,
1999, p. 84 (with
permission from The
Siam Society Under
Royal Patronage)

Figure 4.10 Typical wooden construction on the sea shore, Atlantic zone, Caribbean coast, Costa Rica. Photo: Pepito Torres (by permission of Instituto de Arquitectura Tropical)

consequence of the large amount of data and variables in play. The novelty comes from the pattern given to variables, the surprise from the fact that this pattern is not always predictable and the astonishment occurs because of the revelations that arise.

Is this tropical thought chaotic? It does not seem to be. It is, instead, a diverse thought where, surprisingly (after experiencing and living it), its logic becomes predictable. That is because (in the different cultures that practise it) certain variables are observed with stable weightings or at least regularity and also some variables are recurrent. This is what allows us to recognize attitudes and elements that constitute a tradition.

It can be concluded that the culture of tropical thought possesses distinctive features that distinguish it from Cartesian thought. It happens because people in the tropics practise reason in their own way. Tropical thought is diverse because it embraces many and different variables that coexist in time and space. This practice creates in its cultural expressions an effect of rich diversity that can be unmistakably recognized as a tropical mode of life. Therefore, we can say that if Cartesian thought is linear, tropical thought is spatial or fundamentally holistic.

Figure 4.11 Coulbary, a Galibis Indian city, Mana river, French Guyana, drawn by Laroche, in accordance with M.E. Viaud, Gravure de Best, Hotelin et Cie, in L'Illustration, La France au Dela des Mers, *1843*

LATITUDE AND TROPICAL THOUGHT

Looking at the picture of a humble house in Thailand, I became confused, being convinced that it was in Costa Rica. It had garish colours, eaves, wooden walls and various details and, above all, the architectural expression made it look as if it was Costa Rican. The similarity was so strong that I began to ponder it. How could it be possible that two peoples, located at the antipodes of the planet, with different religions, traditions and histories, had such a similar popular architecture?

Thailand and Costa Rica share the same parallel, they are at a similar distance from the Equator, on the tenth parallel. This implies that there are

Figure 4.12 *Hua Hin, Thailand. Ping Amranand and William Warren,* Heritage Homes of Thailand, *The Siam Society under Royal Patronage, Thailand, 1996, p. 147 (with permission from The Siam Society Under Royal Patronage)*

similarities in their climate, vegetation and, particularly, in the environment that surrounds life. That environment is the sum of all the natural elements that condition life and that mould life experiences in a characteristic manner. The amount of rain, the abundant sunlight, the dancing light, the seductive air, the exuberant vegetation, the torrid temperature and humidity determine and condition life in the tropics as much as anthropological factors, cultural heritage, religious beliefs and historical determinants. The constant presence of these imposing natural conditions brings to our mind a well-known saying in architecture: "The architecture which begins by defying tropical nature ends by deferring to it."

Figure 4.13 *Tropical colours on Kititong Villa in Hua Hin, Thailand. Ping Amranand and William Warren,* Heritage Homes of Thailand, *The Siam Society Under Royal Patronage, Thailand, 1996, p. 142 (with permission from The Siam Society Under Royal Patronage)*

Tropical latitude is something singular and constitutes a species of global regionalism that embraces the entire tropical belt of the planet. It is in this band that conditions prevail for a life which, ruled by the pattern of tropicality, is not only characterized by the portrayal and expression of its cultural identity but also by its way of thinking. Diversity is evident within this region of the planet but it exists in contradistinction to a sameness of responses. This fact can be observed in the architecture because, when we look east and west from our home viewpoint, across the tropical belt, we discover surprising similarities in architectural solutions. This belt, despite being multinational and multicultural, is consistently characterized by the fact that concrete and imaginary realities coexist there and share an alternating hegemony, by way of a constant game of surprises and perplexities that provokes unwonted results.

Life in the tropics is under the permanent dominion of sensuality. This is evoked by the presence of an exuberant vegetation, under a sky inhabited by capricious clouds; by the hammock with its soft swaying; by the importance of the shade that gathers; by the breeze that refreshes and evaporates the sweat of the skin; by the rain, the bracing sun and the multiple mirages. The noises at night come from vigorous nature: the sound of the buds when they blossom, the rustle of animals free and unleashed, the dense, powerful perfume of humidity wafting in the air.

Figure 4.14 Pedregulho Housing Development, Río de Janeiro, 1946, Arch. Affonso Eduardo Reidy. Affonso Eduardo Reidy, *Editions Blau, Instituto Lina Bo e P.M. Bardi, Brasil, 2000, p. 91 (by permission of Editorial Blau and Instituto Lina Bo Bardi)*

The air is laden with moisture that is imbued with the polychromy of sunlight from dawn to dusk, a rainbow being its greatest expression. Everything travels with the air, the smell of moisture, the heat and its solidity that impinges on people as they walk and that we feel as a cloud that enfolds us in lethargy. Air in the tropics is never neutral or indifferent. It is an actor that communicates and arouses sensations and conspires to create this particular atmosphere. Let the air pass and the messages of nature will permeate, as is understood by the builder who allows the breeze to pass through his house.

The tropics are a festival of the senses, a carnival of feelings. Sometimes, this excess of sensations produces, in an outside observer, an overwhelming confusion and bewilderment.

Their way of thought is a determining feature of people from the tropics and is so distinctive that it constitutes a subject for classical analysis, as yet scarcely studied systematically. Tropical thinking encompasses the hallmark traits of tropicality. This provides us with the basis for considering that there is no unique, universal logic and the evidence to prove that various forms of logic exist or cohabit on the planet.

The diversity of tropical thinking is particularly evident in the visual arts, literature, architecture and also the social sciences. An example of this comes from African intellectuals such as Gomdaogo Pierre Nakoulima. In 1997 at his Ivory Coast conference Is Development Still Desirable? (regarding the imposition of a Western model of development by economist and sociologists)

Figure 4.15 *Tropical verandah (photo Bruno Stagno)*

Figure 4.16 *Typical beach of the central Pacific coast, Costa Rica. Photo: Pepito Torres (by permission of Instituto de Aquitectura Tropical)*

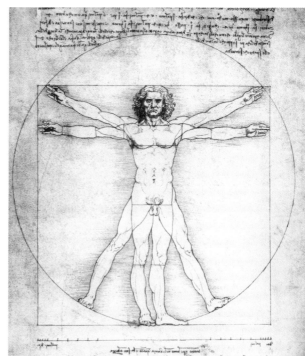

Figure 4.17 *"L'Uomo Vitruviano", 1490, Leonardo da Vinci, Venezia. Gallerie dell' Academia*

he said: ". . . also they never understood that each society seeks to fulfil its own objectives and that we can only measure the degree of satisfaction obtained in relation to those objectives. Finally, they had obscured the fact that each society lives in its own universe and that each universe imposes a particular logic on the cultural expressions of its members and particular objectives to their actions."[6] In this clear statement, philosopher Nakoulima, highlights the root causes for the failure of the mimetic model of development. It refers to the fact that national elites evinced a strong inclination towards standardization along the lines of Western thought, abandoning the intellectual bounty of any variants.

The universally known figure of Vitruvian man became a canonic figure, for the archetype of Renaissance man, as a prosperous and balanced synthesis of the ideal man. Which man was depicted as a frontal portrait against a background according to a geometrical design regulated by rules of proportion that were assumed to be perfect. In other words it was a creation of the intellect (possessing more idealization than reality) which manifested a concrete design that heightened the emphasis on the perfection of being. This led to the exaltation of a human archetype of perfection (proposed by the Renaissance and inherited by Modernity) which is oblivious to externals and only conscious of the inner self.

Figure 4.18 *"Ville Imaginaire", Prefète Duffaut, Haiti. "L'oeil existe à l'état sauvage", André Breton*

This thought, as applied to architecture and urbanism, inspired ideal cities designed in an abstract manner and conceived on the drawing board, according to rules of proportion, within which the behaviour of the inhabitants was as preordained as the geometry of the drawings. The quest was to establish the governance of a divine superorder that was also mundane and constructed to enhance the lives of mankind. This presents evidence of a desire for the domination of a single rationality above all others. In the case

Figure 4.19 "The ideal city", Piero della Francesca, 1470

Figure 4.20 Aula Magna, Universidad Central de Venezuela, 1952. (Architect and photo Carlos Raúl Villanueva)

of the Americas, Europe discounted the Indian peoples as part of mankind, because they had a different way of thinking and reasoning. This is a clear demonstration of the opposition between a rationality guided by divine order and another guided by natural order.

Following the discovery of America, the dominance of European thought began to be challenged by the reflections of Montaigne in France and Thomas More in England. They spoke of the existence of other worlds equally ordered and equally inhabited by humans who, although different, were similarly civilized. In their writings they made specific reference to the peoples of the tropical Americas. While making these references they were taken aback but at the same time acknowledged that such a novel way of life contributed to a harmony of relationships. Within this harmony nature played a significant role. There are even thinkers who attribute to this discovery the creation of egalitarian societies that once lived in social peace.

This harmonious coexistence is expressed with stark clarity in an engraving which depicts a group of American Indians (created by a conquistador artist), in which the concept of the Vitruvian ideal contrasts with the concept of a more relaxed self, in greater contact with daily reality and noticeably tensionless, if compared with the tense muscles of the Vitruvian man in search of the equilibrium of its ideal of perfection.

Figure 4.21 Ford Headquarters, San Jose, Costa Rica
(architect and photo Bruno Stagno)

More than three centuries have gone by, yet the world has still not experienced, and even resists implementing (wholeheartedly and comprehensively) the concepts of Enlightenment. That is in the sense that philosophy and all humanity wanted to be free of ancestral fetters and to adhere strictly to the dictates of reason. For Kant the purpose of the Enlightenment was to rid humanity of immaturity.[7] The predominance of Enlightenment thought in Modernity, the practice of rationalism and that critical spirit, based on analysis and the need of synthesis, became a universal yardstick, paradigm of judgement, intellectual bastion and filter of status acknowledged by the pivotal culture. Exacerbating this tendency, Frederick Schiller declared: "Trust only your reason." Evidently Schiller referred to his brand of reason.

In the field of architecture, German architect Leo von Klenze wrote in 1830 (in order to justify an Enlightenment and "cult" tendency) that: "Ancient Greek architecture should be the architecture of the world and of all times. No climate, no material and no diversity of customs can oppose its widespread application." In fact, during the eighteenth and part of the nineteenth centuries, even in tropical latitudes, the neo-Classical style was applied in the construction of institutional and figurehead buildings, following the desire to demonstrate an affinity with the Enlightenment. Classical Greek architecture became a role model. Its formal language expressed its function and historical prestige. The buildings of the new republics could now not only compete with sacred buildings and princely dwellings, but could even surpass them,

Figure 4.22 *Colegio panamericano – façade*
(architect and photo Bruno Stagno)

architecturally. The Enlightenment found, in neo-Classicism, a style with which to assert its powers in the Americas. The newly independent republics opted for neo-Classicism in order to assert incipient political power (by projecting an image of respectability) and, at the same time, to hide that which the national élites considered to be culturally inferior.

This behaviour was intended as a political measure by the emergent countries, to demonstrate republican maturity. However, from the cultural and especially the architectural perspective those buildings represented an impoverishment; as they negated any possibility of proposing a more engaging and indigenous architecture.

Neo-Classicism is a style that, in order to be appreciated, does not require a sensitive or cultured observer. Because its formal message is absolutely static and direct, no emotion is required in order to understand it. Here we have a reason for its application. It was easy to transmit and this made it readily accessible to the "uncultured masses". As élites imposed this architecture to please the masses, the quality and level of design decayed. In consequence, the number of architectural proposals declined.

With the arrival of sentimental Romanticism and the visionary (which was a reaction against the rational Enlightenment, so insensitive to otherness), the exaltation of nature began. However, architecture from the last third of the nineteenth century onwards, opted for a functional rationalism that drew it into the Modern Movement which, itself, predominated during a large part of the twentieth century.

Figure 4.23 A dwelling house over water from Doreri in the Papuan Gulf, Oceania. Illustration from Duperrey's Voyage of the Coquille 1821.

It is important to highlight that, in Brazil, during the first half of the twentieth century Oscar Niemeyer adopted an attitude that, breaking the ties with pure and arid Modernism, created a fresh architectural expression that incorporated elements appropriate to a tropical latitude. Without parting from the Modern Movement, but with a clear regionalist intention, Niemeyer incorporated parasols, piles, glazed tiles and the open space, in a liberated architecture that combined lightness and transparency. Niemeyer proposed, for the first time, a modern-tropical-Baroque that fires the senses and the imagination.

The attitude of systematically copying architectural styles from the past has returned in recent years; in spite of the variety of other proposals currently emerging and especially in total contrast to environmentalist culture. With the collusion of these architectural falsifications, more appropriate to theme parks, this attitude pretends to escape from the present, or else fabricates a different course of history to cover up its inferiority complex. This retrograde attitude produces an upstart, parvenue architecture that mimics the past, that becomes a false future and patently lacks the will to project itself towards the future. Its buildings reveal the sham and sterility of such an attitude.

Figure 4.24 Centro artistico, San Jose, Costa Rica – courtyard (architect and photo Bruno Stagno)

Figure 4.25 *Centro artistico – exterior view (architect and photo Bruno Stagno)*

TROPICALITY

Tropicality is a mental state resulting from the immersion of the individual in a universe of sensuality, exalted by an overwhelming complexity. The more we consider this reality (very often overcharged and chaotic) the less tropicality is perceived as an extravagant incongruity but instead, as a genuine entity, highly evolved and rich in possibilities. It is, perhaps, this very richness that makes it hard to unravel and probably (in keeping with an attitude typical of tropicality) it is best not to rationalize but simply to submerge yourself in its universe. The biodiversity of life is an evident reflection of the wealth of possibilities that arise in that human life which maintains a close relationship between humanity and nature. Mother Nature is characterized by an uninhibited pleasure of the senses and also by an overlapping, simultaneity of situations and experiences.

Mircea Eliade, who worked extensively on the subject of the logic of Indian thought, wrote about such submersion:

. . . and that gesture of Mother Nature to fling life without rhyme or reason, that gesture of creating for the joy of creation, for the delight of drinking the sunlight and of singing her victory, bewilders and overwhelms you. You close your eyes in order to absorb a little taste of that marvellous richness and when you open them there is another panorama. The battlefield and the sources of rapture have changed, there are new, clamorous, startling, violent, imperious forms, proud of their victory; forms of dreams and desires; fires which burn and extinguish momentarily in that vertiginous kaleidoscope of the jungle.[8]

In order to understand this tropical world you have to plunge into its diverse thought which enables you to understand that all things have multiple meanings and explanations and that neither intuition nor reason can separately exhaust the real. Diverse thoughts are pluralistic, it may seem ambiguous, but certainly they respond to multiple points of view. The tropics are an environment of multiple offerings and this makes it difficult to make any selection or commitment. Octavio Paz says (regarding his experience of tropicality):

. . . the cuisine; to it I owe a first slight intuition that taught me more about India than a whole treatise. I glimpsed its secret, which was not in a mixing of flavours but in a graduation formed of oppositions and conjunctions, simultaneously violent and subtle. Not a succession, as in the West, but a conjunction. It is a logic that governs nearly all Indian creations. The music . . . I learnt in the cuisine, and also the pleasure of meandering along those galleries with echoes and those gardens of transparent trees, where sounds think and thoughts dance. It was something that I found also in the poetry and the thought: the tension between unity and vacuity the continual coming and going between both.[9]

Figure 4.26 Rohrmoser Headquarters – inside/outside relation
(architect and photo Bruno Stagno)

Figure 4.27 *Curridabat*
Headquarters – roof detail
(architect and photo Bruno
Stagno)

This multifaceted experience of reality creates a milieu surrounded by an atmosphere that is full of illusion and enchantment. What Alejo Carpentier called "the marvelous in the real" is effectively a daily experience that particularly characterizes tropicality. Carpentier refers to a milieu that is in contact with the prodigal forces of nature, of exuberant vegetation, lascivious verdure and the phantasmagoria. That ineffable milieu engenders exalted emotional states; this effect is appropriate to the "total work of art". In tropicality it acts independently from the articulating discourse that becomes essential to the understanding of the intellectual work of rationalistic, idealized, abstract thought. What is different in tropicality is that the outrageous stops being a perceived subject and transforms itself into an undifferentiated category of reality. In this way the singular and the outrageous become part of objective reality and cease being distinct from it. The surrealism of Breton captured this reality in Haitian paintings, but, instead of integrating it within its natural state, sought to shift it into an intellectualized and pretentious category whose result was a pale and flat reflection of reality. This surrealism expired because of its artificiality and fictitiousness while the other, the real one continues to enjoy good health.

People in the tropics live in their tropicality and in spite of the influence of "progress", defy discipline and pre-planning. Instead of anticipating events

Figure 4.28 Trigal Apartment House – façade (architect and photo Bruno Stagno)

Figure 4.29 Trigal Apartment House – façade (architect and photo Bruno Stagno)

they wait for them and then resolve them. They have not accepted taming, though they appear to do so. They rebel in many ways; even by covertly looking for the tricks of the trade, to avoid directly opposing the norms, and so remain in coexistence with them in a form of motivating symbiosis. In this way, they live in a world of opportunism and minimal engagement. In the American tropics, it is commonplace to hear, in a serious dialogue, someone putting forward their opinion either by saying "I'm neither in favour nor against, on the contrary" or by saying "I don't know whether it is true or not, but they believe so and therefore so do I". The answer given, by one Costa Rican minister to an exacting question from King Juan Carlos of Spain was "Your Majesty, what is most sure is who knows."

Figure 4.30 Trigal Apartment House – detail of the sun shading (architect and photo Bruno Stagno)

The inhabitant of the tropics customarily greets Enlightenment civiliza-tion with chameleonic adaptability and proudly displays an unlimited versatility that never flags. This adaptive prowess may not actually exist, but it may be the visible result of an opportunistic way of living life and reasoning on it, in an idiosyncratic fashion, without needing absolute truths.

This adaptive faculty is characterized by great skill in improvisation. The tendency is both to evade and weather obstacles and engagements, instead of facing them. However, this state of liberty, produced by the absence of engagement, culminates in fatalism because of the acceptance of destiny and the refusal to take control over it.

Tropicality is lived within an extraordinary labyrinth of the astonishing, in which existence is immersed in the supernatural because it is hyper-natural. This situation, of multiple options, explains the attitude of the inhabitants of a port or an island. This attitude produces a character inclined to the assimilation, or better, the light and rapid acceptance of whatever comes; without establishing any engagement or loyalty, neither with oneself nor with anyone. This essentially two-way disloyalty allows one to adjust to the swings of any situation. It is not surprising that people in the Tropics (with their history of economic deprivation) become, in contrast to their generous nature, adjustable as a necessary resource for survival. This condi-tion is so strong and established that an opportunistic attitude towards life becomes critical whenever we want to characterize tropicality. This attitude comes as the result of choosing from multiple options that arise within the milieu, that is so extensive in variety and opportunity. Such a singular situ-ation makes it difficult to establish stable parameters of conduct; what is really clear is that freedom comes not as a wish but as a daily practice. Though said in relative terms, freedom does end up being a constant. Despite this, we sometimes feel that it is continually adapting and changing.

REFERENCES

* Translated by Jaime Florez.
1. Alejo Carpentier, *El Reino de este Mundo*, Siglo XXI Editores, Mexico, 1994.
2. Eduard Glissant, *Introduction à une poétique du divers*, Gallimard, Paris.
3. Salman Rushdie, *Midnight's Children*, Penguin Books, Harmondsworth, 1995.
4. René Descartes, *Discours de la méthode*, Paris, 1637.
5. Yvonne Vera, "Zimbabwean Lives: the Visual Arts, Books and National Develop-ment", *Prince Claus Fund Journal*, 1, 12–16, 1998.
6. Gomdaogo Pierre Nakoulina, "Faut-il encore souhaiter le dévelopement?" *Prince Claus Fund Journal*, 1, 21–26, 1998.
7. Emanuel Kant, *The Critique of Pure Reason*, 1781.
8. Mircea Eliade, *La India*, Empresa Editorial Herder, Barcelona, 1997.
9. Octavio Paz, *Vislumbres de la India*, Galaxia Gutenberg, Mexico, 1997.

CHAPTER 5

MODERNIZING APPROPRIATIONS/ APPROPRIATING MODERNITY

Tan Hock Beng

> Only if we recognize our tradition as a heritage that is continually
> evolving will we be able to find balance between regional and inter-
> national identities.

In the face of globalization and the transcending power of media, the role of
architecture in place-making and in the evocation of specific traditions has
been questioned. Many architects are producing works that are merely "free-
floating signs", or what critic Michael Hays termed as ". . . purely abstract,
technical signifiers without context which, volatilized by our postmodern
perceptual apparatuses (accustomed as they are to channel flipping and image
sampling), now flow like vapour into what critics call the 'hyperspace' that
consumer capital has constructed for itself".[1]

Yet, despite the perceived homogenization, the assertion of cultural specificity is in no way less vigorous. Manuel Castells suggests that against the
normative trend of the computer-networked world, local societies, territori-
ally defined, must preserve their identities and build on their historical roots,
regardless of their economic and functional dependence upon space of flows.[2]

Traditional architecture is a result of the elemental needs of people and
their intricate relationships to their society and environment. In an era where
the real world appears to sublimate into cyberspace, an explicit desire for a
return to the past is perhaps understandable. In the context of Asia, it has
become quite apparent during the last couple of decades that conscientious
architects are pursuing an engagement with traditions and specifics of locality
with renewed vigour.

Today, issues concerning the growing ecological consciousness as well as
the ideological quest for national roots are extensively debated and inherent
prejudices are examined dispassionately. Regionalism is seen as a counter-
trend to the universalizing force of modern architecture and as a mani-
festation of identity. In Asia, quite a number of architects of opposing persua-
sions have felt the urgent and irrepressible need for previously neglected

cultural introspection and for the formulation of national or even regional identities in design.

But this quest is often associated with a sentimental approach to the regionalism of the past, with its emphasis on contextual reference and ethnicity. Often, this has developed into an architecture of nostalgia – one that is revivalist, scenographic and ethnocentric. An exploitative form in which regionalism resurfaced in the twentieth century was tourism, in which an architecture of tourist commercialism based on a familiarization with the past was produced.

Modern mass tourism has important social consequences for nearly all societies. It is based on two contradictory phenomena: on the one hand, a global homogenization of the culture of the tourists and, on the other, the preservation of local ethnic groups and attractions for touristic consumption. To attract the ever-increasing number of tourists, entrepreneurs and tour operators often use traditions and heritage, both authentic and manufactured, for mass consumption. Resorts are building types that are precisely tailored to fulfil this need. Being intrinsically contrived, many of them are now paradoxically being marketed for their architectural merits, which are hailed for their "being as authentic as the vernacular" (Figures 5.1–5.10).

In many parts of Asia, exquisite works that tangibly draw their scenographic contents from vernacular sources are proliferating. These works, because of their exquisite craftsmanship and offers of luxury in an understated manner, are further challenging the debate of cultural authenticity. Although based on a traditionalist approach, they are not tacky versions of skin-deep treatments of indigenous archetypes. They are distinguished from the arbitrary kitsch agglomeration of vernacular details. Rather, there is a genuine reinvigoration of the wisdoms of traditional crafts.

The term "vernacular architecture" is one of the most commonly used but least understood terms in the region. Vernacular structures, which are in essence "architecture without architects", provide many basic lessons for the latter. These time-proven indigenous shelters were invariably built by anonymous local craftsmen who used local techniques and materials. These indigenous dwellings are well adapted to the extremes of climate and their particular environmental setting. Such dwellings reflect their society's accumulated wisdom and collective images. They are imbued with cosmogonical and religious values, social and political structures, sensibility and attitude towards time and space. Their forms and proportions, craftsmanship and decorations are symbolic and meaningful. They do not have aesthetic pretensions, hence their generating principles are devoid of any straining after originality.

In vernacular settlements, the architectural language is deeply imbedded as tradition. Such tradition assures the continuity of vernacular settings through codified imagery, materials and technology. Forms and symbolism are empirically known and stable while change occurs in an incremental manner.

The term "tradition" comes from the Latin verb *tradere*, meaning to pass on to another. Tradition is elusive and difficult to define in a satisfactory way, although various attempts have been made. Edward Shils sees it as

> . . . anything which is transmitted or handed down from the past to the present. It makes no statement about what is handed down or in what particular combination, or whether it is a physical or a cultural construction, it says nothing about how long it has been handed down or in what manner, whether orally or in written form.[3]

The critical aspect of all definitions of tradition implies that it is something handed down or transmitted from one generation to the next. Implicit in this notion is the double process of preserving and transmitting. Curtis argues that

> Tradition in the obvious sense of a visible past inheritance can only be partly helpful, for reality today is different. The architect must find what is right for the present circumstances and if he is sufficiently probing and profound he will make a valid addition to the stock of forms. There is no place for passeisme or for a bogus, revivalist sentimentality.[4]

The terms "traditional and vernacular" have also been used interchangeably because tradition is synechdochic for vernacular. This is because the qualities that we associate with tradition are also found in the vernacular.[5] Dell Upton has argued that scholars of traditional environments of the so-called First and Third Worlds have comparable limitations in their approaches. Both groups work on theories of tradition and the vernacular that came from European intellectual history, which are static and dualistic in their conception. Both are also "grounded in an elusive faith in the object as authentic sign of its maker".[5]

These concepts of a distinctive social-cultural space termed regional arose in the seventeenth and eighteenth centuries in Europe, where the "picturesque" was the motivating factor in the study of traditional architecture. This acknowledgment of difference not only promoted a circumstantial view of history, it also reinforced the dualistic views of us and them. The positing of a dichotomy between non-Western and Western divides the world into diametrically opposing compartments.

This dichotomy in thinking which views things as "outside" and "inside" includes an implicit opposition – that between stability and change. The vernacular is widely seen as stable, representing enduring values, and therefore authentic. The opposition is between active and passive building traditions. The vernacular is thus seen as traditional. Bernard Rudofsky argues that "Vernacular architecture does not go through fashion cycles.

Figure 5.1 Regent, Chiang Mai, Thailand (photo Tan Hock Beng)

Figure 5.2 Amanpuri,
Phuket, Thailand
(photo Tan Hock Beng)

Figure 5.3 *Club Med Bali, Indonesia*
(photo Tan Hock Beng)

Figure 5.4 *Amandari,*
Bali, Indonesia
(photo Tan Hock Beng)

Figure 5.5 Serai, Bali, Indonesia (photo Tan Hock Beng)

Figure 5.6 Serai, Bali, Indonesia (photo Tan Hock Beng)

Figure 5.7 Ibah, Bali, Indonesia (photo Tan Hock Beng)

Figure 5.8 Novotel,
Lombok, Indonesia
(photo Tan Hock Beng)

Figure 5.9 Novotel, Lombok, Indonesia
(photo Tan Hock Beng)

Figure 5.10 Novotel, Lombok,
Indonesia (photo Tan Hock
Beng)

It is nearly immutable, indeed, unimprovable, since it serves its purpose to perfection. As a rule, the origin of indigenous building forms and construction methods is lost in the past."[6] Upton sees Rudofsky's view as symptomatic of the duality that sets the vernacular aside as a distinct category of experience with a negative aspect. Seen as stable and passive, it is perceived as stagnant, and hence marginalized, in the changing world that characterizes the human landscape.

Current studies of vernacular landscapes and architecture tend to stress continuity and authenticity. Upton suggests that

> . . . we need to contaminate the space of the vernacular and to relocate it in the human cultural landscape. We should turn our attention away from a search for the authentic, the characteristic, the enduring and the pure, and immerse ourselves in the active, the evanescent and the impure, seeking settings that are ambiguous multiple, often contested, and examining points of contact and transformation – in the market, at the edge, in the new and the decaying.[7]

This indicates a need to venture beyond insular and exclusive tendencies towards a more global and inclusive architecture. Jennifer Wicke argues:

> Regionalism also fantasizes a local conversation, a regional "essence" that, however desirable in utopian terms, cannot be located anywhere on the map of postmodern reality. The preservationist and idiomatic references that have arisen out of critical regionalism are all to the good, but a complete regionalist program founders on the politics of the global, which cannot be waved away by the magic wand of a regionally sensitive architecture. The social space, after all, is at least as much constituted by the informational, representational networks of mass culture and media as by anything else, and a regional purism will throw out the baby of social reality with the bath water of internationalism.[8]

The notion of contemporary vernacular can thus be defined as a self-conscious commitment to uncover a particular tradition's unique responses to place and climate, and thereafter to exteriorize these formal and symbolic identities into creative new forms through an artist's eye that is very much in touch with the contemporary realities and lasting human values. Many scholars have rejected the definition of tradition as a set of fixed attributes, and architects in Asia have attempted to define tradition in new ways.

Only if we recognize our tradition as a heritage that is continually evolving will we be able to find the correct balance between regional and international identities. The architect needs to decide which past principles are still appropriate and valid for today's reality and how best to incorporate these into modern building requirements and current constructional methods. The aim is innovation rather than reduplication.

A number of recent projects in Asia have been strikingly successful in this respect. Examples of significant regionalist works in different parts of the world demonstrate a high level of collaboration between architects and the indigenous craftsman. In Asia, this pool of skilled craftsmen is still relatively large. Hence, each of these architects is pursuing his or her own path emanating from the individual's personal philosophy and architectural temperament and sensibility – yet each is consciously urging, through his or her work, a genuine espousing of knowledge of the social as well as a conscious respect for the indigenous culture.

For many architects, a return to the kind of tradition of the preindustrial era is unthinkable. Theirs is an approach which does not accept that there is a fixed and immutable relation between forms and meanings. It tries to understand the traditional typology and attempts to modify the representational systems it inherited. Based upon the difficult attempt at recovering the deeper layers of the architectural tradition through fundamentals abstracted from the past, such an approach aims for a new critical awareness and a reinterpretation of the meanings which belong to the particular tradition.

Sentimental recovery of the past is jettisoned while histrionic gestures are abandoned. Instead, an invigorating Modern idiom is used. However, these buildings are dedicated to place and history without being trapped by the latter. The past is appropriated and transformed in a thoroughly Modernist idiom. Traditional formal devices are not discarded but are transformed in refreshing ways. There is the simultaneous acknowledgement of the past and present through an abstract and usually minimalist statement.

These works demonstrate several ways of dealing with the vernacular and the notion of tradition. Shils argues that

> constellations of symbols, clusters of images, are received and modified. They
> change in the process of transmission as interpretations are made of the tradi-
> tion presented; they change also while they are in the possession of their
> recipients. This chain of transmitted variants of a tradition is also called a tradi-
> tion, as in the "Platonic tradition" or the "Kantian tradition".[9]

Tradition is thus likely to undergo changes in the process of transmission and acts of possession, although important elements remain discernible. The rejection of the imagistic use of symbols does not imply a rejection of tradition. Architecture contributes to tradition in the process of continual transformation.

Raymond Williams points out that what pass off as "cultural traditions" or the "significant past" are actually selective traditions:

> From a whole possible area of past and present, certain meanings and practices
> are chosen for emphasis, certain other meanings and practices are neglected
> and excluded ... Some of these meanings and practices are reinterpreted,
> diluted, or put into forms which support or at least do not contradict other
> elements within the effective dominant culture.[10]

Hence, traditions are always contested, transformed, resisted and invented.

Today hybridity is seen as an important constituent to the sense of cultural identity and architectural tradition. The latter is now accepted as an ongoing process that is fluid – one that changes over the course of time – and inevitably dictated by circumstances of place and programme. The question is how will the compression of time and space by communication technology have an impact on issues of representing and evoking traditions in architectural forms.

REFERENCES

1. Michael Hays, "Frank Gehry and the Vitra Design Museum". In *GSD News*, Harvard Graduate School of Design, 1993.
2. Manuel Castells, *The Informational City*, Blackwell, Oxford, 1993, p. 350.
3. Edward Shils, *Tradition*, Faber, London, 1981, p. 12.
4. William Curtis, "On Creativity, Imagination and the Design Process". In Ismail Serageldin (ed.), *Space for Freedom: The Search for Architectural Excellence in Muslim Societies*, Butterworth Architecture, London, 1989, p. 234.
5. See Dell Upton, "The Tradition of Change", *Traditional Dwellings and Settlements Review*, vol. 1, 1993, pp. 149–65.
6. Bernard Rudofsky, *Architecture Without Architects: A Short Introduction to Non-Pedigreed Architecture,* Doubleday, New York, 1964.
7. Upton, op. cit., p. 10.
8. Upton, op. cit. p. 14.
9. Edward Shils, *Tradition*, Faber, London, 1981, p. 13.
10. Raymond Williams, *Problems in Maternalism and Culture*, New Left Books, 1980, p. 39.

CHAPTER 6

ARCHITECTURE AND
NATIONAL IDENTITY

Severiano Porto

"My house came directly from the jungle."

"I think that faced with the immense technological repertoire of
our century, before the impressive industrial development, we must
place ourselves in a critical selection posture: one must think
when, how and where a determined technical solution must or
must not be used."

"Everything that is pure, that is good, will prevail forever."

Severiano Porto, Brazil

To introduce Severiano Porto is a difficult task, as it always is when we are
before "a great one", since there is always the risk of being incomplete and
omitting characteristics and qualities that we do not know, for which reason
we will turn to Alberto Petrina who, in his interview for *Summa* magazine,[1]
will unveil it for us.

A.P. Your architecture is deeply linked to the regional spirit, to the intrinsic
    quality of the materials, the workmanship features, in respect of local
    building traditions. Is it possible to transfer this type of work to a major
    scale, to cities of intermediate complexity or even to a metropolitan one?
S.P. I believe it is a matter of behaviour, of an attitude towards problems.
    When we try to make "our" architecture we try, really, to think about the
    use of materials of the region and the quality of native workmanship,
    because they are important.
        When I moved to Manaos I came from Rio, bringing with me building
    techniques for wood as they were normally used in Rio, but I found it
    extremely difficult to carry them out in Manaos. This forced me immedi-
    ately to look for new solutions to those techniques, so that they could be
    used by natives in their shops, reducing complexity, cuts, simplifying
    things so as to be able to benefit from the beauty of local workmanship.
    In this way, when planning, I got used to taking into consideration
    the local material and workmanship. I believe that behaviour, vocation,

the best way to work with the local worker – who is ultimately the one who is going to do the work – are very important. In the case of Manaos, a man cuts the trees and works them in a very simple way, without the need of mills or wood-curing industries. In the jungle he cuts the trees himself and prepares them and then works with simple tools.

A.P. Without thinking of mills?

S.P. That is so. My house, for example, came directly from the jungle. These men also build large boats: simply and spontaneously they start building the boats, very easily. Most of these boats are built on the beach by people that could not even draw the plant: they do it out of feeling. This, translated to architecture, means a rich workmanship, and very good resources are available.

On one occasion, one of my students asked me how this could be done in São Paulo. I answered her that the only way was to adapt to local conditions, which, naturally, would be different from those in Manaos.

The investigation of all these simpler building processes, that always worked well, is not taught at the Faculty; it is a subject that is not studied and therefore it is forgotten. Sometimes I think we should compare architecture to the experience of a certain new medicine that is slowly returning to the natural. We are turning again to simple solutions: medicinal plants, humble teas like our "sweet herb". Of course, for some it is easier to prescribe antibiotics but the side-effects, when they are not required, are sometimes harmful. And almost the same happens in architecture.

Now, in the region where I live, it is easier for me to work like this than for you in Argentina, because you go from a harsh winter to a very warm summer. I understand that this contrast between the two climates makes simple planning difficult. You must investigate how people lived before and how they live now in your country. You must try to go back to simple solutions. This does not mean that we cannot sometimes consider different types of solution, but we are always looking for the same thing: to look for the right remedy for each problem. For example, if you are planning a telephone company – in my country we have done several – you must immediately deal with a number of technical considerations: humidity control, low temperature, etc. Notwithstanding, in this case we have to use air-conditioning. For the project in the free zone of Manaos (ZOFRAN), I did not consider using wood, although Manaos is on the Amazon, since I understood that there we had to convey a more solid message of permanence, of a strong government presence.

On the other hand, it is important to understand that architecture must be thought of as following several directions, taking several aspects into consideration simultaneously. When many years ago we built the Manaos soccer stadium it seemed like an investment out of proportion for the city. We were very careful with details, including bathrooms and bars. Then we proved that most of the people – who maybe had never seen a urinal – went into the bathrooms with pride. For years and years not even one fixture was broken. It was the best response from the natives: they showed they could use each and all the spaces of the stadium. We understood then, that it was possible to create identification conditions, that architecture could and should respond in that sense. One has to work on intentions, customs, culture of the people, because they are the ones who give us the more correct guidelines.

A.P. Yes, luckily these concerns have started to be included in teaching. In the faculties of Porto Alegre and Ceará, for example, architecture professors propose matters such as a solution for carpentry without glass, using venetian blinds that complement climatic characteristics.

All this spirit is then reflected, slowly, on the city: in the streets, little bars, seats: all is well done, with taste, there is a lot of green, many plants.

A.P. Is this type of work limited to architects or is it also reflected in the activity of other technicians, master builders, or builders in general?

S.P. Yes, it starts to reflect in their work, and they also look for their own models. I feel that everybody is beginning to like this approach to architecture, that it is starting to be adopted by the community. But, of course, the starting point of this is always the same: teaching. Now, with the exceptions we have stated, faculties still do not have enough awareness to investigate in depth the local building techniques and materials, that are generally the simplest and most economic.

Recently I was in Colombia, in Cali, and there the university is involved in the search for solutions that include the use of wood, bamboo, and other equally regional techniques; there is a great concern in this sense. I think that faced with the immense technological repertoire of our century, and the impressive industrial development, we must place ourselves in a critical selection posture: we must think when, how and where a determined technical solution must or must not be used.

A.P. Knowing your architecture so well it is almost rhetorical to ask you this, but I do not want to deprive myself of doing so for the sake of regional proselytism and because returning to the subject can never be sufficiently reiterative. Do you think that a determined architecture for each region or, on the contrary, international architecture can solve all the problems in all of the places for all of the people?

S.P. I think I can give you an example on this matter. Some years ago a Portuguese businessman, linked to the cement business, invited me to plan a large tourist complex in Mexico.

I answered that I would accept the commission on one condition: that I spend two months prior to doing so living in the region – not in the Mexico City area – to learn the climatic characteristics, the quality of workmanship of the place, in short, the "local colour". He then told me, that he only wanted me to work as I normally did. But that, for me, was not possible. I told him it was necessary for me to spend some time over there, since it was essential to really get to know the people, materials and building processes, local resources, anything that was part of the very interesting and specific lifestyle of the region.

I even suggested to my client that maybe it would be better to look for a local architect, someone who would value all this in his work. Finally he said good-bye, told me he would come back, and . . . he never did. As for me, it was only an attitude of conviction I had about the problem. I believe it does not make any sense to build an identical building in Manaos, Acapulco, Miami or in any other part of the world. I do not believe in a universal architecture; I simply have a concern for the regional. I do not understand that there would be reasons – beyond those sustained by multi-national industries of central air-conditioning, aluminium carpentry, reflecting glasses, modulated dividing panels – for a building built in Buenos Aires to be the same as one built in São Paolo, Rio, or New York. Instead, what a difference can be found in a building such as the Bank of London for South America![2] I have visited it; it is lovely, a beauty. In it there is a break, a rupture of the patterns of rigidity: the dimensions of the accesses, the heights, everything was altered. And this is important since creativity has been relegated, blocked out by the process of accelerated industrialization.

A.P. On the other hand, there is in Rio de la Plata a proven tradition of the use of reinforced concrete, a highly specialized workmanship in this technique that, in the Bank of London, reaches a superlative excellence.

S.P. Yes, sometimes it is understood that in the face of the new realities and the other arguments and cost revisions, most architects prefer to stop thinking, creating, and enter into a much easier and safer modality in which there are no risks, no danger of error. However, I still believe that the creative approach is important to architecture and that it is also necessary that this creativity be referred to its roots, to the local building traditions. When young architects leave the Faculty they find themselves in a situation of great indecision on how to behave professionally. Then they believe, if they follow the patterns indicated in magazines, they will avoid all error, that in this way they are half way there. It is a fact that in Brazil we are going through a phase of neo-Colonial architecture that we call *coloniosa*. Well, this architecture was perfectly acceptable when Brazil was a colony, but today it shows a total lack of creativity, although local materials such as tiles, ceramics and wood are used.

A.P. While I was listening to you I was thinking of something very strange. We have been talking for a long time and, if we were having this conversation with an Argentinian colleague or, better yet with a native of Buenos

Aires, there would have already been at least twenty references to European and North American architects, we would have only talked about theory, criticism or the last works that were built (or drawn) in New York, Paris, Tokyo, Milan, etc. . . . or else all those cocktail party banalities. Rather, you have not stopped talking about your town, your city, your region, your country; of the building techniques or materials of your country, of the teaching problems of Brazil and your own experience. Severiano, would you like to move to Buenos Aires? But, no, it might be taken here as chauvinism.

S.P. The thing is I do not like to talk lightly, to give my opinion about things I do not know in depth or criticize having no basis. I think the moment has come to make proposals, to look for solutions researched by ourselves. We must concentrate on the search for new technological answers using our materials, the architectonic elements of our building traditions, and with consideration for our climates. I see in Buenos Aires the tremendous European influence in buildings, shops and restaurants. This is a phase that definitely existed, and we are still marked by it. But we must also assume our Americanship and begin the search that we mentioned before, to investigate our own problems. That is why we have to be coherent with ourselves, as were the Egyptians, the Greeks, the Romans. They accomplished, in this way, authenticity and beauty, and permanence. Everything that is pure, that is good, will prevail forever. This is the spirit of Classicism. The search for quality, good design, beauty, technical solutions, is something we have to assume as an important task of our time. And for this you only need coherence: coherence with possible technology, with available materials, with the workmanship of our people. More than searching in the examples of the great masterpieces, of the great ideas, sometimes we should look back to popular houses, to the opinion of the people who live in them, to the voice of the community. Maybe our main task would thus be to concern ourselves with our life, our city and our moment. From here we can accept, now, the experience of others; if it is good and can be adapted, and if it agrees with the purpose of the work, . . . why not? But to start by immersing ourselves in European and North American magazines I do not believe is the best course. That is fine for them. They are concerned with the styles . . . fine, that is their approach. I do not think it has anything to do with our needs or our reality.

A.P. Now I see that, for you, the real metaphoric synonym when you refer to antibiotics, is the International Style, whether from the past, the present or the future. Of the international styles we require only small doses, and that would be only if there is no other remedy available. Considering the price we must pay to the pharmaceutical multinationals, or the achitectural profession for their products, . . . well your prescription seems very healthy.

S.P. I think so.

A.P. Changing the subject, where did you study?

S.P. In Rio.

A.P. But you are mineiro.[3]

S.P. That is so.

A.P. And your family?

S.P. Pernambucan; but my family lived in Rio, where I studied. Now I have been in Manaos for twenty years. I have identified with the region and sometimes I am introduced as an architect from the Amazon. For a long time the local people have granted me the title of citizen of the Amazon.

A.P. There must be very few Brazilians as Brazilian as you: of Pernambucan father, born in Minas, educated in Rio, living in Manaos. But, returning to your studies, how were your training years, the atmosphere of the university at that time?

S.P. The Faculty operated in the Art Museum. Attendance was not mandatory, which was excellent because we could move around freely. The lectures were carried out in the museum's dining rooms; the senior students placed their easels there and the junior students would sit next to them and watch them drawing their perspectives with ink and paints. All the time we had a global vision, we learned by watching the more advanced, asking and experimenting. We had good teachers, some very valuable, of whom I have pleasant memories. Also, since the Municipal Theatre was across the street from the Museum, we participated in a broader world. At night we would cross the street and attend acting and scenography courses, we helped paint the sets, participated in all the ballets and symphonic concerts. They were very good years, experiences that provided a really complete training.

A.P. Severiano, what is your work method? Do you solve building problems in the plans or do you rather outline them there and define them in the work?

S.P. Well, it depends on the type of work. If it is a government commission I solve everything beforehand, in the plans. But generally I do the preliminary studies and from then on I develop the project almost only based on the details. In the case of a house, for example, most of these details evolve with the work, there are changes that emerge and are added during the process.

A.P. Your modality of work must demand a fair amount of time being present at the site, doesn't it?

S.P. Yes, depending on who is building it. Once the sketches, project, design are made I collaborate with the architect in charge of following the work and I control the process. Of course we never have enough time to develop certain research that is sometimes important for the resolution of the work; also, the client would not understand it, unless he were a very enlightened person. This is not Europe or the United States ... but it is more exciting, much more creative. One is doing this, following the work and solving problems at the moment when they arise, meanwhile trying to sort out a number of possible details. Of course, there are limits fixed by cost and time that one must not exceed.

A.P. Regarding this last remark, how is your relationship with your clients? Because I suppose the people that look for Severiano Porto have – at least in most of the cases – a very clear idea of your architecture and, for this reason, what they want for themselves.

S.P. The people who come looking for me, at least in Manaos, are normal people. I listen to them, and try, to the best of my knowledge, to answer their questions in the most faithful way. I try to make a project tailored to the person who requests it; I do not make projects for my own satisfaction: I am not the one who must be happy in that house.

A.P. Your idea that it is the client who must be satisfied with the work seems to me basic in a time where the theoretical principles are handled compulsively. Many architects start by imposing a theory on themselves and from there automatically try to impose it on the client.

S.P. Yes, it is not always easy to deal with clients; you have to be very patient, one has to give in. Sometimes, it can happen that I feel a project would not come out well because I have had to deprive myself of a lot of things, because in order to obtain them I must get angry. In this case I prefer not to accept the work. In other cases I have been wrong, and, since I chose a certain course of action, I have had to change it because I found out it was not the right one. And there is also the type of client who halfway through the work announced that they have ordered something of their own to be done, and that we should run and solve the problem ... well, there are certain limits. It is as if you were given a pink coat: maybe you could feel excited fixing it, adapting it, but ... you would never use it. Anyway, I believe that the relationship must be the most flexible and human possible, don't you?

A.P. What do you think of the unexpected emergence of architecture "to be published"?

S.P. Well, I do not make projects to be published in magazines. I am not interested in this.

A.P. I think you are still speaking a strange language. Here we have some colleagues – ethics commands amnesia – and all they do is flood us with projects whose only destiny is to be published. But, in the last years, there has been an international epidemic. At this point there is no immunization known.

Severiano, some last comment on the transfer of the architectural experience, on the transfer of knowledge, namely, what does teaching mean to you?

S.P. Let us go back to what we mentioned before. It is necessary to commit to the work; architectural work must be committed to the time and available techniques, and to the local people. Building processes must be studied and felt in depth. As was true with popular architecture, so it is with the works that have transcended.

Regarding the students, it is important that they feel safe. If they know all the available technology, the resources, all the possible choices, they will have more time to create, conceive, project, research. They could build well. Is this not the work of the architect?

On the other hand, I believe that architectural language must be simplified, translated to a real, everyday language. Currently there are too many terms. We should talk about architecture with the students as we do when we refer to any other common thing, using words that everybody understands. As if we were speaking of rice and beans.

NOTES

1.   *Summa*, No. 210, 1997.
2.   Clorindo Testa, Argentina.
3.   From Minas Gerais.

APPENDIX

Severiano Porto

Manaos is the centre of a particular area, the State of Amazon, located in the north of Brazil. The city is closer to Colombia, Perú or Venezuela than

Figure A6.1 Balbina Environment Protection Center, Minas Girais (architect Severiano Porto)

to the centre of its own country. It is a jungle region, in which the force of nature is really powerful and this obliges the inhabitants to use the resources with ease. The city of Manaos has a fundamental importance in the life of the state and its growth in recent decades has been steady.

My insistent use of local materials and techniques is due to my conviction that faced with the immense technological repertoire of the twentieth century and with its impressive industrial development, we must place ourselves in a critical selection posture: we must think when, how and where a determined technical solution must or must not be used, and thus, together with the wise and rich use of wood, I use concrete, metallic materials, brick, whenever required by the circumstances and character of the work.

CHAPTER 7

ARCHITECTURE AND CITY IN THE CARIBBEAN: THE REINVENTION OF PARADISE*

Roberto Segre

TROPICAL IDENTITY

The twenty-first century got off to a start under the sign of globalization in a world minituarized by instant mass communication. We all awaited the arrival of the new millennium with a degree of anxiety, whether huddled under a horse blanket or sharing in the collective hopes that were being celebrated all around us in city streets and squares. Television made it possible to simultaneously observe the start of the year 2000 in the kingdom of Tanga and on the beach of Copacabana; to partake in the celebrations before the pyramids of Egypt, inside Red Square and beneath Richard Rogers's Millennium Dome in London. Celebrated by the Pope at St Peter's Cathedral in Rome, Midnight Mass was seen in five continents and reached the biggest television audience of the century. The economic, political and cultural homogenization created through computers and the Internet has not, however, reached all inhabitants of the planet. Access to the possibilities opened up by the new electronic and digital technologies remains limited to certain social groups, in both "north" and "south." Millions of people in the world subsist in conditions much closer to prehistory than to modernity.[1] For this reason the debate concerning cultural and architectural identity continues unabated, as recognition that there are communities that have not received – or do not wish to receive – the supposed benefits of globalization promoted by those countries that are highly developed.

One does not have to subscribe to the thesis of geographical fatalism upheld since the time of Isabel, Catholic Queen of Spain,[2] by generations of thinkers, to see that countries that have been antithetical in terms of social and economic development coincide with cold and hot climates. Europe, the cradle of Western civilization, did not begin to concern itself with atmospheric conditions of the tropical zone until its possessions began to include the tropics. With the arrival of Columbus in America, the conquistadores addressed the particularities of the local habitat and applied technical and constructional solutions based on those of the original inhabitants; however, in establishing the first cities, they imposed their own models and lifestyles. Although there are instances as early as the eighteenth century, following the added colonial expansion of France, England and Holland, where architecture was studied in relation to climatic conditions,[3] only the twentieth century can be seen as defining "tropical" attributes in specific formal terms.[4] What emerges from this definition is an equation of architectural identity with a new International Style for hot countries based on the use of louvers, filters, brises-soleil or bamboo roofs. Can we accept the existence of a *Caribbean Style*[5] reduced to a common denominator applicable to all Caribbean islands and countries? Of course, the response of the human habitat is conditioned by geographical and climatic determinants, but there are other factors involved, embodied in lifestyle, customs, beliefs, social and economic ties and symbolic values identified with a given community.[6] It is from the intersection and interaction of these factors that cultural identity must be considered if it is to be taken in the full sense of the term.

We will not apply the concept of cultural identity here in a restrictive sense but in one forged by the dialectical relationship between internal processes and external influences; between the attributes linked to the persistence of historic memory and modernizing transformationing elements of traditional culture. During the 1980s, the term "Critical Regionalism," coined by Alexander Tzonis and Liane Lefaivre then widely diffused by Kenneth Frampton,[7] to identify the architecture outside of the economic and cultural mainstreams – creators of the anonymity and alienation of the artefacts introduced in the urban environment – amplified its standing as a "subcategory" that included only "peripheral countries".[8] Although the founders later substitute "regionalism" for "critical regionalism", it was severely questioned in Latin America by Ramón Gutiérrez, Alberto Petrina and other participating members of the Seminarios de Arquitectura Latinoamericana. Recently (1997) Ignasi de Solá Morales buried it in lapidary form, denouncing the restrictive contents of the term, sometimes associated with neo-conservative positions or a thinly veiled, exclusionary nationalism.[9]

This does not imply falling into the other extreme, denying the identity of place, its community and the heritage of local history, as Rem Koolhaas proposes in his theory of the Global City,[10] but rather integrating the dynamic of a universal avant-garde with local particularities. Always, the periphery was considered as a reflection of achievements of the "centre", whose artistic and architectural manifestations revealed a "provincial" character, following the definition of Graziano Gasparini.[11] However, reality demonstrates the error of such an affirmation: Santa Prisca de Tasco in Mexico emerges as the equal of any German baroque church of the eighteenth century; the Kavanagh Building of Buenos Aires (1936) is more innovative than the towers of

Rockefeller Center in New York; Mario Romañach's Noval House in Havana (1949), preempts by several decades the formal and spatial experiments of Michael Graves's "white" architecture of the 1970s.

I have persistently criticized Charles Jencks for his mania for classifying contemporary styles and tendencies. The consumerist obsolescence of images and objects in the developed world produced an almost pathological multiplication of short-lived architectural movements: International Style followed by Brutalism, Postmodernism, Deconstructivism, High Tech, Super-modernism and Minimalism. Fortunately, the new century opened with a diminishment of frivolous fashion, and some recent works indicate the value of function, constructional techniques and the reduction of aggressive symbolic attributes to a minimum, regaining to some extent a certain conceptual and moral dimension inherited from the Modern Movement.[12] In the return to the essential containers of architecture, multiple languages come together in the centre of a critical modernity that assimilates the multiple differences in a Deleuzian sense. In this context, Ricardo Legorreta borrows the telluric codes of Barragán in the buildings of IMB in Texas and José A. Choy deploys the deconstructive experiments of the Terminal of Executive Flights in Santiago de Cuba without losing the intrinsic attributes of local traditions. There is more at stake here than mere architectural style. What counts is the appropriateness of the response to the complex surrounding reality, which it tries to renew and transform.

The Caribbean is a microcosm within Latin America. The constellation of islands is both a factor of union and disunion. From the continent, people long to come to the magic world of secret and unknown islands. On the other hand, the hell of slavery and the age-old eradication of transplanted Africans came from the continent. Hence the latent contradictions: the isolation generated by insularity; the superposition of races and social groups; the desire to be integrated into a universal culture. For this reason, the definition of the Caribbean as a crossroads implies a persistent necessity of confrontation of the inhabitants of the islands with the universal avant-gardes in order to form their own identity.[13] From this reality emerges the category of "Caribbean environmental syncretism" that we elaborated along with Bruno Stagno[14] in order to identify the inherent content of "tropicalism" without imposing the canons or formal restrictions associated with temporary stylistic trends. It involves, more precisely, the particular combination, interaction, articulation and innovation inherent in the multifaceted and multinational Caribbean kaleidoscope that generated an urban and architectural system suited to the natural and geographical conditions of the tropics, to the idiosyncrasy of its population in constant mutation – marked from the beginning by the asymmetric relationship between masters and slaves; between subjugation and the yearning for liberty – to the values of a culture caught between the popular culture and professional Modernity that defines its identity.[15]

THE PERSISTENCE OF MODELS

When Christopher Columbus arrived in the West Indies, he was surprised to find a dissimilarity between the landscape and the native population with respect to the dominant models of Europe. On one hand, exuberant nature, trees, flowers and countless birds; on the other, human beings of a rare skin colour, semi-naked, communicating with each other in a strange language, dwelling in primitive huts, who possessed no cities, churches or palaces.[16] At the beginning of the occupation of the islands, the Spanish imposed peninsular urban schemes, without any relation to local climates. Nevertheless, the integration of this new reality of the first appearance of the first villas in Hispaniola, Cuba and Puerto Rico as not inappropriate. The medieval inheritance, combined with the presence of the traces left by the Arabs in Extremadura and Andalucia and the Renaissance ideas filtered through the military encampments that arose from the Reconquista, joined the flexibility of adaptation with local.[17] This is why Santo Domingo, the seven Cuban towns and San Juan, founded at the beginning of the sixteenth century, were characterized by the dominance of a semi-regular plan and the adaptation to the topography of the actual site.[18]

Appearing between 1500 and 1520, the first Spanish cities in the Caribbean symbolized the possession of the territory on the part of the conquistadores and the establishment of ports for the supply of ships arrived from the peninsula in search of dry land. The early presence of nations sent by the crown – France, England and Holland – eager to grab their share of the American booty, means that military constructions assumed first place within urban structures. Between 1550 and 1770 on the islands of Cuba, Puerto Rico and La Hispaniola, the greatest fortifications of America were built, integrated into the grand defensive system of the Greater Caribbean that protected territories, cities and ports.[19] Given the constant wars in the "Mediterranean of the Americas", the war infrastructure expanded in the archipelago, built by the French, the Dutch and the English. Because of the presence of numerous troops, they adapted the buildings occupied by the soldiers to the tropical climate: the barracks of the Nelson Dockyard in English Harbour, Antigua, and the Naval Hospital of Port Royal, Jamaica, adopted the transparent walls of wooden slats and the ample colonnades that fostered shade and breeze for the interior spaces.[20]

From the very beginning of the conquest, Spain created in Santo Domingo symbols of the central power – the Casas Reales, the Alcázar, the Cathedral – built in stone from the dominant building codes of the Peninsula. Once the continent was conquered, however, the Caribbean Islands themselves took on a secondary importance. The defensive and commercial significance of the harbour outweighed its urban dimension. Thus, in Havana, following two centuries of a lack of a Plaza Mayor, the social functions were spread throughout the different areas of the city.[21] Although the streets were narrow, prefiguring the later norms of the Leyes de Indias, no porticos existed in the public squares that were essential for protecting against both the torrid sun and surprise tropical rainfalls.[22] The Oficios and Mercaderes of Havana, or in Las Damas of Santo Domingo were lined with primitive introverted dwellings still dominated by the Moorish influence of Andalucia. Then, gradually, in the seventeenth century, rooms began to open up around an interior patio, with widening doors and windows in order to permit the passage of refreshing breezes.[23] Everyday life of the population and its activities were a function of the port and of the temporary presence of the fleet, concentrated once a year in the harbour awaiting the return to Cadiz.

At the beginning of their occupation of the smaller islands, settlements placed *ex-novo* – there were no urban antecedents or original settlers – by England, France and Holland followed the grid as the base of the configuration of central areas, a plan that facilitated the distribution of lots and functions. However, the adaptation to irregular river basins or harbours necessitated in most cases – for example Bridgetown, capital of Barbados; Saint George in Granada; Pointe-à-Pitre in Guadeloupe – could not be accommodated by the regular character of the grid. Exceptions began to multiply: in Jamaica, the irregular plan of Kingston originated from the expansion of a meeting point of two commercial streets into a square – King's Street and Queen's Street; and Basseterre in Saint Kitts – recalls the heritage of London squares. In Curaçao, Willemstad was called "Little Amsterdam" because of the resemblance of the administrative buildings to those of the capital of the metropolis. The cities were conceived basically as centres for commercial transactions and for storage of agricultural products for their exportation to Europe. The white landowners and the black slaves alike resided in plantations that were far from urban centres. From that time, that is from the end of the eighteenth and beginning of the nineteenth centuries, with the diversification of urban functions, the increase of the white population and the elimination of slavery, the "Caribbean" personality consolidated itself in most cities. Absentee landlords reproduced the rural in brick and stone residences of England and France on their properties, conserving the Classical attributes established by Andrea Palladio and Inigo Jones. The Rose Hall Great House in St James Parish, Jamaica, the Versailles-inspired palace of De Poincy in Saint Kitts, and the Chateau Murat in Marie Galante, are most representative.[24]

There is no doubt that the primitive hut constitutes the symbol of Caribbean "tropicality" in force even today among the original inhabitants of the islands: Arawaks, Caribes, Taínos and Siboneyes, among other ethnic groups. The huts made of palm leaves, guano, mud and bamboo, either circular, oval or rectangular in plan, with steep, two or four sloped roofs still survive in the shacks, *caneyes, carbets* and *ajoupas* that survive as the

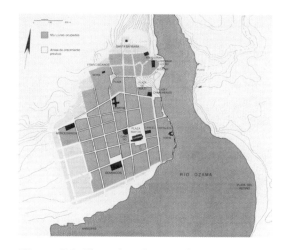

Figure 7.1 Plan of the city of Santo Domingo in the sixteenth century. From Aníbal Sepúlveda Rivera, San Juan. Historia ilustrada de su desarrollo urbano, 1508–1898. Carimar, San Juan, 1989 (reproduction by Ithaca Urban Plans)

Figure 7.2 The urban layout of Santo Domingo and its main monuments in the sixteenth century. From: Eugenio Pérez Montás, La ciudad del Ozama. 500 años de historia urbana. Patronato de la Ciudad Colonial de Santo Domingo. (Source: Centro de Altos Estudios Humanísticos y del Idioma Español. Universidad Católica de Santo Domingo, Santo Domingo, 1998, p. 74)

Figure 7.3 Engraving of the eighteenth century, with the reconstruction of the primitive huts in the Caribbean

Figure 7.4 Engraving of Martinique, eighteenth century

Figure 7.5 Engraving with a "romantic" view of a Cuban sugar plantation, nineteenth century

Figure 7.6 View of Falmouth, by Adolphe Duperly, 1844. Reproduction of the engraving by Martin Mordecal, courtesy of University of the West Indies Library. (Source: Marcus Binney, John Harris, Kit Martin. In Marguerite Curtin (ed.), Jamaica's Heritage. An untapped resource. The Mill Press, Kingston, Jamaica, 1991, p. 14. Typical urban structure in the English and French Caribbean, with individual residences along the street)

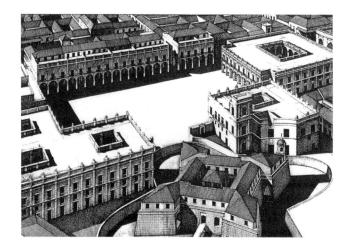

Figure 7.7 *The Plaza de Armas of Havana. Design proposal with the porticoes in the buildings that surround it, directed by the Marqués de La Torre, 1773. (Source: drawing by Francisco Bedoya, Havana)*

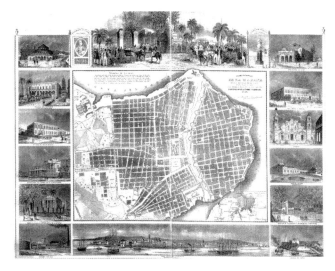

Figure 7.8 *Picturesque map of Havana, 1848 by Antonio de La Torre y Cárdenas. Apparent is the system of avenues and tree bordered streets in the new urban extension of Extramuros*

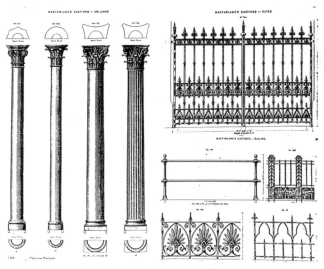

Figure 7.9 *Prefabricated iron elements imported from England in the nineteenth century used in the Caribbean*

(a)

Figure 7.10 a and b *Drawings by John Newel Lewis that show the innovations introduced by the architect George Brown in the city of Puerto España, Trinidad, Tobago, at the end of the nineteenth century. The iron introduced into the construction allowed for a lightness in the building. (Source: John Newel Lewis,* Ajoupa, Architecture of the Caribbean. Trinidad's Heritage. *Republic of Trinidad and Tobago, Port of Spain, 1983, pp. 194/195)*

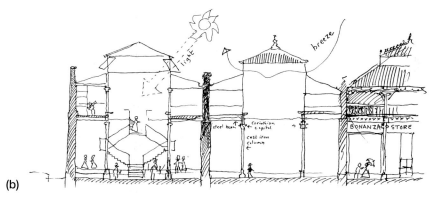

(b)

Figure 7.11 *Typical façade of commercial buildings with the wooden structure and ample openings onto the street in the Caribbean. Commercial Building, Frederiksted, St Croix. (Source: Robert Douglas (drawings),* Caribbean Heritage. Architecture of the Islands. *Darkstream Publications, Trinidad Tobago, 1996, p. 49)*

Figure 7.12 Example of the wood and brick residences built in the neighbourhoods of Pacot and Bois Verna, end of the nineteenth century and beginning of the twentieth in Port au Prince, Haiti. Casa Amélie Rivière, Bois Verna, 1913. Designed by León Mathon. (Source: Drawing from Anghelen Arrington Phillips, Gingerbread Houses. Haiti's Endangered Species. *Imprimerie Henri Deschamps, Port au Prince, 1977, p. 46*)

Figure 7.13 Maison Zévalos, Grand Terre, Pointe-à-Pitre, Guadeloupe, 1870. Prefabricated residence in iron designed by Gustave Eiffel and meant for New Orleans. (Source: Robert Douglas (drawings) Caribbean Heritage. Architecture of the Islands. *Darkstream Publications, Trinidad Tobago, 1996, p. 80*)

Figure 7.14 Typical residence of the administrator of the sugar plantation called Central Azucarero "Las Delicias", early twentieth century. The province of Matanzas, Cuba

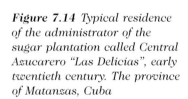

Figure 7.15 *View of the Paseo del Prado in Havana during the decade of the 1920s, before the intervention of Forestier*

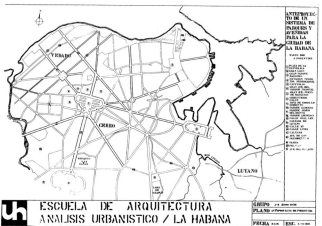

ESCUELA DE ARQUITECTURA
ANALISIS URBANISTICO / LA HABANA

Figure 7.16 *Master plan of Havana, Cuba. J.C.N. Forestier, 1925–1930*

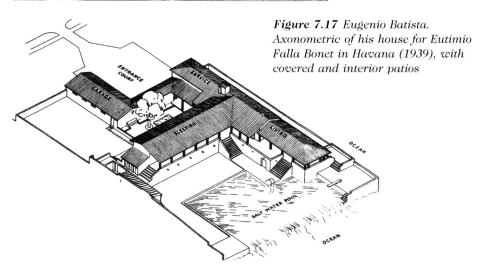

Figure 7.17 *Eugenio Batista. Axonometric of his house for Eutimio Falla Bonet in Havana (1939), with covered and interior patios*

Figure 7.18 *Antonin Nechodoma, Georgetti Residence, Miramar, Santurce, San Juan, 1917 (demolished). This is the tropicalization of the Wrightean Prairie House*

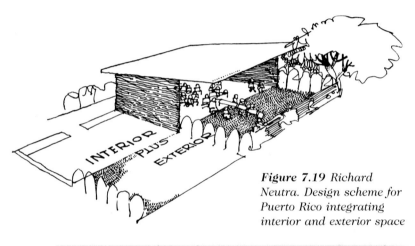

Figure 7.19 *Richard Neutra. Design scheme for Puerto Rico integrating interior and exterior space*

Figure 7.20 *Waterfront of Bridgetown, Barbados. The 1980s. The traditional architecture hostage to maritime tourist development (photo Roberto Segre)*

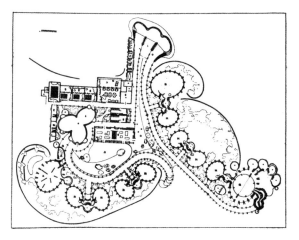

Figure 7.21 *Ricardo Porro. Ground plan of the Escuela Nacional de Artes Plásticas, Cubanacán, La Habana, 1961–65*

Figure 7.22 *Gustavo L. Moré, Grand Café, Santo Domingo, Republica Dominicana. View of the open stage with the entrance on to the interior aedicula (photo Roberto Segre)*

(a)

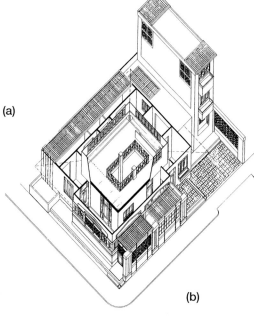

(b)

Figure 7.23 *(a and b) Luis Flores, court and axonometric of his private residence. San Juan, Puerto Rico, 1990. The theme of the zaguán and of the interior transparencies is a constant of Caribbean architecture*

SECTION B

habitat of the most humble peasant inhabitants today both as a demonstration of the environmental "identity" and as reappropriated in "vernacular"
resorts and hotels all along the islands. This typology was used by the
colonizers in establishing the first settlements and integrated it in the design
of their own buildings for African slaves on their plantations. Soon, with the
use of wooden planks in the inside and outside walls, the houses assumed
a rectangular plan, with a roof clad in zinc with two or four slopes. This
abstracted became the "shotgun house" characteristic of Haiti.[25] The universal significance of this typology appears in the reappropriation of the
Caribbean hut on the part of neo-Classical treatises in search of the original
sources of architecture.

It is not for nothing that at the end of the seventeenth century, Juan
Caramuel associates the birth and development of the Classical orders with
the Caribbean shack.[26] More recently, Le Corbusier sought the inspiration
for the pure forms that identify his works of the rationalist period[27] in
the primitive hut, and even among the current Latino students of the
Architecture School of the University of Miami this recycled image from their
collective subconscious crops up in materialized projects.[28] It must be said,
on the other hand, that these materials proved to be particularly well suited
to the local ecology in terms of thermal isolation and resistance to torrential rains and constant earthquakes. Moreover, the closed and introverted
character of the buildings responded just as well to the wish on the part of
slaves to create a sense of psychological protection against an adverse outside
world, as to the search for that particularly sociable public space in cities
that became a distinctive feature of urban "tropicality".

BREEZE AND SHADE IN THE URBAN SPACE

From the middle of the eighteenth century on a distinctive image of the
Caribbean city began to develop due to the political social and economic
transformations. The consequences lasted to the end of the nineteenth
century. In the Spanish colonial order the system of the fleet came to an
end. Each island acquired its autonomy, consolidating the productive structure of the plantation, just as in the English, French and Dutch islands, and
based on the cultivation of sugar cane and on the work of slaves that began
to overtake the former at this time. The local wars and the exchange of property of the islands stopped – the last great attempt by the English to take
over Spanish territories occurred in 1762 when they occupied Havana for a
few months – a peace that aided in the consolidation of functional structures and their architectural containers in cities. Local rich bourgeoisies
appeared that imposed a social life with their own cultural patrons and
expanded considerably the urban and commercial activities. The plantations

got modernized with the advent of the steam engine that in turn produced a crisis in slave labour. The slave trade was suspended by England and France. The black population of Haiti rose up and liberated itself from the limits of work related to the plantation, bringing on a great immigration from the country to the city on the part of the African population.

The portico, the defining trait of the tropical city, appears in Havana in the last third of the seventeenth century in luxury residences located around Plaza Nueva (today Plaza Vieja), then extended to other areas in the city such as the Plaza de la Ciénega (today Plaza de la Catedral), the Plaza de San Francisco and the administrative buildings of the government in the Plaza de Armas.[29] Finally, porticos were applied in cities through the norms fixed by the Leyes de Indias of two centuries earlier. In addition, the medieval walls fell as the constant danger of corsair and pirate attacks disappeared. In 1770, the governor of the island, the Marques de la Torre, laid down the plan in Havana of two Alamedas or boulevards, the Paula, inside the city and next to the harbour, and the Extramuros (later called Isabel II) outside the city walls.[30] Trees and vegetation alien to the Hispanic urban structures made a timid appearance and found themselves converted into an indispensable element along with the portico, the coolness and shade protecting from the torrid Caribbean sun.

Havana quickly spread beyond the historic centre, requiring the substitution of the original model of narrow streets by avenues and boulevards suited to coaches and pedestrians. Once the possessions of the American continent were lost (1824), Spain wished to convert Havana and San Juan into two urban showcases through the beauty and monumentality of their buildings then impossible to equal given the Bolivar-inspired republican convulsions of the time. In the capital of Cuba, the Governor General Miguel Tacón (1834–38) set forth with ambitious plans of urban development. He brought in a team of talented military engineers who, in addition to laying down avenues and putting up public buildings, defined the building codes borrowed from the Spanish.[31] From them are born the porticos along the main streets and, in the suburban extensions, the obligation to arrange trees in front of the residential lots.[32] The protecting galleries, previously restricted to the introverted spaces of the squares, spread throughout the city, unifying all the avenues and boulevards under a single continuous portico. The established norms for the incipient residential neighbourhoods of the Vedado and the area of Las Murallas that articulated the old city with the new are in keeping with this same *Havanero* character. On one hand, we have the first garden neighbourhood of Latin America informed by Anglo-Saxon initiatives and the ideas advanced by Idelfonso Cerda for Barcelona and Madrid; on the other, the compact texture of the centre is lightened by the high colonnades of the luxurious palaces and monumental tobacco factories.[33] Hence the "city of columns" immortalized by Alejo Carpentier.[34] In addition to being the only

Caribbean city with European traits, it was already in the early nineteenth century distinguished by the transparency of its urban spaces and the mixture of races and social groups happily interrelated in the streets and squares. A Spanish visitor affirmed in 1866: "In contrast with Madrid that slips between dark shade and dark colours, Havana is the other side of the coin. There everything is diaphanous, light, like the atmosphere that covers her . . .".[35]

The concentration of wealth of the urban population and the existence of a strong central power – Cuba was colonized until 1898 – allowed Havana to have a monumentality in its buildings and public squares as well as a differentiation of residential and productive functions that did not occur in the smaller islands. Although San Juan in Puerto Rico also reflects the crown's intention to promote to the maximum one of its only two American possessions, the only buildings that are significant are the neo-Classical buildings in the city centre. Outside, the public spaces lack coherence. The plans for extending the city and to create tree-shaded avenues in La Puntilla and in Puerta de Tierra, as well as the Bulevar with its view of the Atlantic coast close to the historical centre, never got off the drawing board.[36] In Curaçao, on the other hand, the rich Dutch merchants, although faced with the pressures of the climate, accepted the presence of low porticos in the streets of Willemstad, and never abandoned the architectural and decorative typologies imported from the Netherlands.

The expressive image of the Caribbean city was reinforced in the English and French islands. Its character was rooted in the economic and cultural limits of the local bourgeoisies, the disinterest of the central countries in building monuments and the strong integration of popular traditions and professional knowledge. There was one exception, the cluster of public buildings built around the square in Spanish Town, Jamaica (1765).[37] The centres remained tied to the economy of the plantations, and its development remained linked to them. A great deal of the black population freed from slave work had scant means but rapidly integrated itself within the dynamics of offer and demand of goods and services. As a result, narrow passageways linked dwellings, commerce and the warehouses of the port into one continuous structure whose architectural identity was based on the priority for wood and iron over stone and brick. There begin to appear colonnaded streets with light columns in both materials, used as much in the primary commercial arteries – King's Street and Queen's Street in Kingston – as in the harbours where they became two storey buildings with dwellings and shops on different levels. This is also to be found in Cap Haitien and Jacmel in Haiti, Castries in St Lucia and Point-à-Pitre in Guadeloupe.

The most significant example of transparency and urban continuity based on iron structures appears in Puerto España, Trinidad Tobago. The Scottish architect George Brown transformed the image of the historic centre, whose wood buildings were destroyed by fire in 1895. In his reconstruction project, he created commercial streets, shops and offices with colonnades and interior spaces ventilated and illuminated from above, thus defining a clear Caribbean urban typology.[38] After two centuries of isolation of the enslaved population in barracks and primitive shacks of the sugar plantations, the city now knew the happiness of sociability, of urban fiesta, of free consumption and of interpersonal meetings in streets and squares. An urban image that was repeated in Fort-de-France after the destruction caused by the great fire of 1890 and the cyclone of 1891. The iron, brick and wood constructions conformed to the image of the tropical "modern" city. It was a sequence of shops and dwellings, accentuated by "monuments" such as the church, the market and the Schoelcher Library, housed in an iron and glass pavilion from the World Exhibition of Paris (1889) and transplanted in Martinique.[39]

The marketplace was the paradigm of social participation in the Caribbean urban space for most of the islands. Although Havana and San Juan are defined by solid buildings of stone or brick inserted in the homogeneity of the surroundings, in the cities where English or French is spoken, it forms the main focus of social life. "It is the place and the moment of the organization of community celebrations, the public place where news is diffused, the seat of the secret organizations." It is the "centre of the city" where the everyday activities reunite thousands of people.[40] This is why there is no contradiction between the two Byzantine church towers of the market of Puerto Príncipe that symbolize its existence far away, not its location in the square of the Cathedral of Jacmel. As in Paris, where the formal and spatial innovations introduced by Baltard in Les Halles do not transcend urban life and maintain a scale similar to the symbolic attributes of Garnier's Opera, in Jacmel, the covered space of the market constitutes the "megastructure" that protects the daily to and fro of the square, defending the climax of urban centrality. The same phenomenon is to be found later in Pointe-à-Pitre, Cap Haitien, Castries, Charlotte Amalie and in Puerto Plata. They constitute clear examples of the cultural and architectural assimilation of the High Tech of the time to house the various functions of popular life.[41]

THE ATTRIBUTES OF THE CARIBBEAN HABITAT

From the second half of the eighteenth century transformations occur in villas and in ordinary dwellings that gradually adapt to the forms of local life and climatic conditions. The peninsular models of Extremadura and Andalucia are mechanically translated to Cuba and Porto Rico, based on the introversion of the Roman and Arabic houses, alien to the tumult of street life, and the articulation between public and private spaces.[42] So much so that in the interiors of the dwellings there are the grids and filters of the Moorish tradition according to Francisco Prat Puig (1906–97) who restored the mansion of Diego Velázquez in Santiago de Cuba.[43] Emerging in Havana under the economic requirement of that time, the "house-warehouse" grew vertically around the patio and horizontally to the road through balconies and galleries. It concentrated the stock of agricultural products, such as cigar, coffee and tobacco, on the ground floor. Above were the administrative activities and the slave dwellings, with the residence of the master and his family placed on the floor above, away from the hustle that permanently occurred at street level produced by the constant passage of people and coaches.

The Havana patio was intended as a means of creating interior shade. Its transparency was possible thanks to the extensive surrounding galleries. Windows and openings opened to the maximum to accommodate the circulation of breezes and the expulsion of hot air. The protection of family life behind screens was guaranteed through various shutters, nets, grids, filters, screens and gratings[44] that established a complex system of closures between intercommunicating rooms. The French wooden slatted blinds were adopted in the nineteenth century, halting the entrance of the rays of the sun while allowing in the indispensable refreshing breeze. The last "tropical" element of the dwelling was the centre of the arch closed by a polychromatic system of filtering crystals that attenuated the oppressive exterior light and charged the atmosphere of the interior penumbra with sweetness.[45] The house of the Count of Jaruco in the Plaza Vieja; of Lombillo and of the Marques de Arcos on the Cathedral Square constitute the principal paradigms of this typology. These models multiply in the nineteenth century in the interior of the island from the cities and towns, while diffusing the use of European neo-Classical codes. If a part of the new residences in the neighbourhood of the Cerro in Havana and the Brunet and Cantero palaces in Trinidad represent the peak of the architectonic language overlaid on luxurious mansions,[46] the identifying attributes of "tropicality" appear in the modest Italianesque villas, laid out along the streets that make up the dominant urban grid of Cuba.[47] In addition to the stylistic components, one must add the orthogonal importance of the continuity of the interior space, reducing to a minimum the autonomy of the rooms. The integration of the living rooms and other rooms, separated by arcs and columns, reappears constantly, from the grand residences, such as the Cantero Palace, to the modest dwellings of the middle class. Only in the eastern provinces do the use of wood and the presence of the bungalow dominate, revealing the relations of Santiago de Cuba with the neighbouring islands.

During the nineteenth century the canonical sway of the metropolis weakens in the residences of the landowners in the English and French colonies. Although stone and brick construction remains, it co-exists with verandas and transparent galleries, as, for example, in the Villa Nova House in St John Parish, Barbados (1834). The radical change occurs from 1850 on, with the spread of balloon frame construction in the United States and

the appearance of luxury wood mansions designed by Samuel Sloan, George
E. Woodward, Andrew Jackson Downing and other North American businessmen in the Caribbean. Its aesthetic attributes, although originating in
dominant styles, acquires a renewed expression with the so-called "gingerbread" ornamentation. Thus, wood and iron, used basically in plantations
and systems of production, distribution and consumption, end up being
assimilated under the theme of the residence. Lightness, transparency and
provisionality that characterize the surrounding Caribbean structures,
conform definitely to the image of tropical architecture, adapted to the artisan
and cultural particularities of each island, in a strong symbiosis between the
popular traditions of the plantation and the professional knowledge that dominates in the city.

The norms of the Classical orders canonized by Palladio are substituted
by the catalogues of metal and wood parts with their filigreed and ornamented
surfaces, that convert the heavy walls into virtual screens. In Guadeloupe,
the rationalist heritage of Eiffel and Labrouste persists in, among others, the
Maud'Huy residence (1873) prefabricated in wood in Louisiana, which
protects the ventilated interiors with a deep perimetric gallery. The Maison
Zévalos, totally metallic and designed by Eiffel – for a rich businessman of
New Orleans and then erected in Point-à-Pitre – with its filigree railings and
intense shade produced by transparent upper galleries supported on fragile
columns, appears almost suspended in the air over the ground floor.[48] In
Haiti, the medieval rationalism of Viollet le Duc influenced the local architects trained at the École des Beaux-Arts in Paris – Eugène Maximilien,
Georges Baussan, Léon Mathon – invent little medieval castles with pitched
roofs and attics, finished with a lace-like trimming. The climax of the
medieval gingerbread style occurs in the house of Demosthése Sam (1887)
(today the Oloffson Hotel), whose outside walls seem to become immaterial,
subjected to airy shade.[49] Georgian Classicism comes to its apex in Kingston,
Jamaica, in Devon House (1881) that remains one of the most translucid,
best ventilated of all the Caribbean architecture. Between guillotine windows,
walls of wooden slats, Classical gingerbread ornaments, shaded galleries and
protective pitched roofs, traditional monumentality of stone is displaced by
fragile surfaces.

But mansions and villas do not define the Caribbean urban tissue, they
are just isolated and autonomous examples of it. The specialty of the grid
consolidates itself before the urban expansion of the island cities, once initi-
ated to the rapid growth of the slaves in Haiti (1804), the English possessions
(1838)[50] and French ones (1848). The progressive insertion of poor farmers
and the formation of an Afro-Caribbean middle class established a typolog-
ical variety of houses that included the most elemental schemes: the Haitian
shotgun house, the Jamaican bubble house and the chattel house of the
migrant workers of Barbados to the complex and diverse configurations of

the bungalow.[51] In all these cases, the interior cell maintained a compact configuration, because of the replacement of the interior patio by the *zaguán*, a central shaded nucleus illuminated and ventilated from above. It was part of the modalities that affected the original bungalow spread throughout the Asian colonies of England.[52] The predominance of the individual isolated house, both the classic box covered with a pitched, four-sloped roof and the bungalow with its multiple zinc sheet roofs and surrounding verandas, embodied the same fragmentation which characterizes the urban space and the irregularity of the peripheral labyrinth whose free and spontaneous plan disintegrates the regular grid of the centre.[53] The fragmentation associated with this space is only enhanced by the proliferation of the Caribbean garden, attached to each unit without any strict plan in order to ensure the livelihood of the family.

On the basis of fundamental models many variations appeared defined by the cultural heritage of ethnic groups of African origin as well by the lifestyle and the traditional crafts of local carpenters and builders. It is possible to establish the specific attributes of humble dwellings in each one of the islands from the ornamental components, such as locks and screens, to the distribution of the interior spaces and the formal and structural organization of the roofs.[54] Thus the vivid colouring of the main façade can be seen as an expression of the syncretic religious contents in Haitian dwellings. The small protective eave above each window is typical of Barbados and the Persian blinds with slats that tilt upwards, allowing the breeze in and keeping the sun out – the demerara window – originates from Guyana. In addition, the major or minor use of social spaces depends on the degree of introversion and extroversion of the family, and on the internal ties of the social group or religious communities that interact between public and private space. From this comes the system of the housing for those of precarious and small means up to our own time, in spite of the aspirations for modernization and collectivization in residential urban structures.

NATURE, OPULENCE AND PRECARIOUSNESS

It is legitimate to affirm that the distinctive attributes of urban and architectural tropicality of the Caribbean were defined in the nineteenth century. The basic variations of public and private space of the Caribbean city include the schemes of neo-Classical urbanism, forging the infinite continuity of the porches of Havana, as well as the proliferation of the individual bungalow and the balloon frame present in most of the islands. From 1898 on, with the intervention of the United States in the Cuban War of Independence, the Caribbean turned into a "North American lake" before the permanent intervention of that country in the internal affairs of many islands such as Cuba,

Haiti, the Dominican Republic, Granada and Puerto Rico. The latter was transformed into a colony, euphemistically called a "Free Associated State", like the Virgin Islands that were bought by the United States from Denmark. This means that the urban and architectural models arrived mostly from the North, in the wake not only of economic interests but also of the progressive increase of tourism.

The California–Florida axis is the greatest source of images and fantasies that make up the modern tropical lifestyle associated with millionaires, Hollywood actors and luxury cruise passengers and informing neighbourhoods, dwellings, buildings and design objects.[55] Among the most significant elements let us point out the formation of outlying suburban neighbourhoods with individual houses and the adoption of the neo-Colonial style throughout the first half of the twentieth century as an expression of Hispano–Caribbean identity.[56] The hotel model spread, characterized by the use of Classical or neo-Colonial codes, the 1950s kitsch Miami style associated with Morris Lapidus and the promotion of the sporting life in the out of doors. To these were added the landscape components to be found in the islands, in particular the sea and the beach, the obsessive proliferation of the car as a symbol of economic status and, from the 1970s on, the creation of business centres and shopping malls. Only Cuba, with the changes that occurred from 1959 on, stayed clear of these influences.

Havana had a predilection for new urban proposals that took the particularities of the climate into account. With the arrival of the republic, the local bourgeoisie displayed its wealth and its identification with modernistic architectural and urban models. Between 1900 and 1930, the city grew by a quarter of a million inhabitants. This led to the need for new outlying neighbourhoods, infrastructure and urban plans. The great availability of financial resources of a restricted part of the population encouraged the spread of residential areas with generous green spaces, wide streets and luxurious mansions. El Vedado, already laid out in the previous century, turned into the paradigm of tropical urban space, with its compulsory tree-lined street, green lawn in front of the houses and porch at the front of each house.[57] This was a norm that excluded inhabitants of scarce means, and whose application became more rigorous in later areas with the "garden city" typology in Miramar and in the Country Club. On a smaller scale, there emerged at the beginning of the century in Santo Domingo, the Dominican Republic, the leafy neighbourhood of Gazcue occupied by residences in the neo-Colonial style.[58] In San Juan de Puerto Rico, there was Condado, along the coast, full of mansions and later hotels, and in the interior suburbia, the remote neighbourhood of Floral Park in Hato Rey was developed for middle-class housing.[59]

Invited by Carlos Miguel de Céspedes, the Minister of Public Works for the government of Gerardo Machado, the French urban planner and landscape designer J.C.N. Forestier directed the master plan of Havana between

Figure 7.24 An eighteenth century house in Havana. Porch taken from the interior with French blinds and chromatic glass (photo Roberto Segre)

Figure 7.25 Nelson Dockyards, English Harbour, Antigua, eighteenth century. The outside walls are made of wooden blinds (photo Roberto Segre)

Figure 7.26 Old House of Assembly, Spanish Town, Jamaica, eighteenth century. Portico along the square (photo Roberto Segre)

Figure 7.27 Sagua La Grande, Provincia de Las Villas, Cuba. Typical neo-Classical house of the nineteenth century with shops on the ground floor. The porticoed entry is to be found frequently in the area (photo Roberto Segre)

Figure 7.28 Typical Cuban interior mampara of the nineteenth century. This kind of wood and glass allows for ventillation of the interior spaces (photo Roberto Segre)

Figure 7.29 Neo-Classical façade of La Quinta de San José, El Cerro, Havana, nineteenth century, with its shaded galleries aligned with the street (photo Roberto Segre)

Figure 7.30 The buildings located on the main avenues of Havana had to keep the entrance accessible to pedestrians all along the façade. View of a tobacco plant on the Avenida Belascoaín, Havana, nineteenth century (photo Roberto Segre)

Figure 7.31 Market place in the main square of Jacmel, Haiti, nineteenth century (photo Roberto Segre)

Figure 7.32 The Club Fé y Esperanza en el Porvenir, Puerto Plata, Dominican Republica, 1908. The wood construction is applied to domestic architecture and to public buildings (photo Roberto Segre)

Figure 7.33 The tree-lined steets of the neighbourhood of El Vedado, Havana, Cuba. Beginning of the nineteenth century (photo Roberto Segre)

Figure 7.34 The continuous portico between the houses on the Paseo del Prado in Havana, early twentieth century. In the foreground, the redesign of the Paseo by Forestier (photo Roberto Segre)

Figure 7.35 Luis Flores, Centro de Transportación de Río Piedras, San Juan, Puerto Rico, 1985. View of the perimetric wall that borders the surrounding neighbourhood (photo Roberto Segre)

Figure 7.36 Patrick Stanigar, Jamaica Conference Center, Kingston, Jamaica, 1983. View of a conference room with a false roof of bamboo (photo Roberto Segre)

Figure 7.37 Ricardo Porro. Escuela Nacional de Artes Plásticas, Cubanacán, Havana, 1961–1965. The work refers both to colonial tropical architecture and to the African heritage (photo Roberto Segre)

Figure 7.38 José A. Choy, Executive Flights Terminal, Santiago de Cuba, Cuba, 1988. Deconstruction of the image of the colonial residence (photo Roberto Segre)

Figure 7.39 Oscar Imbert. International Airport of Puerto Cana, Dominican Republic, 1995. The first airport made of bamboo, wood and thatch in the Caribbean (photo Roberto Segre)

(a)

(b)

Figure 7.40 a and b Plácido Piña. Exterior view of the Finca in La Cuaba, Santo Domingo, Dominican Republic, 1998. Example of the integration of the Classical Palladian heritage and of elements of vernacular architecture (photo Roberto Segre)

Figure 7.41 Luis Flores. Interior view of his own residence in San Juan, Puerto Rico, 1990. The filters of light and screens create a system of transparencies in the interior of the building (photo Roberto Segre)

1925 and 1930. Thanks to the basic general scheme, formed by avenues and diagonals borrowed from Haussmann's model, it gave special importance to the vegetation inside the city as a protective element for pedestrian pathways. By favouring the integration with nature, the spaces of encounter and Sunday walks carried out with the rhythm of the *flâneur* he set up an opposition to the invasive presence of the car. The Paseo and the De los Presidentes avenue in El Vedado that was lined with royal palms, the Avenida del Puerto near the historical centre, the Parque de la Fraternidad and, most especially, the Paseo del Prado covered with leafy laurel trees, formed urban living rooms, resonances of Barcelona's *ramblas* and the Mediterranean streets of European cities, thanks to the exploitation of the local vegetation.[60] Coinciding with these "tropical" responses, the proliferation of elegant shops in the narrow streets of the historic centre in turn generated the multiplication of awnings that, one next to the other, collectively formed protective tunnels of shade. Another positive element was the creation of the exuberant Parque Metropolitano along the Almendares River, providing wonderful infrastructure to absorb the free time of the population. The sea front also acquired a significant importance in Havana and Santo Domingo following the construction of coastal boulevards – the Malecon – massively utilized by the populations of both cities. In the first, buildings with gallerias appeared at the beginning of the twentieth century providing it with a strong identity – the Malecon was defined as the "Entrance to Havana".[61] In the second, the all-year-round calm sea allowed for a long row of palms bordering the maritime boulevard.

The residences built in the first decades of the century abandoned the sobriety of the previous period and gave way to the influence of historicism from Europe and the United States. Wealthy businessmen, landowners and politicians valued the aggressive ostentation of their fleeting riches above the functional and climatic aspects of their buildings. Some examples did, however, reveal a search on the part of the architects to put forth their own interpretation of local conditions. In Puerto Rico, the economic flourishing of the cities of Poncho and San German produced mansions – the house of Juan Orates Perch (1920) for example – with interiors that were extremely refined, with great multicoloured stained glass panels, dividing screens with lacy woodwork that prefigure the shaded and ventilated *zaguán*, the heart of the house.[62] During the decade of the 1920s the architect Antonin Nechodoma tropicalized the Wrightean Prairie House by building mansions shaded with extensive overhangs in San Juan.[63] Less coherently, the so-called Magnificent Seven in Puerto España, Trinidad Tobago, emerged, combined with exotic houses in different styles, from neo-Hindu to Tudor castles in a free mix of forms and ornaments, in harmony with the syncretic exuberance of the Caribbean.[64] The diminutive Havana *palacetes*, rigorous in their Classicism without giving up their transparencies and their special interiors, were more successful. The Pablo de Mendoza de Leonardo Morales residence (1918) in El Vedado, Havana, articulates a deep, shaded terrace that contains the first Pompeian swimming pool built in Cuba.[65] Later, in the Country Club, the Mark A. Pollack mansion reuses the colonial heritage of the porticoed patio, smothered in vegetation.

Without doubt, the most authentic expression of the Caribbean dwelling of the first part of the twentieth century goes back to the poorest layers of the population. These people were radically indifferent to the external models of behaviour assumed by the local middle classes. Involved in migrating from the country to the city, motivated by the irregularity of work in the sugar plantations, they were obliged to live in collective buildings built by urban speculators, thus facing the impossibility of ever having a "cabin" of their own. Thus the continuity between the *lakous* in the French islands, the yards in the English islands, and landscapes of Havana or San Juan. Surrounding a central patio, along a narrow corridor or in buildings of various levels, in the small living quarters workers lived in multifamily clusters, often with collective sanitary facilities.[66] Distributed in the central or peripheral areas of the city, they shaped a collective lifestyle with an intense use of public space, inherent to the *mestizaje* or mixing that also expressed itself through music, dance, the oral cultural tradition, the art of cooking and religious syncretism. This reality that has survived up to today has kept the Caribbean cultural identity alive, as opposed to the values of the "petit bourgeois" identified with the "American way of life", the consumer style and the imported individualistic social attitudes that dominate a large part of present Caribbean society. Because of this, new forms of organization of the environment were not sufficiently studied or applied or adapted by the state bureaucracy of revolutionary Cuba that for decades has insisted on maintaining solutions based on anonymous schemes of apartment blocks with functional and spatial structures alien to the community relations that were born there.[67]

TROPICAL, MODERNITY AND TRADITION

The accelerated growth of the Caribbean cities in the second decade of the twentieth century proved antithetical to the establishment of the tropical identity. In fact, the distinctive traits that survived up until the 1940s were eliminated by the importation of foreign urban models that were alien to local traditions. The automobile became the first factor to transform urban life and limit the expansion of suburbia and alienated residential private "modern" housing blocks cement-clad and aglow with the interior heat, the so-called *vaho-haus* (1998) according to the Puerto Rico author Urajoán Noel.[68] The aggressive and fast sports cars and covertibles[69] facilitated communication between the habitat, the isolated shopping centres and the glass towers of the "business cities" appearing in the main cities. This is the case with New Kingston in Kingston, Hato Rey in San Juan, and the accelerated relocation of bucolic individual houses by apartment towers, hotels and offices in the neighbourhoods both of Gazcue in Santo Domingo[70] and El Vedado in Havana. This is a phenomenon that extends throughout the 1970s, with the insertion of hotel and office in the district of Miramar, upsetting the traditional residential make-up of this section of the city.[71] In addition, the need to meet the massive demand for housing narrowed the possible design responses to the climate. Anonymous apartment blocks proliferated during the 1970s, in socialist Cuba as much as in the "federal" neighbourhoods of San Juan or in the subsidized HLM housing projects built in the periphery of Pointe-à-Pitre or Fort-de-France.

In Havana, the progressive Miamization did not keep the ideas of Forestier from being realized. In spite of the erroneous planning ideas in Jose Lluis Sert's master plan for the historical centre (1956), one must recognize the validity of the system of parks that cross the different neighbourhoods of the city, counterbalancing the overpowering and reverberating concrete jungle imposed by local speculators.[72] Interrupted before the occurrence of the revolution, as private property disappeared from the urban land, there was a plan for great open green spaces in the city centre and in the free spaces of the periphery. Millions of trees were planted in the part of Havana contained between the Parco Metropolitan, the Lenin Park, the Botanical Gardens and the Zoological Gardens.[73] The upgrading of the urban environment occurred on the waterfront in most of the islands because of the immense influx of maritime tourism, private yachts and cruise ships alike, in Kingston, Bridgetown, Willemstad, Fort-de-France, Charlotte-Amalie and Castries to name only a few.

With the rise of the Modern Movement during the 1940s and the importance it granted to economic and functional aspects of design, the theme of the adaptation to the climate and the search for an expressive language of "tropicality" made itself felt in the region. Alberto Sartoris had already, in his desire to demonstrate the "mediterranity" of Rationalism, associated the pure forms created for loggias, terraces, balconies and pilotis with the strong Italian sun and its ramifications in Latin America.[74] But it was Le Corbusier who developed a mature typology through the use of the brise-soleil, a key feature for an architecture located on the geographical belt of the hot climate. The first projects of Argel (Cartago, 1928) and the Ministry of Education and Public Health in Rio de Janeiro (1936) are the first to adopt it internationally, converting it into a "regionalist" stereotype.[75] Nevertheless, in the Caribbean, it was Richard Neutra who established himself as the reference of the modern architectonic language for creating the solution to the problems of ventilation and insulation. His projects for schools and hospitals in

Puerto Rico, houses in California and the Schultess residence in Havana
(1956) constitute a creative and innovative response to the local particularities, and provide a mature expression of Caribbean architecture free of any
historicist connotation.[76]
    Faced with the desolate panorama of a great part of Caribbean cities domi-
nated by kitsch architecture[77] imposed by the moneyed parts of the
population, by pharaonic government buildings,[78] by the proliferation of
commercial activities, by the banalization of the fake-vernacular design of
hotels and tourist facilities, and by the rise of extensive and chaotic anonymous peripheries combining workshops and shops, small industries and poor
self-help housing, the search for serious and mature architectural responses
was limited to a minority of the local professionals. Between the 1940s and
the 1950s among the pioneers in Puerto Rico were Henri Klumb, who synthe-
sized the influences of Neutra and Wright to the conditions of the island and
the firm of Toro y Ferrer, designers of the Caribbean Hilton (1949), the second
tropical modern hotel in the region, after the pioneering Jaragua hotel in
Santo Domingo by Guillermo González (1942). In Cuba, Eugenio Batista integrated the colonial heritage to the codes of the Modern Movement in the
house of Eutimio Falla Bonet in Havana (1939) – defined by the three "P"s:
patio, Persian blinds and the *puntal.* Mario Romañach attained the climax
of this tropical synthesis in the 1950s in individual residences with wood or
ceramic screens on the exterior and interior openings, chromatic filters and
spatial transparencies that allowed cross-ventilation and breeze in the rooms
reducing the need for air-conditioning.[79]
    In the last two decades of the twentieth century, countless works expressed
the search of local designers to develop an architectural language capable of
integrating tradition and modernity, local historical memory and a universal
avant-garde. Call it regionalism or a contextual Caribbean syncretism,
it represented the anxieties of renewal of the talent and creativity contained in the islands, in search of an original Caribbean discourse based on
the particularities of the site, the integration of multiple facets of social
culture and the respect for the habits and customs of the inhabitants, the
resources, materials and local building techniques, related at the same time
to multiple tendencies of universal architecture. Nevertheless, as we said at
the beginning, it is not a matter of establishing a *Caribbean style,* but to
assimilate the conceptual foundations – not the stylistic cosmetics – of the
many currents that inform the expression of contemporaneity in the present
world. Hence the "peaceful" coexistence of divergent tendencies, without
abandoning the architectural attributes of Caribbeanness: the openness,
transparency and lightness dictated by the climate, the geographic and
ecological conditioners (humid tropics, torrential rains, cyclones, tidal waves,
earthquakes); the limited availability of resources and the general poverty of
the region; the practical and symbolic meaning of covers; the use of local

materials; the use of colour; the integration with nature; the control of natural light and the omnipresence of interior shade; the narrow border between public and private space; the constant reworking of the original spatial ancestor and the historical memory of the different social groups of the region.[80]

To conclude, it is possible to isolate certain essential elements of Caribbean architecture today. The theme of housing maintains its narrow connection with Bachelard's psychological and sociological interpretation of the primitive hut,[81] as much as with the Classical Palladian heritage. Components of memory and the subconscious are apparent in the *finca* or farm house in La Cuaba, Santo Domingo (1998), designed by Plácido Piña, whose rigid plan that reproduces the layout of palm enfilades decomposes specially in the virtuality of filters and wooden screens of the local interiors. In turn, the persistence of the bungalow and the *zaguán* is integrated in the redesign of the private house of Luis Flores in San Juan (1990), who transforms a typical introverted San Juan house into a succession of units differentiated by light and shade. The subtle equilibrium between Classical and vernacular, present in the Grand Café of Gustavo L. Moré (1992) in Santo Domingo, disintegrates and transforms the hardness of an urban stage into the lightness of a Bramantesque *aedicula*. The rejection of any contamination with Western culture, descending to the depths of the indigenous past, appears in the first vernacular airport in the world: Oscar Imbert designed with wood, bamboo, guano and palm leaves, the tourist terminal of Punta Cana (1995) in the Dominican Republic. Located at the other formal antipode, there is the image of the airport for executive flights by José A. Choy in Santiago in Cuba (1988), that, without renouncing the tropical identity, "deconstructs" the stereotype of the primitive hut. This, in its African version, is sublimated in the cupolas of the School of Artes Plásticas by Ricardo Porro in Havana (1961–65), affirming the ancestral context of liberated slaves.[82]

In the institutional buildings, the functional and symbolic bonds limited the expressive liberty and the transgressions to stereotypes. Nevertheless, the distinctive traits of creativity appear in the headquarters of the Banco Central of Rafael Calventi (1972–80)[83] in Santo Domingo, characterized by the light golden colour of the cement and the system of openings with brises-soleil in order to keep the use of air-conditioning to a minimum. Example of rigour and perfection it is followed a quarter century later by Gustavo L. Moré's Supreme Court (1999), located in the "Feria de la Confraternidad y del Mundo Libre", whose transparencies, interior patios and volumetric articulations reach a synthesis between monumentality and tropicality; between lightness of the screens and the weight of the marble cladding. The anonymous and introverted character of the convention centres – typical example of the "non-places" of Marc Augé[84] – is transformed to express the attributes of the centre and the local culture of Cuba and Jamaica: Antonio Quintana creates a succession of interior patios in the Convention Hall of Havana (1978)[85] and eliminates the candles in the principal entry, integrating the building with the exuberant surrounding nature by means of the great windows protected by eaves and extensions. In contrast, Patrick Stanigar in his Jamaica Conference Center in Kingston (1983), develops the totality of the functions around an interior porticoed patio and expresses the vernacular identity of the conference halls by covering them with light bamboo vaults.

Although the paradisical image of the Caribbean, seen as the sum of its natural features, is exploited by tourism, the greatest part of the local life of the Caribbean is actually spent in cities. Hence the importance that urban interventions assume if one really wishes to reinvent the lost paradise. It is not an easy task, faced with the persistent social disequilibrium, the traditional poverty of great tracts of the population and the myopic economic and political vision of the local bourgeoisies. Nevertheless, the fragmentary government initiatives attempt to rescue the lost urban significance of those original spaces that resound with shadows and poems. In San Juan, Santo Domingo and Havana, the last two decades have witnessed a significant effort towards rescuing the historic centres, and revitalizing monuments and public spaces in order to reintegrate them into the modern life of the city, not merely to serve tourism but also for the use of the local population. In Havana, site of three decades of isolated apartment block projects, the city of Villa Panamericana (1991) is being built, preserving the typology of the traditional block, with its interior patios and covered galleries along the principal avenues. The pedestrianizing of the commercial streets, such as the El Conde in Santo Domingo and San Rafael in Havana, and the creation of public streets, such as the recent corridor of the 27 of February avenue in Santo Domingo (1999), the Paseo del Parque associated with the government centre of Bayamón in San Juan (1998) and the design of the Sierra, Cardona y Ferrer studio for access to the Caribbean National Forest in El Yunque, Puerto Rico (1998)[86] all demonstrate the interest of governments and municipalities in upgrading the quality of the urban context. These are interventions that aesthetically upgrade circulation points and nodes that define the entry points to the city for thousands of people, such as the transportation centres of Río Piedras (1985) and Ponce (1986) in Puerto Rico, by Luis Flores, the transparent airport of Bridgetown, Barbados (1980) by Víctor Preus and the contextualized train terminal of Santiago de Cuba (1998) by José A. Choy.[87]

It is not by chance that the theme of the anxious city of the twenty-first century is also crossing through the Caribbean universe. Two important international conferences were organized in France and Spain during the year 2000 integrating the Caribbean into the global world of architecture and urbanism. One was the Europandom in Paris, that brought together the urban

146

centres of Guyana, Martinique and Guadeloupe. The other was promoted by the city hall of Santiago de Compostela with the title of The European Model of the City: History, Force and Projection into the Future, in which Santo Domingo and Santiago de Cuba participated along with six other Latin-American cities. Finally, Vincent Scully, in observing the balance sheet of the millennium in an article published in the *New York Times*,[88] singled out the perspectives for the future of the humanized city with a "tropical" model. What he was referring to was the New Urbanism promoted by Andrés Duany and Elisabeth Plater-Zyberk in Florida which attempts to articulate the dispersion of the built environment with the metropolitan concentration, to make design responsive to the identity of the site, and to integrate nature and the built environment, individuality of private space with the sociability of public space, and architecture with the urban texture. Perhaps this is the way to reinvent paradise.

REFERENCES AND NOTES

* The present chapter is based on research carried out in the PRORB/FAU/UFRJ, Río de Janeiro, under the auspices of the CNPq. (*Conselho Nacional de Desenvolvimento Científico e Tecnológico*, Brasilia), on the theme "*Categorização de Cidades Sustentáveis nos Trópicos*". Translation by Liane Lefaivre.

1. Tomás Maldonado, *Crítica de la Razón Informática*. Paidós, Bacelona, 1998, p. 104.
2. Upon receiving the accounts of travellers to the Caribbean the queen commented: "In that part of the world where trees do not take root, little truth and less constancy will spring up between people." Antonello Gerbi, *La Disputa del Nuevo Mundo. Historia de una Polémica (1750–1900)*. Fondo de Cultura Económica, México, 1960, p. 37.
3. In 1776 M. D'Albaret published the first treatise of architecture with a reference to the tropical climate: *Différents Projets au Climat; et la Manière la Plus Convenable de Batir dans les Pays Chauds, et Particulièrement dans les Indes Occidentales*. Engraved by CRG Pouleau, Paris.
4. Richard Neutra and Maxwell Fry, after the end of the Second World War carried out serious studies in order to define the attributes of "tropical" architecture. Richard Neutra, *Architecture of Social Concern in Regions of Mild Climate*. G. Todtmann, San Pablo, 1948; Maxwell E. Fry and Jane Drew, *Tropical Architecture in the Humid Zone*. Reinhold, New York, 1956.
5. I am referring to the book by Suzanne Slesin, Jack Berthelot, Stafford Cliff, Martine Gaumé, Daniel Rosensztroch, *Caribbean Style*. Clarkson N. Potter, New York, 1985, whose images of Caribbean architecture went around the world in the format of a delectable coffee table book.
6. Rafael E. J. Iglesia. "Identidad cultural y arquitectura: orientándose en el laberinto". In Enrique Vivoni Farage and Silvia Hernández Curbelo (eds), *Hispanofilia. Arquitectura y vida en Puerto Rico, 1900–1950*. Editorial de la Universidad de Puerto Rico, San Juan, 1998, pp. 3–23.

7. Alexander Tzonis and Liane Lefaivre, "The Grid and the Pathway", *Architecture in Greece*, No. 5, Atenas, 1981; Kenneth Frampton, "El regionalismo crítico: arquitectura moderna e identidad cultural". In Hal Foster (ed.) *The Anti-Aesthetic Essays in Post-Modern Culture*, Bay Press, Port Townsend, 1983, pp. 101–109.

8. Alexander Tzonis and Liane Lefaivre continued defending the validity of "critical regionalismo" in papers presented at the Encuentro de Arquitectura Tropical, organized by the Instituto de Arquitectura Tropical (San José, 1998). They claim it as a universal category that emerged with Vitruvius, reaffirmed by Lewis Mumford and prolonged up to the present with works carried out in the post-war period on a global scale, in Spain, Scandinavia, and in tropical frameworks such as Brazil, Sri Lanka, Florida and Africa.

9. Ignasi de Solá-Morales, "Identidad y diferencia. Regionalización versus regionalismo". In *Memorias*, Tercer Seminario de Arquitectura y Urbanismo de América Latina y el Caribe "Erwin Walter Palm". "En torno al entorno común". Intentions, references and self-references in Latin America and the Caribbean. Universidad Nacional Pedro Henríquez Ureña, Santo Domingo, 1997, pp. 41–51.

10. Rem Koolhas, Bruce May and OMA, *Small, Medium, Large, Extra-Large*. Monacelli Press, New York, 1995, p. 1238.

11. Graziano Gasparini, *América, Barroco y Arquitectura*. Ernesto Armitano, Caracas, 1972, p. 28.

12. The "Mies van der Rohe" prize awarded by the Art Museum of Bregenz to Peter Zumthor (1999), reaffirms the return to essential values of architecture. *6° Premio Mies van der Rohe de Arquitectura Europea*. Mies van der Rohe Foundation, ACTAR, Barcelona, 1999.

13. "The Caribbean is the natural and unpredictable queen of the marine currents, of the waves, of the churning flux, of fluidity and sinuousness; it is, in the end, a meta-archipelagic culture, a chaos that turns everything upside down, a detour without a way out, a continuous stream of paradoxes; it is a feedback machine of asymmetric processes, like the sea, the wind and the clouds, the Milky Way . . .". Antonio Benítez Rojo, *La Isla que se Repite. El Caribe y la Perspectiva Posmoderna*. Ediciones del Norte, Hanover, 1989, p. XIV.

14. Roberto Segre, "Sincretismo ambiental caribeño: una definición", *De Arquitectura. Cuaderno de Ensayo y Crítica*, No. 2, Novembre 1991, Mexico, pp. 19/22.

15. Jorge Rigau, "No longer islands: dissemination of architectural ideas in the Hispanic Caribbean, 1890–1930", *The Journal of Decorative and Propaganda Arts*, No. 20, The Wolfson Foundation, Miami, 1994, pp. 237–251. The author defines this particularity as a process of "alchemy".

16. Beatriz Pastor, *Discurso Narrativo de la Conquista de América*. Ediciones Casa de las Américas, Havana, 1983, p. 64.

17. *La Ciudad Hispanoamericana. El Sueño de un Orden*. CEHOPU, Ministry of Public Works and Urbanism, Madrid, 1989. Graziano Gasparini, "Las Leyes de Indias. La Retícula Hispanoamericana: Una Forma Urbana Burocrática", *The New City*, No. 1, "Fundaciones", University of Miami, School of Architecture, Miami, Fall, 1991, pp. 7–17.

18. Eugenio Pérez Montás, *La Ciudad del Ozama. 500 Años de Historia Urbana*. Sponsored by the colonial city of Santo Domingo, and its Centro de Altos Estudios Humanísticos y del Idioma Español, Universidad Católica de Santo Domingo, Santo Domingo, 1998, p. 48. In founding Santo Domingo in 1503, Nicolas de Ovando, made the streets parallel with the Ozama, utilizing the levels of the terraces bordering the river banks.

19. Roberto Segre, "Significación de Cuba en la evolución tipológica de las fortificaciones coloniales de América". In *Lectura Crítica del Entorno Cubano*, Roberto

148

Segre (ed.), Editorial Letras Cubanas, La Habana, 1990, pp. 25–65. Ver también, Eugenio Pérez Montás (Org.), *Monumentos y Sitios del Gran Caribe*, Carimos, Santo Domingo, 1995.

20. Edward E. Crain, *Historic Architecture in the Caribbean Islands*. University Press of Florida, Gainesville, FL, 1994, p. 134.

21. Roberto Segre, *La Plaza de Armas de La Habana. Sinfonía urbana inconclusa*. Editorial Arte y Literatura, Havana, 1995.

22. "Las Leyes de Indias. Ordenanzas de descubrimiento, nueva población y pacificación de las Indias dadas por Felipe II en 1573", in *The New City*, No. 1, "Fundaciones", University of Miami, School of Architecture, Miami, Fall, 1991, pp. 19–33. Paragraph 115 establishes that " the entire square around and the four main streets, that have porticoes because they are most comodious for the traders that wish to gather there." And no. 116 indicates that "the colder streets and squares should be broad and the hot ones narrow, although for reasons of defense where there are horses, they should be wide."

23. Joaquín E. Weiss, *La Arquitectura Colonial Cubana. Siglos XVI al XIX*. Instituto Cubano del Libro, Junta de Andalucía, Havana, Seville, 1996, p. 88.

24. Alissandra Cummins, "Architecture, Caribbean Islands". In Jane Turner (ed.) *Encyclopedia of Latin American & Caribbean Art*. Grove/Macmillan, New York, London, 1999, p. 149. The author cites the book of Richard Ligon, *A True and Exact History of the Island of Barbados* (1657), which reveals the lack of assimilation of the climatic conditions in the residences of the plantations.

25. John Michael Vlach, "The Shotgun House: An African Architectural Legacy". In *Common Places: Readings in American Vernacular Architecture*. University of Georgia Press, Atlanta, GA, 1986, pp. 58–78.

26. Roberto Segre, *Habitat Latino-Americano. Fogo e Sombra, Opulência e Precariedade*. Faculdade de Arquitetura Ritter dos Reis, Porto Alegre, 1999, p. 39. Caramuel, in his *Arquitectura Civil Recta y Oblícua* (1678), reproduces the Palladian palace of a Dominican administrator – *Palatium Reguli in S. Dominici Insula ab Hispanis inventi* – and the figures that show the hut as the antecedent of the wooden doric column.

27. Adolf Max Vogt, *Le Corbusier, The Noble Sauvage. Towards an Archeology of Modernism*. MIT Press, Cambridge, MA, 1998, p. 158. The maestro claimed to see the primitive huts of Swiss fishermen in these terms: "*Mais ces maisons sont des palais . . .*" (trans. "but these houses are palaces").

28. Vincent Scully, *Between Two Towers. The Drawings of the School of Miami*. The Monacelli Press, New York, 1996.

29. Joaquín E. Weiss, op. cit., p. 210 ff.

30. Emilio Roig de Leuchsenring, *La Habana. Apuntes Históricos*. Tome II. Consejo Nacional de Cultura, Havana, 1964, p. 121.

31. Abel Fernández y Simón, "The Different Types of Urbanization that Were Established in the City of Havana during Colonial Times". In Felipe J. Préstamo y Hernández (ed.) *Cuba. Arquitectura y Urbanismo*. Ediciones Universal, Miami, 1995, pp. 163–196.

32. "Ordenanzas de Construcción para la Ciudad de La Habana y Pueblos de su Término Municipal", *CyTET, Ciudad y Territorio. Estudios Territoriales*, No. 116, XXX, Madrid, winter 1988, pp. 515–536. Estas Ordenanzas promulgadas en 1861 y elaboradas por el ingeniero militar Antonio Mantilla, resultan de una extraordinaria modernidad, al coincidir con las propuestas de Ildefonso Cerdá para Madrid y Barcelona. Transcribamos algunos artículos importantes: *Art.* 36: En todas las casas de las plazas y calles de primero y segundo orden de los nuevos

repartos se establecerán precisamente portales, a expensas de los terrenos de los solares, pero quedando los portales abiertos al tránsito del público, y debiendo desde luego proponerse y marcarse éstos en el plano del reparto. *Art. 37*: El ancho de los portales será de 3.50 m. en las calles y plazas de primer orden y de 3 m. en las de segundo. *Art. 40*: En las plazas y calles de primero y segundo orden se propondrá arbolado, representándolo en el plano, y todo el que adquiera solares, y en su defecto el dueño del reparto, quedará obligado en el sitio que se designe por el Excmo. Ayuntamiento, la colocación de los árboles correspondientes al frente de sus terrenos.

33. Carlos Venegas Fornias, *La Urbanización de las Murallas. Dependencia y Modernidad*. Editorial Letras Cubanas, Havana, 1990.
34. Alejo Carpentier, "La ciudad de las columnas", in *Tientos y Diferencias*, UNEAC, Havana, 1966, p. 51. "[with the columns] ... go to the outskirts of the city, crossing the whole center of the settlement, covering the old roads of Monte or of de la Reina, climbing the roads of Cerro or of de Jesús del Monte, following the same and always renewed colonnade ...".
35. Manuel Fernánde Miranda, "La Habana, ciudad de América". In *La Habana Vieja. Mapas y Planos en los Archivos de España*. Ministerio de Asuntos Exteriores de España; Ministerios de Cultura de España y Cuba, Madrid, 1985, p. 14.
36. Aníbal Sepúlveda Rivera, "Puerto Rico: Territorio y Ciudad", *CyTET. Ciudad y Territorio. Estudios Territoriales*, No. 116, XXX, Madrid, winter 1998, pp. 321–50. See also by Aníbal Sepúlveda, *San Juan. Historia Ilustrada de su Desarrollo Urbano, 1508–1898*. Carimar, San Juan, 1989.
37. David Buisseret, *Historic Architecture of the Caribbean*. Heinemann, London, 1980, p. 84.
38. John Newel Lewis, *Architecture of the Caribbean and its Amerindian Origins in Trinidad*. American Institute of Architects Service Corporation, Washington DC, 1983, p. 194.
39. Françoise Bonnat, "Espace, culture et societé en Martinique", *Concours International Urbano-Architectural. Thème & Règlement*. Europandom, Paris, 1999, pp. 132–134.
40. Georges Anglade, *Atlas Critique d'Haiti*. Erce & CRC. Groupe d"Etudes et de Recherches Critiques d'Espace. Département de Geógraphie, Université du Québec à Montréal, Montréal, 1982, p. 37.
41. Roberto Segre, "La arquitectura antillana del siglo XX. El síndrome de la plantación", *AAA, Archivos de Arquitectura Antillana*, No. 4, Vol. 2, Santo Domingo, May, 1997, pp. 103–109.
42. Enrique Vivoni Farage, "La Arquitectura de la Identidad Puertorriqueña". In E.V.F. and Silvia Álvarez Curbelo, *Hispanofilia. Arquitectura y vida en Puerto Rico, 1900–1950*. Editorial de la Universidad de Puerto Rico, San Juan, 1998, pp. 119–154. The well-known architect Henry Klumb claimed in an interview in 1962: "There does not really exist a true architecture of the tropics in Puerto Rico.... The Spanish enclosed everything behind bulky and latticed walls. No existe verdadera arquitectura de los trópicos en Puerto Rico. ... Their women were to be not admired but protected."
43. Alicia García Santana, "Francisco Prat Puig y los Estudios Sobre Arquitectura Cubana Colonial", *AU, Arquitectura y Urbanismo*, No. 1/94, Instituto Superior Politécnico José Antonio Echeverría, La Habana, 1994, pp. 19–27; Francisco Prat Puig, *El Pre Barroco en Cuba. Una Escuela Criolla de Arquitectura Morisca*. Burgay y Cía., Havana, 1947.

150

44. Alejo Carpentier, op. cit., p. 55. "De ahí que la obsesión de tener amaestrado algún *lugar de fresco* originara la multiplicación de las mamparas. Porque la mampara, puerta trunca a la altura del hombre, fue la verdadera puerta interior de la casa criolla durante centenares de años, creando un concepto peculiar de las relaciones familiares, y en general, de la vida en común".

45. Alejo Carpentier, op. cit., p. 59. "El medio punto cubano – enorme abanico de cristales abierto sobre la puerta interior, el patio, el vestíbulo, de casas acostilladas de persianas, y solamente presentado con iluminación interna, palaciega, en las ventanas señeras de edificaciones de mucho empaque – es el *brise-soleil* inteligente y plástico que inventaron los alarifes coloniales de Cuba . . . había que instalar en la casa, un enorme abanico de cristales que quebraran los impulsos fulgentes, pasando de lo demasiado amarillo, lo demasiado áureo, del incendio sideral, a un azul profundo, un verde de agua, un anaranjado clemente, un rojo de granadina, un blanco opalescente, que dieran sosiego al ser acosado por tanto sol y resol de sol. . . ."

46. Rachel Carley, *Cuba. 400 Years of Architectural Heritage*, photos by Andrea Brizzi. Whitney Library of Design, New York, 1997, p. 104. See also Lilian Llanes, *Maisons du Vieux Cuba*, photographs by Jean-Luc de Laguarigue. Arthaud, Paris, 1998, *The Houses of Old Cuba*. Thames & Hudson, New York, 1999.

47. Joaquín E. Weiss, *La Arquitectura Cubana del Siglo XIX*. Junta Nacional de Arqueología y Etnología, Havana, 1960.

48. José A. Gelabert-Navia, "La Villa Antillana y los Complejos Vientos de la Historia", *Plástica. Revista de la Liga de Arte de San Juan*. No. 15, Año 8, Vol. 2, San Juan, Sept. 1986, pp. 12–23.

49. Anghelen Arrington Philipps, *Gingerbread Houses. Haiti's Endangered Species*. Imprimèrie Henri Deschamps, Port au Prince, 1977.

50. David L. Cuthbert, "The Jamaica Bungalow. An Archetype of the Caribbean Style", *Axis. Journal of the Caribbean School of Architecture*, No. 0, Introductory Issue, The University of Technology, Kingston, March, 1997, pp. 22–27.

51. Anthony D. King, *The Bungalow. The Production of a Global Culture*. Routledge & Kegan Paul, London, 1985.

52. Gilles Deleuze and Félix Guattari, *Qu'est-ce que la Philosophie?*. Les Éditions de Minuit, París, 1991, p. 101. "Los ingleses son esos nómades que tratan el plan de *inmanencia* como un terreno móvil y cambiante, un campo de experimentación radical, un mundo en archipiélagos donde se conforman con plantar sus tiendas, de isla en isla y sobre el mar. . . . Los ingleses nomadizan sobre la vieja tierra griega fracturada, fractalizada, extendida a todo el universo."

53. Albert Flagie, Laurent Charré, "Modes d"habiter dans les villes caraïbes. Le damier et le labyrinthe", *Concours International Urbano-Architectural. Thème & Règlement*. Europandom, Paris, 1999, pp. 23–27.

54. Jack Berthelot and Martine Gaumé, *Kaz Antiyé. Jan Moun Ka Rété. L'Habitat Populaire aux Antilles*. Éditions Perspectives Créoles. Pointe-à-Pitre, Guadeloupe, 1982.

55. The links established are documentedd in the recent issues of *The Journal of Decorative and Propaganda Arts* published on behalf of The Wolfsonian-Florida International University. Issue 22 is devoted to Cuba (1996) and 23 (1998) to Florida.

56. Roberto Segre, "Preludio a la Modernidad: Convergencias y Divergencias en el Contexto Caribeño (1900–1950)". In Aracy Amaral (ed.), *Arquitectura Neocolonial. América Latina, Caribe, Estados Unidos*. Memorial de América Latina, Fondo de Cultura Económica, San Pablo, 1994, pp. 95–112.

57. Roberto Segre, Mario Coyula and Joseph Scarpaci, *Havana. Two Faces of the Antillean Metropolis*. John Wiley & Sons, Chichester, 1997, p. 54.
58. Onorio Pérez Montás, op. cit., p. 259.
59. Anibal Sepúlveda, op. cit., p. 346.
60. Heriberto Duverger, "El Maestro francés del urbanismo criollo para La Habana", in Bénédicte Leclerc (ed.), *Jean Claude Nicolas Forestier (1861–1930). Du jardin au paysage urbain*. Actes du Colloque International sur J.C.N. Forestier, Paris, 1990. Picard, Editeur, Paris, 1994, pp. 221–240; Jean-François Lejeune, "The City as Landscape: Jean Claude Nicolas Forestier and the Great Urban Works of Havana, 1925–1930", *The Journal of Decorative and Propaganda Arts*, No. 22, Cuba Theme Issue, Miami, 1996, pp. 151–185.
61. "El Malecón de La Habana. Un proceso de transformación y cooperación. Programa Malecón España+Cuba", *Ciudad City*, No. 3, COAVN, Colegio Oficial de Arquitectos Vasco Navarro, Pamplona, 1998, pp. 6–65.
62. Jorge Rigau, *Puerto Rico 1900. Turn of the Century Architecture in the Hispanic Caribbean, 1890–1930*. Rizzoli, New York, 1992, p. 41.
63. Thomas S. Marvel, *Antonin Nechodoma Architect, 1877–1928. The Prairie School in the Caribbean*. University Press of Florida, Gainesville, FL, 1994.
64. Eugenio Pérez Montás (ed.), *Monumentos y Sitios del Gran Caribe*. Carimos, Santo Domingo, 1995, p. 336.
65. About the particularity of the *palacetes* and the festive life of the high Cuban society see: Emma Álvarez Tabío, *Vida, Mansión y Muerte de la Burguesía Cubana*. Editorial Letras Cubanas, Havana, 1989; Nancy Stout and Jorge Rigau, *HAVANA/La Habana*. Rizzoli, New York, 1994.
66. Jorge Rigau, "La Lámpara de Benina y la Ilusión de Ostentación en la Arquitectura del Caribe Hispano". In Enrique Vivoni Farage and Silvia Álvarez Curbelo, *Hispanofilia. Arquitectura y Vida en Puerto Rico, 1900–1950*. Editorial de la Universidad de Puerto Rico, San Juan, 1998, pp. 94–115. In recognizing some environmental qualities of these buildings in Havana, the author assumes a romantic vision of the life of its inhabitants.
67. Lourdes Ortega Morales, "La Habana. Barrio de Atarés". In H. Harms, W. Ludeña, P. Pfeiffer (eds) *Vivir en el "centro". Vivienda e Inquilinato en los barrios céntricos de las metrópolis de América Latina*. Technische Universität Hamburg-Harburg, Hamburg, 1996, pp. 97–134.
68. Aníbal Sepúlveda, op. cit., p. 348.
69. Havana of the 1950s, replete with brand new North American cars, was master-fully described by Guillermo Cabrera Infante in *Tres tristes tigres*. Seix Barral, Barcelona, 1987, p. 298.
70. "La Construcción de la Ciudad de Santo Domingo", monograph of *AAA, Archivos de Arquitectura Antillana*, No. 8, Año 3, Santo Domingo, January, 1998.
71. María E. Martín Zequeira, "Una Ciudad con Vista al Mar. Conversación con Andrés Duany", *La Gaceta de Cuba*, No. 2/3, UNEAC, Havana, March/April, 1999, pp. 10–13.
72. E. N. Rogers, J.L. Sert and J. Tyrwhitt, *El Corazón de la Ciudad: Para una Vida más Humana de la Comunidad*. CIAM, Editora Científico-Médica, Barcelona, 1961, p. 11. "En estos centros deben encontrarse árboles, plantas, agua, sol y sombra, y todos los elementos agradables al hombre. Las calles cubiertas, los pórticos, los patios, etc. – todos ellos elementos muy frecuentes en las ciudades del pasado –, han desaparecido de nuestros pueblos y ciudades". See also Jaume Freixa, *Josep Ll. Sert*. G. Gili, Barcelona, 1979, p. 77.

73. Roberto Segre *et al.*, *Transformación Urbana en Cuba: La Habana*. G. Gili, Barcelona, 1974, p. 108. The master plan of 1970 claimed: "El *Verde* debe ser considerado como uno de los elementos de diseño fundamentales para la estructuración de la *ciudad* y la realización del concepto de *espacio único*. . . . La Habana es una ciudad que ha desconocido en su organización y relación espacial su clima tropical. Por lo tanto, se debe llegar a un nuevo concepto del área verde: 1.– La mayor cantidad de recorridos peatonales totalmente sombreados (verdaderos túneles verdes) que unan puntos de la ciudad. Estos recorridos permitirán al ciudadano caminar en sombra total y continua, alternando con portales que lo harán sentirse servido en cualquier punto de la ciudad y no abandonado en un desierto de asfalto."

74. Sartoris, in his *Encyclopédie de l'Architecture Nouvelle. Ordre et climat américains* (Hoepli, Milan, 1954) devoted much space to the architecture of the regions, from Mexico to Argentina. The book, however, ignored the Caribbean, which remained a marginal and unknown world for European architects.

75. "Después de pasar veinte años estudiando un nuevo (y sin embargo, básicamente tradicional) elemento, éste quizás se ha incorporado definitivamente a la arquitectura de acero, hormigón y vidrio. El *brise-soleil* introduce una nueva tecnología: el control solar . . . [se trataba] de instalar sobre la piel de vidrio, el diseño de un elemento regulado por el movimiento cotidiano del sol y sus variaciones entre solsticios y equinoccios. El evento arquitectónico del *brise-soleil* había nacido." Cited in Jacques Guitton, *The Ideas of Le Corbusier. On Architecture and Urban Planning*. George Braziller, New York, 1981, p. 55. See also: Luis Fernández-Galiano, *El Fuego y la Memoria. Sobre Arquitectura y Energía*. Alianza Editorial, Madrid, 1991, p. 44.

76. Roberto Segre, "La Arquitectura Antillana del Siglo XX. Regionalismo y Modernidad", *AAA, Archivos de Arquitectura Antillana*, 9, 4, September, 1999, Santo Domingo, pp. 98–110.

77. "El 'neototumismo': Brea, Gómez-Tagle, Gutiérrez, Moré y Rancier en la redacción de *AAA*". *AAA, Archivos de Arquitectura Antillana*, 6, 3, Santo Domingo, January 1998, pp. 34–35.

78. In the 1950s, the local dictators erected monumental administrative complexes: in Cuba, Fulgencio Batista carried out the project for the Plaza Cívica in Havana and the monument to José Martí, while Leónidas Trujillo in Santo Domingo, fathered the complex called the "Feria Mundial de la Fraternidad y el Mundo Libre" (sic.). More reproachable was the project carried out in the 1990s in Santo Domingo of the mediocre Faro de Colón, supported by President Joaquín Balaguer, at a cost of over $100 million. Omar Rancier, "*Batman forever* y el Faro de Colón: de Fritz Lang a Melnikov", *AAA, Archivos de Arquitectura Antillana*, 1, 1, Santo Domingo, May 1996, pp. 77–80.

79. Eduardo Luis Rodríguez, *La Habana. Arquitectura del Siglo XX*, photographs by Pepe Navarro. Blume, Barcelona, 1998, p. 269 and following. Among the works, let us cite the Noval house (1949); the Vidaña house (1953) and the La Sierra apartments of Miramar (1956).

80. Bruno Stagno, "El Ejercicio de la Libertad". In *Bruno Stagno, arquitectura para una latitud*, Menhir Libros, Mexico, 1997, pp. 15–35.

81. Gaston Bachelard, *The Poetics of Space*, tr. John R. Stilgoe, Beacon Press, Boston, MA, 1994. See also Joseph Rykwert, *La Casa de Adán en el Paraíso*. G. Gili, Barcelona, 1974.

82. John Loomis, *Revolution of Forms. Cuba's Forgotten Art Schools*. Princeton University Press, New York, 1999.

83. Rafael Calventi, *Arquitectura Contemporánea en República Dominicana*. Banco Nacional de la Vivienda, Santo Domingo, 1986.
84. Marc Augé, *Introduction a une Anthropologie de la Surmodernité*. Éditions du Seuil, Paris, 1992.
85. Roberto Segre, *Arquitectura y Urbanismo de la Revolución Cubana*. Editorial Pueblo y Educación, La Habana, 1995, p. 236.
86. Sierra, Cardona, Ferrer, "De Expo Sevilla al corazón del Yunque: el oficio de arquitectura", *AAA, Archivos de Arquitectura Antillana*, 5, 2, Santo Domingo, September 1997, pp. 53–63.
87. Only work selected in the first Mies van der Rohe competition in Latin America in 1998, *1er Premio Mies van der Rohe de Arquitectura Latinoamericana*. Mies van der Rohe Foundation, Actar, Barcelona, 1999, pp. 66–69.
88. Vincent Scully, "A Cidade Tornou-se o Templo do Século 20", *O Estado de São Paulo*, Caderno 2/Cultura, São Paulo, 2 January 2000, p. D11.

CHAPTER 8

THE ARCHITECTURE OF THE PANAMA CANAL: COLONIALISM, SYNCRETISM AND COMING TO TERMS WITH THE TROPICS

Eduardo Tejeira-Davis

The Panama Canal is renowned as one of the great engineering feats of the twentieth century, but its effects on architecture have not attracted the attention they deserve.[1] In fact, the building of the waterway, which lasted from 1880 to 1914, produced a vast and ingenious array of building types adapted to the tropics. Two world powers (France and the United States) took part in this enterprise, not to forget people from the most diverse origins and backgrounds. The uniqueness of Panama Canal architecture could be preserved for decades due to the existence of the Canal Zone, a *de facto* possession of the United States which lasted until 1979. The heritage of the now defunct Canal Zone, whose reversion to Panama was completed in 1999,[2] includes thousands of buildings, vast forests and other natural reserves, and as such it is one of the most outstanding architectural, urban and landscape settings in Latin America. The future of all of this is presently at stake.

Given the quality of Panama Canal architecture, one is tempted to speak of an absolutely unique and exemplary "tropical architecture" applicable without much ado to the world of today. Here it should be clear, however, that this peculiar "tropicalness" is related to a specific phase of colonialism that bore similar fruits in other areas, mainly in the Caribbean, Asia and Africa.[3] Panama, in fact, has a feature it shares with countries such as the Philippines – Western colonialism appears not in one, but in several guises and time frames. Whereas the architecture of the Panama Canal was possible in the wake of the Industrial Revolution (which made the canal possible in the first place), there is another, earlier type of European-style tropical architecture in the country, this time of pre-industrial origin: that of Spain. The important thing, in any event, is that in the end, neither of these experiences may be repeated today. In this sense, Panama faces the challenge of integrating this complex colonial heritage with today's needs.

ARCHITECTURE IN PANAMA BEFORE THE BUILDING OF THE CANAL

The architecture that developed in Panama from the moment the first Spanish settlers arrived at the beginning of the sixteenth century was, among other things, a response to an environment considered adverse by Europeans. Before the invention of air-conditioning, European-style architecture on the isthmus had to be "tropical" in the sense that it had to adapt to the harsh local climate, where temperatures invariably hover around 25–33°C, rain is abundant during eight months of the year and humidity comes close to 100 per cent. This process of adaptation continued in a trial-and-error process until modern times, when air-conditioning and the increasing globalization of design standards made the climate less and less important as an architectural issue.

The three centuries of Spanish domination produced an architecture comparable in many respects to that of other areas in the Caribbean basin: multiple-storey houses built of masonry, wood or wattle-and-daub, inner courts, overhanging balconies, tile roofs. The balconies, building materials and generous room heights lessened the negative effects of the climate. Houses, on the other hand, were dark and had poor ventilation; it was believed that the flow of air could have deleterious effects on health, especially during the night.[4] Doors were generally planked and had neither louvers nor glass, although often they did have small windows and tiny ventilation holes. Plazas and streets were clearly defined by closed rows of houses built wall to wall, and within the towns there was little vegetation.

In spite of its many similarities with other Spanish American countries, Panama is unique for being a so-called "transit area" ever since European presence in the Western Hemisphere was consolidated. This fact made the country a melting pot for the most diverse cultural influences. During the colonial period, the isthmus owed its transient character to the flow of people and goods between the Pacific seashore of South America and Europe; this traffic was managed through the port cities of Panama and Portobello. A canal of some sort, for that matter, was proposed several times, above all the 1786 proposal by the Frenchman Defer de la Nouerre,[5] but conditions at the time were not yet ripe for such an ambitious enterprise, at least not in Spain.

Things changed dramatically in the nineteenth century. What was first built, however, was not a canal but a rail line across the isthmus (1850–55). The Panama Railroad was the product of American entrepreneurs taking advantage of the famous Gold Rush, which began in 1848. Thousands of fortune-seekers were pouring into California as best as they could, and the detour across Panama was a good option. The rail line, however, did not start from colonial Portobello, but from a new port established by the railroad company on the island of Manzanillo some 30 km to the west. In 1852, the new settlement was named Colon in honour of Christopher Columbus.[6] The modern route across the isthmus was thus established, since it is practically the same as the one chosen later for the canal.

The Panama Railroad dramatically changed Panama's architectural landscape, which up to that time had been a kind of latter-day continuation of the colonial situation described above. To begin with, immigrants in significant numbers arrived, mainly Americans but also Europeans, many of whom bought land, invested money and settled down in the country. The flow of capital and the use of bank credits, both of which were new in Panama, favoured real-estate speculation and encouraged imports of industrially produced building materials. The Panama Railroad also furthered a hybridization process comparable to what was happening in other boom areas of the Caribbean basin and the Gulf of Mexico. The main influences came from the United States, where vernacular building traditions applicable to warm-humid climates already existed. In New Orleans, for example, which had been both French and Spanish before being passed to the United States, the townscape of wall-to-wall houses, balconies and patios would have seemed familiar to a Panamanian; besides, New Orleans was easy to reach from the isthmus. The modernization of the Panamanian capital, in any event, produced strikingly similar effects: although houses from the 1850–1900 period are built of colonial-style rough masonry, doors have louvers and fanlights, decoration is of industrial origin, wood was imported from the United States or Canada and roof tiles are of French origin. Such houses, which are generically described as "French" in Panama, are usually better lit and ventilated than their colonial predecessors.

What happened in Colon also deserves some discussion, since it represents the first important US urban venture in Panama. Land in this Atlantic port city belonged almost wholly to the Railroad Company, and as such it was laid out according to the latter's priorities.[7] The starting point, for instance, was neither a plaza nor a church (as it would have been in Spanish colonial times), but the railroad tracks, which ran close to the wharves. Most houses were of light construction and prefabricated materials imported from the United States were used, since local materials were difficult to obtain and delivery was protracted. The town had a distinctly provisional character and a dismal infrastructure: streets were unpaved, full of refuse and often muddy. For years, the only area worth seeing was Front Street, which faced the main tracks and the wharf. Lots were deep and narrow, and the houses had wide porches towards the street. Eventually, such porches were required by law throughout the town.

The railroad brought to Panama much of what is often (and perhaps misleadingly) called "Caribbean" architecture, which sprang up above all in work camps, stations and small towns along the route. Nothing of this remains today, but this was an architecture of free-standing houses with porches (also called verandas or piazzas), light wooden construction and corrugated metal roofs; all of this fits well into the customary picture of the non-Hispanic colonial world, where the élites approached the climate issue in a way radically different from the Spanish. This architecture was the hybrid heir of two centuries of British, French and Dutch colonial expertise in the plantations and factories of the tropics. The British seem to have been the first (in the Caribbean at least) in promoting well-ventilated building types raised from the ground,[8] an example that was later emulated in other colonies; one should keep in mind that it was long believed that malaria ("bad air") was caused by unhealthy miasma seeping out of the ground.[9] Great Britain, France and the Netherlands also had a strong presence in Asia, where their architecture profited by the contact with that continent's ancient civilizations; the characteristically tropical-colonial roof combining the hip and saddle form, for instance, which is called *techo a la holandesa* ("Dutch-style roof") in Spanish, was common in India and China centuries before the arrival of Europeans.[10] The veranda supposedly also comes from India – from the so-called bungalow, a one-floor house with large roofs, that spread out throughout the tropical colonial world based on the British example.[11] No less important, France, Great Britain, the Netherlands and the United States industrialized at a very early date, a fact which opened the door to production methods beyond the reach of pre-industrial societies: the use of prefabricated materials, simple wood joints and corrugated metal translated into substantial benefits for large companies. Racial segregation was yet another aspect of colonial experience in the tropics, which was put into practice by the Railroad Company in Colon and the various communities along the route.[12]

THE ARCHITECTURE OF THE FRENCH CANAL, 1880–1900

The building of the Panama Canal began in 1880 with the celebrated Compagnie Universelle du Canal Interocéanique: a protracted, difficult and enormously expensive affair which ultimately ended in failure.[13] Led by Ferdinand de Lesseps, the French company attempted to follow the example of the Suez Canal. Significantly, it also bought up most of the Panama Railroad stock, which from that moment formed part of the canal enterprise. The important thing is that the Compagnie Universelle laid out a number of communities on strategically located sites along the route, not to forget extensive residential, administrative and health-care installations in Panama City and Colon. Digging work progressed with great impetus from 1882 to 1889, the year the company went bankrupt. The initial plan envisaged a sea-level canal, although later a lock-canal option was grudgingly accepted. In 1894, five years after the financial collapse of the Compagnie Universelle, not to forget the thousands who died of malaria and yellow fever, a new company (the Compagnie Nouvelle du Canal de Panama) was patched up, but it only did minor work and was sold to the United States in 1903.

During the French company's heyday in the 1880s, tens of thousands of immigrants arrived in the country. The communities built for these masses of people repeated the example of what the Railroad Company had done 30 years earlier, but very little of it is left: most of the buildings were wooden and in time they rotted away and were demolished. On the other hand, French building plans and records, which are very detailed, are preserved in United States government archives, a fact that at least permits a mental reconstruction of the situation.[14]

What is known today about French canal architecture shows a number of distinct features. The norm was represented by standardized, easy-to-build barracks comparable to those that the Panama Railroad or any other great European or American industrial enterprise in the tropics would have envisaged. A well-documented example of French wooden architecture in Panama is a house for four employees the plans for which were published in 1887 in the magazine *La Semaine des Constructeurs*.[15] It was a prefabricated building with four two-room apartments, each room measuring 13 × 16.4 ft. The house was raised 5.6 ft from the ground and it had a porch (called veranda in the plans) on all four sides. The corrugated metal roof was a combination of a hip and saddle, and there was a wooden ceiling for lessening the heat. The wood was imported pine. The boxes with the materials were shipped from the French port of Le Havre, and the building process took no more than 25 days; the house could even be dismantled and rebuilt on a new site, supposedly "without any loss". Although the article does not mention it, each house was clearly separated from its neighbours, and the ensuing arrangement seemed vaguely suburban, very different from Panama's customary crowdedness.

In order to distinguish French from United States concepts, it helps to know that the Compagnie Universelle was not state-owned; neither did it acquire all the land along the route, which is what the American administration later did. Although communities for Canal employees and workmen were laid out, the French never created a closed colonial society, and in this sense the communities were comparatively heterogeneous. Apparently there was also little segregation.[16] The long-disappeared town of Empire, for example, which was one of the main French camps, consisted of houses of many different types and built close to each other, a townscape impossible to imagine in the later United States Canal Zone. The French enterprise was also quite international, and there were subcontractors from many countries, including the United States.

The Architecture of the US Canal, 1904–14

The vast installations and landscapes preserved to this day throughout the Panama Canal area are the product of the United States, whose presence on the isthmus began officially in 1903 with Panama's independence and the signing of a treaty between both countries.[17] The terms of this treaty brought about profound political and administrative changes. To begin with, the Canal Zone was created in 1904 as a separate entity. It had roughly 1400 km^2 and its own government responsible to Washington. The Canal Zone was clearly distinct from the Republic of Panama, although the border was fluid; in Panama City and Colon you merely needed to cross a street to be in the "Zone", as it was generally called.

"Zonian" society arose in the wake of the Panama Canal's construction, which opened in 1914 at a cost of about $350 000 000,[18] and it could flourish given the waterway's elaborate administration, maintenance and defence apparatus. The Canal Zone, which had a population of more than 60 000 in its heyday, had both civilian and military sectors, but in practice the military always had the upper hand: from the beginning, the President of the United States placed the affairs of the canal under the orders of the Secretary of War. From 1907 onwards, in fact, it was the military who actually directed the actual construction of the waterway – standards were set by Colonel George W. Goethals, who had studied at West Point and was a member of the United States Army Corps of Engineers. Both as president of the Isthmian Canal Commission (ICC) and chief engineer, Goethals enjoyed almost dictatorial powers. In fact, Goethals began a long tradition of high-ranking officers from the United States Army Corps of Engineers serving as Canal Zone governors.[19] Army engineers wielded decisive influence in the structuring and layout of the Canal Zone, even if what was actually built depended on the corresponding government agency for its detail, be it the ICC, the later Panama Canal Company or the War (later Defense) Department.

Given its quasi-military origins, it comes as no surprise that the Canal Zone government had complete and absolute control over the land: areas were rigorously allotted in view of the various administrative and military functions or for the maintenance and management of the waterway. Beginning in 1904, for that matter, the notorious Gold and Silver Rolls were established, terms that were initially meant to reflect the currency types used for paying salaries, but which in everyday practice implied a strict caste system defined by the rank and race of canal personnel (United States-born white employees, European or black labourers, etc.).[20] Races and salary ranks were rigorously segregated throughout the Canal Zone, a situation that was kept until the Civil Rights Law was passed in the United States in 1964. Segregation ultimately had important effects on Canal Zone building codes and the quality of construction, both of which were adapted to the various ranks within the hierarchy.

Zonian architectural policies evolved in the course of time. When French property was taken over in 1904, one of the initial priorities was simply to inventory and take advantage of existing buildings and installations.[21] More than 2 000 buildings belonging to the Compagnie Nouvelle were still standing, and 1 500 of these were ultimately repaired and reutilized. Speaking of architectural standards, the first decisive change with respect to the French legacy came in the wake of the health and clean-up campaign that began in 1905. By 1900 it was a known fact that yellow fever and malaria were not "filth diseases", as they had long been called, but were transmitted by mosquitoes. Colonel William C. Gorgas, who was in charge of public health in the Canal Zone, decided to stamp out mosquitoes from the area, and at the same time he opted for sealing off buildings with copper screens. Such screens, which were applied to windows, doors and above all porches, radically changed a building's appearance, which now seemed almost ethereal, enveloped in a kind of fuzzy lightness.

Given the growing lack of housing for the great number of labourers and employees coming to the isthmus (by 1913 there were about 65 000), construction of new barracks was begun as early as 1906. A Department of Architecture had been created in 1904, although initially it only dealt with adapting existing buildings to the new health codes. When opting for new types of barrack, chief architect P.O. Wright Jr mentioned several priorities: meeting the requirements of the climate, choosing materials that would withstand delivery from the United States and low cost.[22] By 1907, 24 new types of house had been developed for the white personnel, and these were clearly based on French experience: they were all wooden and raised from the ground, had porches (albeit screened) and corrugated metal roofs. That same year specific building codes were brought out.[23] These were later perfected and amended; they specified street widths and the dimensions for rooms, doors, windows, balconies and porches. Any new building would have to be erected either wall to wall with its neighbours or separated by a strip of land 15–50 ft wide depending on the case. If the building was wooden, the ground floor would have to be raised at least 3 ft from the ground.

The original community of Pedro Miguel, which was located close to one of the locks, was typical of Canal Zone architecture. The buildings from the French era and barracks built after 1906 were all free-standing, although the French housing had just one floor. Today, for that matter, the only place where wooden architecture from the early years of US presence may still be seen is Quarry Heights, which was formerly a military base. These houses were erected on this site from 1919 onwards, but they actually date from 1906 and initially stood somewhere else.[24]

Zonians, by the way, began to value their lush tropical environment once the dreaded fevers became a thing of the past: from hell on earth, Panama became a paradise. Artist Joseph Pennell, who visited the canal works in 1912 and published a collection of drawings in a handsome book, suggests precisely such an idyllic vision in one of his sketches, where he writes: "I never saw a man who wanted to 'go home' – and some hadn't been home for seven years, and dreaded going – and rightly. The Canal Zone is the best-governed section of the United States."[25] Gold-roll employees, in fact, led a life of great privileges, with high salaries and lavish subsidies.[26]

Not all early Canal Zone architecture was strictly utilitarian. Some buildings showed the influence of United States monumental academic architecture, and as such they were symmetrical, axial and had a historicist air, albeit maintaining the lightness of timber construction. One of the first landmarks in this sense was doubtlessly the long-gone Tivoli Hotel on Ancon Hill which was built from 1905–07 as an official guest house; P. O. Wright Jr – already mentioned above – was the architect. The emplacement of this luminous building on a hill, precisely on the avenue bordering Panama City and facing one of the latter's poorest slums, was not only a masterpiece in adapting to the tropics, but also an obvious statement of American presence on the isthmus. Comparable buildings were soon erected, mainly hotels and club houses in the various communities. A good example was the hotel at Corozal, which was likewise demolished long ago; it had a three-floor porch on all sides and a central pediment.

Official architectural and urban design policies changed around 1912, when a strategy for permanent United States occupation was worked out. By that time it seemed clear that the canal enterprise would be successful, and the Canal Zone seemed viable as a permanent political entity, not as a land of fleeting camps and barracks. This intention is reflected in the Panama Canal Act passed by the United States Congress on 24 August 1912, which gave the Canal Zone its definitive legal framework. A further step was taken soon afterwards: President William H. Taft decided that all the land within the Canal Zone was necessary for running the canal, and he gave Colonel Goethals the authorization to take formal possession of it in the name of the United States.[27] Most of the people living in the area were driven out, including the native population in the old towns and farms along the transisthmian route, some of which harked back to colonial times. A great number of canal workers was forced to move to Panama City and Colon, where they usually ended up living in crowded tenement buildings. At this moment, United States control over Canal Zone lands became complete, and all private property within it disappeared. Land-use policy envisaged a reduced number of communities within the Zone, each one with specific functions. Some communities replaced earlier ones flooded by the rising waters of Gatun Lake. Goethals's idea was to leave most of the

Canal Zone as a huge forest reserve, a step he justified out of strategic considerations.[28]

The new Canal Zone required a monumental backdrop, with buildings erected in massive, durable materials. The star project in this sense was the new government and administrative centre at Balboa, built in 1914–15. Given the proximity of Panama City on the other side of Ancon Hill, this was a kind of parallel American capital. The old hospital inherited from the French (Ancon Hospital, later renamed Gorgas Hospital), located picturesquely on the hillside nearby, was also monumentalized. The same applies to the port terminals, the main schools and other significant buildings. Housing was also improved and landscaping became a priority. Enormous tracts of unused land were transformed into gardens – another substantial difference between the Canal Zone and the Republic of Panama.

The new architecture of the Canal Zone was characterized on the one hand by great severity and economy in decoration and – on the other – by lavishness in the use of available land. An attempt at adapting to the environment (not only functionally but also visually) is also evident. Much remains to be discussed about the underlying principles and concepts. The United States had recently become a colonial power (in 1898, it had divested Spain of some of its last possessions), and in élite circles there was much discussion about how to demonstrate American power, efficiency and order. In 1913, in any event, a Fine Arts Commission established by the government sent a committee to Panama in order to make recommendations "regarding the artistic character of the structures of the canal".[29] Although the original idea was to embellish the canal works, the committee – made up of sculptor Daniel C. French and landscape architect Frederick Law Olmsted, Jr – was impressed by the grandeur and simplicity of the canal as it was. In their opinion, the most an artist could aspire to achieve was to "aid in selecting, as between alternative forms of substantially equal value from the engineering point of view, those which are likely to prove most agreeable and appropriate in appearance".[30] In the end, the commissioners simply made general suggestions about landscape design and achieving high quality of execution in the new installations.

The easiest thing to say about Canal Zone architecture is that its sobriety reflects Anglo-American protestant traditions, the utilitarian character of the waterway and, of course, the standards of the United States Army Corps of Engineers. The École des Beaux-Arts in Paris, on the other hand, was also an important point of reference. The élite among US architects had largely studied there, and the celebrated City Beautiful movement, which had started in the wake of the 1893 World's Columbian Exposition in Chicago, was also based on École principles. A more specific precedent is to be found in the newly acquired Philippines with the plans for refashioning Manila and creating a summer capital at Baguio (1905), projects promoted by William

H. Taft based on his experience as governor of the archipelago. Planning was in the charge of Daniel Burnham, one of the architects of the Chicago fair, who believed in the importance of creating formal urban centres and generous recreational facilities which would serve as palpable lessons in civic virtues.[31] Baguio, then, was designed according to garden-city principles and the centre of Manila acquired a monumental architecture adapted to the local context by means of tiled roofs and Spanish-style porches.[32] Another certain point of reference for the new tropical American architecture overseas was the historic southern plantation, not only because of its dignified appearance and hierarchical use of space, but also because the idea of the "southern gentleman" served as a convenient archetype and symbol of supremacy and capacity to civilize.[33]

The Administration Building and the avenue leading to it, originally called El Prado as the famous boulevards in Havana and Madrid, are the most outstanding symbols of the new Canal Zone. Moreover, they show how the Classical vocabulary could be adapted to the needs of a climate with lots of sun, rain and humidity. The huge building, which makes one think of a royal palace, was designed by Austin C. Lord, the ICC architect, who had his office in New York. The building was erected on top of an artificial hill with a view of the canal; its most outstanding feature is the huge overhanging roof, which is clearly visible from the distance. The plan is E-shaped and the structure is made entirely of steel, although concrete blocks were used for the outer walls to give the building a sense of solidity. Behind the colonnade there are open corridors which initially helped screen the office areas from the sun and rain.

In order to understand this design one must reflect on its sources. For one thing, the Classical orders had long shown their adaptability to the tropics, so their use here requires little comment. The inner rotunda, with its allegorical paintings showing the heroism of the canal enterprise, is likewise to be expected in an American context. According to the magazine *Canal Record*, the building "adapts the Renaissance of the fifteenth century in Italy to modern building conditions and materials",[34] a somewhat enigmatic comment if one thinks of the architecture of Brunelleschi or Alberti, which has little in common with it. On the other hand, if one thinks of the Villa Medici in Poggio at Caiano near Florence, built around 1485 for Lorenzo de' Medici, one comes across a great roof with wide eaves; the villa is likewise free-standing and placed harmoniously in a natural setting. This is not the only place in the Canal Zone, by the way, where the Italian villa had direct offshoots: part of Gorgas Hospital harks back to the Villa Medici in Rome, and the Elementary School built near the Administration Building also looks like an Italian villa. In this sense, the "tropicalness" of Canal Zone architecture ends up being quite European after all.

El Prado led to the true centre of Zonian civilian life: a plaza where there was a club house for white canal employees, a commissary, a post office and other (mostly recreational) installations. This avenue is a true axis of symmetry, and from it the Administration Building may be viewed in all its splendour. The palatial overtones are underscored by the monumental stairs, which are frankly Baroque. The buildings on both sides of the avenue, by the way, look mostly alike.

Whereas Canal Zone public architecture echoes Greek, Roman and Renaissance precedents, housing largely reflects a Spanish-colonial idiom of tiled roofs, porches and white masonry walls. The Gothic revival appears in many a church, and there is an early modern building here and there, such as the Commissary in Balboa (1914–15), which reminds one somewhat of Josef Hoffmann. This stylistic pluralism, of course, was pretty common at the time throughout the United States.

The Spanish-colonial revival, which includes the so-called Mission Style and is usually called *"estilo neocolonial"* in Spanish, deserves a closer comment. In the United States, interest in Spanish colonial architecture had arisen as a regionalist trend, initially in California and later on in other states.[35] This revival could echo anything from an exquisitely simple eighteenth-century Franciscan mission in California to a lavish Baroque church in central Mexico. In Panama, the starting point for the Spanish-colonial revival was the Washington Hotel in Colon (1911–13), which belonged to the Panama Railroad and, by implication, to the Canal Zone. The architect was the renowned Bertram G. Goodhue, champion of the Spanish-colonial revival in the United States. Within the Canal Zone proper, the popularity of the style shows the attempt to visually echo the area's Hispanic setting – as we know, something similar was being done in the Philippines and, for that matter, also in Puerto Rico. This approach became the rule. From 1914 onwards, housing for upper-echelon white employees largely acquired a Spanish look. One of the most important examples is a bachelors' quarters in Ancon erected in 1915–16, which is used today as a cultural centre. Built in reinforced concrete, typologically it echoes the wooden barracks of the previous era, except that the roof is tiled, the massing is heavy and the finial is "suggestive of the Mission Style".[36]

Although timber construction in the Canal Zone was relegated more and more to a lesser rank, as late as the 1930s many an outstanding wooden building was still being erected. Lower-rank housing was often wooden, although by now ground floors were built in reinforced concrete. Such installations looked somewhat like housing quarters from the canal construction era, albeit without porches, which were replaced by conventional windows. Substantial housing from this period is preserved in the town of Gamboa, the maintenance centre for the canal.

THE MILITARIZATION OF THE CANAL ZONE, 1914–45

With the conclusion of the Panama Canal in 1914 (its opening took place two weeks after the outbreak of the First World War), the need for defending the waterway from potential aggressors became apparent. This was to be the beginning of the last important phase of Canal Zone architecture and urban design.

The presence of the US military in Panama had existed since 1903, but at the beginning few troops were permanently stationed in the country. In 1913, Congress assigned a substantial budget for the defence of the waterway and the establishment of large military bases on the isthmus was discussed for the first time. The initial idea was to station an army of 3 000 men, and the plans for the corresponding installations were formally presented to Congress by the Secretary of War in November of that year.[37] Extant plans show buildings of many types: officers' quarters, barracks for troops, administrative offices, etc., all made of reinforced concrete and concrete blocks. In this, Col. Goethals' recommendations were followed.[38] As shown in Fort Grant at the Pacific entrance to the canal, the architecture was still mostly classical in inspiration and it exemplified the influence of the southern plantation archetype.

At the end of the First World War, the Department of War enlarged its installations and a veritable chain of military bases was laid out around Panama City and Colon, all within the territory of the Canal Zone.[39] The military population ended up exceeding the civilians, a trend reaching its apogee during the Second World War. Military barracks and quarters still followed traditional typologies, although beginning in the 1920s – as shown by the ubiquitous tiled roofs and arched openings – Spanish-colonial echoes were discernible. In former Fort Sherman near Colon there are still many barracks with their original screened fenestration, whose long strips have – somewhat surprisingly – a Wrightean air. The ensuing urban design concept, which was applied in both military and civilian contexts, may be loosely described as low-density suburban. Much has been said about the purported "garden city" concept employed, although in retrospect this seems misleading. What is certain, on the other hand, is that landscape design won great importance and was perhaps the only thing giving some warmth to an architecture that was extremely simple in itself.

ECHOES OF THE CANAL ZONE IN PANAMA CITY AND COLON

What was happening in the Canal Zone could not remain unnoticed in Panama City and Colon. In spite of territorial separation there was much Zonian influence in both cities, mainly because the Panamanian economy depended on the United States at all levels. Besides, Canal Zone authorities enjoyed certain prerogatives in Panama. The Zonian Health Office, for example, controlled building permits, garbage disposal and the supply of drinking water.

Architecture in Panama City and Colon reflected this dependency in many ways, some of them quite creative. The first evident Zonian influences were felt in tenement housing built in both cities for canal workers who had to abandon the Canal Zone after 1912.[40] Often erected on deep lots with narrow fronts, tenement buildings followed models developed in Colon during the nineteenth century. They were usually built of timber and had two floors, with rooms arranged in rows along open corridors towards the front and at least one of the sides. Such houses were built according to Panamanian codes derived from Zonian norms and, as such, great emphasis was put on health and hygiene. A minimum separation of 3 ft was required between each house, and rooms had to have a minimum of 100 ft^2, all (at least in theory) with sufficient natural light and ventilation. In Panama City, the most outstanding example of this was the Casa Müller (1911) in the working-class neighbourhood of El Marañón. It is worth noting that after a fire ravaged Colon in 1915 (22 blocks went up in flames) the use of concrete or other non-combustible building materials was made compulsory in that city.[41] Front Street was completely rebuilt and acquired a neo-Classical air, with widely-spaced colonnades in concrete that remind one of Havana. It is worth remembering that porches had been compulsory since the nineteenth century.

As the tenement districts grew, the Panamanian government built a number of monumental public buildings.[42] As in other countries in the region, the models were both European and North American; given the example of the Canal Zone, the climate and natural surroundings had some effect on many a design. Of all Canal Zone-inspired projects, the most outstanding was doubtlessly the huge Santo Tomás Hospital in Panama City, which was begun in 1920. Evidently echoing the Gorgas Hospital in Ancon, the project was in the charge of James C. Wright, an American architect who envisaged a historicist vocabulary of porticoes and great roofs comparable to that of the Administration Building in Balboa. The buildings are arranged in such a way that the main one (built 1920–24) is located at the centre and dominates the composition. The great garden, which faces the sea, permits a good view of the whole.

In suburban architecture the influence of the Canal Zone is likewise evident.[43] As the century began, upper-class residential areas in both Panama and the rest of Latin America echoed the US experience of picturesque houses of irregular silhouette and sophisticated gardens. This was amply known through magazines and motion pictures. In Panama, the effects of the Spanish-colonial revival and Mission styles, which took California, Texas and Florida by storm beginning in the 1910s, could be appreciated early through highly publicized projects such as the Washington Hotel in Colon, already mentioned earlier. The mixtilinear finials, white-plastered walls and tiled roofs of the Mission Style, which were widely used in the Canal Zone beginning in 1915, made their appearance in Panama City in the 1920s; since the country was a melting pot of architects and clients, many mixtures and combinations were possible.

The most unexpected mixture was between the luxurious Spanish-colonial revival mansion found in Beverly Hills, Pasadena or Coral Gables and Zonian military housing. Since many contractors working in the Canal Zone also worked in Panama, it seemed only natural to adapt the mass housing concepts of a military base to a civilian apartment building. Some typically Zonian details, such as the heavy tiled eaves supported by concrete brackets of Spanish-colonial design, proved so functional that they were adopted throughout the country, and the same applies to the screened porch. Although the term "Spanish-colonial revival" may be used generically to describe many a building and residence from the 1930s and 1940s in suburbs such as Bella Vista and Campo Alegre in Panama City, in fact this is a new synthesis that goes beyond established style categories. Unfortunately, real-estate speculation has seen to it that much of this legacy has been destroyed in recent years.

LATER DEVELOPMENTS AND TODAY'S CHALLENGES

The "golden age" of Canal Zone architecture concludes with the heyday of military architecture in the 1940s. Once the Second World War ended and the Cold War began, the Panama Canal passed, strategically speaking, to a second rank. Given the growing importance of air forces, missiles and nuclear warfare, the canal became impossible to defend. The waterway, in any event, required widening to allow the US Navy's largest ships to pass, but this step was never taken. In the 1950s, moreover, there were substantial budget cuts that affected the privileged lifestyle of the Zonian élite. Finally, there was growing resentment in Panama against segregation and the offensive treatment given to Panamanians in the Canal Zone. In 1959, there were violent clashes between Panamanians and Zonians, a trend culminating in the bloody 1964 crisis.[44] After all of this the Canal Zone was never to be the same. Washington decided to negotiate with Panama and search for an alternative to the 1903 treaty. The need for replacing the quasi-colonial Canal Zone with a more equitable arrangement was admitted, a fact ultimately leading to the Torrijos-Carter Treaties of 1977.

The unmistakably Zonian architecture of overhanging roofs and porches remained valid as a standard until the arrival of air-conditioning. With technological progress, however, this character was lost, since cross-ventilation became obsolete. Zonian authorities began closing up porches and windows or reducing their size, and ungainly panoramic windows with aluminium frames replaced wood-framed copper screens; usually there was little interest in finding aesthetically acceptable solutions for these changes. Beginning in the 1950s, in any event, a kind of watered-down, staid International Style became the norm. Zonians, who now lived in air-conditioned houses and apartments, lost their contact with nature.[45] In this sense, the Canal Zone that reverted to Panama from 1979 onwards was, architecturally speaking, very different from what it had been initially.

Today, the future of the architectural legacy of the old Canal Zone is at a crossroads. As a whole, this legacy is the remnant (not to say the corpse) of a very peculiar colonial world. Secure, orderly and rigidly stratified, Zonian society could only exist on the basis of absolute control over the population and the land; the latter, in fact, was completely excluded from the real-estate market. Since the extinction of the Zone, however, these lands are being slowly introduced into Panama's real-estate market, which has long been defined by rampant speculation and where urban and regional planning are commonly subservient to vested interests.[46] Doubtlessly, privatization will lead to great changes in the landscapes of the old Canal Zone. Some forest areas will certainly survive, and older buildings will be preserved only if they can be adapted to the requirements of new market conditions and the ambitious development strategies promoted by the Panamanian state.

The manner in which Canal Zone installations have reverted since 1979 deserves some discussion. The first installations – mostly housing – were handed over to the Ministries of the Treasury and Housing without an overall concept or strategy. Many buildings, for example, were offered for ridiculously low rents or were arbitrarily allotted to government institutions. In 1993, however, the Autoridad de la Región Interoceánica (ARI) was created, and strategies changed.[47] The ARI hired a number of specialized planning companies to work out management plans for the canal area. In this sense, in the last few years the ARI has systematically privatized installations for industrial, commercial, residential, educational and tourism-oriented uses, depending of course on the characteristics of each area. Most of the forests will supposedly be preserved, and ecotourism may bring some profits from them. Gamboa, for example, a maintenance centre in the old Canal Zone, had turned into a veritable ghost town while in the hands of the Ministry of Housing. Gamboa, however, has a spectacular natural setting, and the remains of the colonial royal road are to be found nearby. In view of this asset, an ecotourism resort has recently been established there, although it remains to be seen whether it will turn out profitable. Another example is the City of Knowledge, a technological park laid out in Clayton, formerly a military base.

Architecturally speaking, privatization has brought few promising results. In Albrook, for instance, which was formerly an air force base and where housing installations have been for sale since 1997, many new owners "improve" their standardized houses with decorative details associated with gentrification and social prestige: vaguely Classical columns, arches, coach lamps and other forms of kitsch inspired by US suburban culture.[48] It must be kept in mind, however, that pastiches of this kind sell well in the new middle- and upper-class suburbs throughout Panama City. Given this popularity, one could argue that this is precisely the kind of "tropical architecture" of overhanging roofs and porches that has a place in today's real-estate market.

In spite of the enormous popularity of US suburban models (of which the Canal Zone was arguably the first example in Panama), one can scarcely overlook the fact that the legacy of US presence in Panama fails to awaken much interest in local public opinion – besides, the ARI is interested in privatizing, not preserving. This situation stands in marked contrast with Panama City's historic downtown district, which is on UNESCO's World Heritage List and is protected by precise legislation; the same applies to the colonial fortresses on the Atlantic side. In the canal area context, in any case, it is not easy to decide what deserves to be preserved. Although the historic value of some sites – the Administration Building, El Prado, Gorgas Hospital, Quarry Heights – seems obvious, the same cannot be said of the military bases.

A "critical mass" of people genuinely interested in the colonial legacy of the United States in Panama is probably still lacking. Although some Panamanian élite groups feel nostalgic about the old Canal Zone (in view of Panama's chaotic, crowded and fragmented urban culture, the old Zone easily seems a paradise of order, ampleness and tranquillity), others cannot forget that Zonian society was based on inequality and segregation. Some go to the extreme, in fact, of seeing the conservation of the canal area's forest reserves as a latter-day continuation of Goethals' plan and, by implication, of US colonialism.

The ambiguity of this legacy makes it difficult to integrate into modern Panama's realities. In Panama City's Zonian-influenced suburban areas, of course, such a problem does not arise. Even so, the low-density urban design concepts and generous green areas promoted during the first half of the twentieth century are very difficult to reconcile with *laissez-faire* or maximum profit.

REFERENCES

1. This study is due to a an initiative on the part of the Institute of Tropical Architecture in San José, Costa Rica, and it has likewise benefited from an exchange programme between the University of Panama and the University of Arizona. The best sources for studying the architecture of the Panama Canal are the actual plans and documents preserved in the US National Archives. The magazine *Canal Record*, official organ of the Isthmian Canal Commission, is also of great importance for understanding the American phase of canal construction. Among modern studies, see, above all, Samuel Gutiérrez, *La Arquitectura de la Época del Canal, 1850–1914* (Panama City, 1984) and Richard M. Houle (ed.), *An American Legacy in Panama* (Panama City, c. 1994). See also Ralph E. Avery, *The Greatest Engineering Feat in the World at Panama* (New York, 1915).
2. Following the Torrijos-Carter Treaties signed in 1977.
3. This subject is discussed at length in Anthony D. King, *The Bungalow. The Production of a Global Culture* (London, 1984).
4. David McCullough, *The Path Between the Seas* (New York, 1977), p. 142.
5. On this, see Ramón de Manjarrés, "Proyectos Españoles de Canal Interoceánico", *Revista de Archivos, Bibliotecas y Museos* (Madrid, 1914), pp. 3–12.
6. Colon's original name was Aspinwall in honour of William H. Aspinwall, president of the Panama Railroad, but the name was changed when the city was formally founded with government approval.
7. On Colon's early history, see Robert Tomes, *Panama in 1855. An Account of the Panama Rail-Road, of the Cities of Panama and Aspinwall, with Sketches of Life and Character on the Isthmus* (New York, 1855) and F.N. Otis, *Illustrated History of the Panama Railroad* (New York, 1862).
8. These characteristics are described in Sir Richard Ligon, *A True and Exact History of the Island of Barbados* (London, 1650).
9. McCullough, op. cit., p. 142; King, op. cit., p. 210.
10. See José Ramón Paniagua, *Vocabulario Básico de la Arquitectura* (Madrid, 1985).
11. This is precisely King's subject (see op. cit.).
12. Velma Newton, *Los Hombres del "Silver Roll". Migración Antillana a Panamá, 1850–1914* (Panama City, 1995), p. 171.
13. See McCullough, op. cit., pp. 45ff.
14. That I know of, no systematic study of this legacy has been yet published.
15. Paris, November, 1887, p. 224.
16. Newton, op. cit., p. 171.
17. Panama was part of Colombia from 1821 to 1903. The treaty is the Hay-Bunau Varilla Treaty of 1903.
18. According to McCullough, op. cit., p. 610.
19. On the government, administrative system and first governors of the Canal Zone, see Avery, op. cit., pp. 69ff. and 240f.; Michael Conniff, *Panama and the United States: The Forced Alliance* (Athens, Georgia, 1992), pp. 85f.; McCullough, op. cit., pp. 450, 459ff. and 508ff.; "Five Years of Canal Work", *Canal Record*, vol. II, no. 4, Balboa Heights, 2 June 1909, pp. 316ff.; Willis Abbot, *Panama and the Canal in Picture and Prose* (New York, 1914), pp. 354ff. On Goethals, see Joseph B. Bishop and Farnham Bishop, *Goethals, Genius of the Panama Canal. A Biography* (New York and London, 1930). During the first decade of the Canal Zone's existence, by the way, there were many changes in its administrative and judicial structures.

20. The subject of segregation in the Canal Zone is dealt with at length in Michael Conniff, *Black Labor on a White Canal. Panama, 1904–1981* (Pittsburgh, 1985).

21. P. O. Wright Jr., "What the French Did: Development of the American Type", *Canal Record*, vol. I, no. 15, Balboa Heights, 11 December 1907, p. 117.

22. *Ibid.*

23. "New Zone building laws", *Canal Record*, vol. I, no. 4, Balboa Heights, 25 September 1907, p. 4.

24. Johnson, op. cit., p. 33.

25. Joseph Pennell, *Joseph Pennell's Pictures of the Panama Canal* (Philadelphia and London, 1913). The quote corresponds to Figure 8.10 (pages are not numbered).

26. First-hand testimony on this is found in Abbot, op. cit., pp. 320ff.

27. The complete text of the Panama Canal Act of 24 August 1912, may be found in the *Canal Record*, vol. VI, no. 1, Balboa Heights, 28 August 1912, pp. 3–5; Taft's decree of 5 December 1912, appears in the *Canal Record*, vol. VI, no. 17, Balboa Heights, 12 December 1912, p. 135.

28. *Ibid.*, pp. 213–16.

29. *Panama Canal. Message from the President of the United States*. Washington, DC, US Senate, 1913, p. 5.

30. *Ibid.*

31. Ron Robin, *Enclaves of America. The Rhetoric of American Political Architecture Abroad, 1900–1965* (Princeton, 1992), p. 24.

32. *Ibid.*, pp. 24–29.

33. This subject is discussed in detail in ibid., pp. 63ff.

34. *Canal Record*, vol. VIII, no. 19, Balboa Heights, 30 December, 1914, p. 181.

35. I discuss this subject at length in "Raíces Novohispánicas de la Arquitectura en los Estados Unidos a Principios del Siglo XX," *Jahrbuch für die Geschichte von Staat, Wirtschaft und Gesellschaft Lateinamerikas*, vol. 20 (Cologne and Vienna, 1983), pp. 459ff.; likewise see my doctoral dissertation, "Roots of Modern Latin American Architecture: the Hispano-Caribbean Region" (Heidelberg, 1987), pp. 319ff.

36. "Quarters for Bachelors", *Canal Record*, vol. IX, no. 16, Balboa Heights, December 8, 1915, p. 135.

37. Henry Breckinridge (Secretary of War), *Construction of Barracks and Quarters on the Island of Oahu and in the Panama Canal Zone* (Washington, 1914).

38. *Ibid.*, p. 2.

39. For a summarized history of these bases, see Houle, op. cit.

40. For more details on tenement housing in Panama, see Eduardo Tejeira-Davis, "Panamá: Barrios Céntricos y Vivienda de Alquiler", in Hans Harms (ed.), *Vivir en el Centro. Vivienda de Inquilinato en los Barrios Céntricos de las Metrópolis de América Latina* (Hamburg, 1996), pp. 187ff.

41. See *Canal Record*, vol. VIII, no. 37, Balboa Heights, 5 May 1915, p. 330; vol. VIII, no. 51, 11 August 1915, p. 444; vol. IX, no. 48, 19 July 1916.

42. On this subject, see Samuel Gutiérrez, *Arquitectura Panameña: Descripción e Historia* (Panama City, 1966), pp. 197ff.

43. See Eduardo Tejeira-Davis, "El Neocolonial en Centroamérica", in Aracy Amaral (ed.), *Arquitectura Neocolonial* (São Paulo, 1994), pp. 113–123.

44. All these subjects are discussed in Conniff, *Panama and the United States* . . . , pp. 92–121.

45. On this see Kurt Dillon, "La nueva región metropolitana y los espectros del canal", daily newspaper *La Prensa*, Panama City, 25 January 1992, p. 4B.

46. On Panama City's real-estate market, see Alvaro Uribe, *La Ciudad Fragmentada* (Panama City, 1989).
47. Law 5 from 25 February 1993.
48. On this, see Eduardo Tejeira Davis and Margot López, "Entre lo pintoresco y lo banal hay un trecho muy corto," suplemento *Talingo*, daily newspaper *La Prensa*. no. 301, Panama City, 28 February 1999, pp. 18–21.

CHAPTER 9

DESIGNING AND BUILDING IN THE TROPICS*

Bruno Stagno

In that vast moment I saw millions of actions, some pleasurable, some horrible; none of them amazed me as much as the fact that they all existed at the same point, not superimposed, and not transparent. What my eyes saw was simultaneous.

Jorge Luis Borges, *El Aleph*

TRADITION AND AVANT-GARDE

Traditional architecture and the avant-garde tendency are usually thought of as two opposed extremes. Because we are accustomed to defining tradition as something fixed, immovable, and the avant-garde position as what is progressive, we relate traditional architecture to a specific, pre-existing style and avant-garde architecture to the use of new technologies.

When tradition plays a part in contemporary architecture it is most frequently as an aesthetic consideration in which the most obvious element is the use of some style from the past. And at the other end of the spectrum is the avant-garde tendency, where the latest technology is the means architects use to achieve novel forms of expression.

Both these perceptions are limited. Not only are they presented to us as two extremes of one thing, opposed to one another, but also as excluding one another. An architecture that follows a given style cannot be avant-garde because it makes use of compositional rules derived from the past; it is backward-looking and dependent on various forms of counterfeit to create the look of a bygone era. It is this tendency which, starting in the 1970s, has gained momentum as an option and has now become the universally accepted norm, with examples of buildings that show considerable ingenuity in the way tradition has been interpreted. The result, however, is a proliferation of architectural styles lacking in cogent ideas and which, in addition, have ended by debasing the very cultural values on which traditional architecture depends.

Even when embarking on a purely technological or structural appreciation of a building, it is the outward effect produced by the use of new materials
and construction techniques which dictates to what extent the resulting
architecture is "avant-garde". The architecture centred on technology which
was at the forefront in the 1980s was called Hi-Tech. It was then followed in
the 1990s by "showcase" architecture, where the emphasis was on displaying
technological advances in various ways. In both cases, but more obviously
in the 1990s, architectural space was overtaken by the use of this space to
display big advertising logos, giant monitors, strobe images, or by the use
of several materials at once to achieve various finishes, with multicoloured
neon tubes, and the like, alongside music, speeches, advertisements, voices,
sounds and smells, all thrown together in a chaos of superficial sensation. If
Hi-Tech architecture was the expression of innovation in construction, then
the architecture of the 1990s simply abandoned the idea of architectural
space and replaced it with mere technological and commercial exhibitionism.

These two extremes of definition – traditional and avant-garde – have given
rise to enormous confusion in contemporary architecture, since they are
freely used as yardsticks to distinguish between various architectural forms,
or as a means of marking the limits of one or the other tendency, as either
retro or technological. The architects representing each tendency portray
themselves as two irreconcilable factions competing for first place, and, in
competing for the support of the journals in each case, have succeeded in
impoverishing the whole field of critical architectural debate.

On the one hand the retro or traditional tendency attempts to eulogize
its expression of the architecture of the past, weighing it down by direct,
subjective allusions that are supposed to awaken in the spectator a feeling
of aesthetic "belonging". By repeating stylistic motifs such as cornices,
turrets, cowls, niches, embrasures, exposed brickwork, and others, the architects of retro try to reproduce a past that is in reality dead and gone.
To achieve this they employ structural deceptions such as imitating the
materials used in previous eras with present-day materials, for example
making beams, cornices and balustrades, out of polyurethane to simulate
wood or concrete, stone or brick. In other words it is an architecture of
pretence.

The architecture centred on technology, by way of contrast, has become
an expression of the way new materials can be used to accord with the idea
of progress. The architects of this tendency are motivated by a fundamental
desire to be the mouthpiece of innovation, of the latest fashion, to be the
first ones to popularize it. This attitude leads to the creation of an architecture embodying technological innovation which can only be put into practice
in those countries that possess the latest technology and the resources to
finance it in their buildings. For example, in most countries of the world it
would not be practicable to use 3 m × 6 m plate-glass sections mounted

in high-resistance stainless steel frames, or to use thin sheets of titanium as exterior cladding, since this would be beyond both the country's techno-logical capacity and the financial resources available. Underlying this technology-centred architecture is the desire to channel its structural capabilities and organization in a way which demonstrates its real possibilities. There is a wish to startle people, to excite admiration. Strangely, however, the capacity of these new styles of architecture to startle is short-lived, since in reality the latest generation of a product stops being the latest almost from the minute it sees the light of day, because it will be supplanted by a more efficient and even newer generation of the same product.

An extreme (internal) paradox contemporary architecture is wrestling with is that on the one hand, the architecture of pretence, aspiring to recreate past glories and, on the other, an architecture that is attempting to establish its position by means of feats of technological daring. The present appears to be becoming detached from both, the previous eras and the future.

These considerations – questions of tradition versus avant-garde tendencies, based solely on the form taken by their expression – have resulted in a conception of architecture which is at the same time limited and dualistic, and hence have led to an impoverishment of contemporary architecture. An impoverishment which has manifested itself in a tendency to perceive architecture in terms of its aesthetic image alone, leaving to one side any considerations of practical life common to all contemporary societies, such as shelter, or a cohesive social and economic, environmental and ecological environment. It is a preoccupation which, above all, has made us forget that architecture is the rational creation of a structural form intended to help us live more in touch with the essence of poetry. Any dualistic interpretation cannot fail to have a limiting and impoverishing effect on life, on the individual and on society as a whole.

So will it be possible to make tradition evolve, or to conceive of an avant-garde architecture without technology, or will this mean we end up with a complete intellectual contradiction?

If tradition is having an origin, or roots, in past eras, as well as the action of transmitting this tradition, then it also implies the assimilation of the successive lessons society teaches us as individuals. If we consider tradition in those terms we are including in it a dynamic element which, when it is left out, limits tradition to a purely custodial role with regard to the past, excluding the possibility of evolution.

Similarly, in the last few decades of the twentieth century the avant-garde position reduced itself to the mere application of the latest technology and the use of novel materials, thus excluding the possibility of a non-techno-logical interpretation of this position. If we say that the word "avant-garde", in the broadest sense, means to move ahead of the majority in any activity in which progress is implicit, then it should be possible to consider other forms of architecture as avant-garde that are not centred on technological advances.

So we have two tendencies regarded as irreconcilable according to architectural criticism. One looks to the past, attempting to imitate the reality it finds there, while the other is probing the future in its attempts to create effects. As things stand at present both tendencies reveal a lack of concern for the people, for their real situation, because they are in effect trapped between the past familiar to them and a future about which they have some intuitions but of which they are mainly ignorant. In such a situation the architecture which is suitable for us as people, in other words contemporary architecture, has not reached any comprehensive decision as to the course it should take.

If we could broaden the scope of the traditional tendency by adding to it some force or current which would develop and evolve as it incorporated and assimilated lessons from the past, enriching it by introducing the concept of a progression from one stage to the next, we could then rely on a new meaning of avant-garde to resolve the doubt still inherent in our present situation.

Such a conception of avant-garde which starts with tradition and forces it along the road of evolution is particularly compatible with those regional architectures which have been able to integrate the notion of progress into their values without abandoning a balanced interrelation between the architecture and the environment in which it is placed. Nevertheless, it is these regional architectures which are being forgotten, or shelved, because they are considered as not relevant to either of the two extreme tendencies so much at the forefront of our attention today. This neglect has led to a lack of interest in looking at the dynamic relationship that exists between the past and the present, and the way this could serve as a base for the future. We are forgetting or ignoring architectural traditions that are rich in content and stored knowledge, and implicitly the bearers of cultural content, given that they have found the right harmony between (a) the necessities of living, (b) the environment, (c) material resources and (d) ideas on the use of space.

If we study traditional architectures, using the four criteria mentioned as guidelines, we will be in a position to formulate serious propositions as to the direction contemporary architecture should take, one where cultural continuity and adaptability take pride of place. We will probably then be able to resolve the problem of denial of present and future which is at the heart of our present situation, and which has produced a vacuum in which very few real propositions exist.

The challenge will then be to call on both tendencies – the traditional and the avant-garde – to create a true contemporary architecture.

EXPERIENCE OF TROPICAL LIVING

The Spanish word *vivencias* is used to describe those experiences which are everyday and yet permanent, those which both form and express our personalities. In the tropics the *vivencias* that have the most power and character are those which arise from the relation created between man and his surroundings, rather than those that arise from man's metaphysical introspection.

In tropical latitudes people live out their relationships with the environment in a particular way. Existing in a benevolent climate, but where coolness is a sought-after relief, the body becomes sensitive to slight changes of temperature and humidity. If someone wants to rest he or she will move their chair to take advantage of any breeze, until the most favourable spot has been found. This constant search for breeze and shade means that there is no one place in the house set aside for social intercourse. This close relationship of dependency between people and the natural elements has given them a fund of natural wisdom which, as their surroundings become more artificial, has gradually disappeared.

The modern city is planned using a methodology which is becoming more and more detached from the limitations imposed on it by climate and the environment. The examples we have of uncontrolled urban expansion, both horizontally and vertically, are a testimony to the complete absence of consideration given to these aspects. This is particularly regrettable in tropical latitudes, given that it is precisely here that the benefits the climate offers could be exploited in a more profitable way. Here, urban planning has disregarded the existence of such things as the winds and rains of the tropics, the tropical sun, the brightness, the vegetation, the dust, the shadow, the local topography. In some cases, this was because it was thought that an urban environment could be created artificially by squandering available resources, while in other cases not enough attention was paid to the natural environment, because the aim was not to create a culturally acceptable urban environment but simply to create housing and infrastructure.

The use of artificial microclimates to create comfortable living conditions is indispensable in areas where extreme conditions prevail, and can be considered necessary if one is to populate certain areas of the planet, but its application has been much more widespread than necessary. Much of today's architecture makes wasteful and undisciplined use of these artificial microclimates. Two of the consequences of this, apart from the deterioration of the environment, are the loss of the knowledge handed down by the local populations on how to create habitable urban space which uses its natural resources properly, and also the appearance of a population which becomes increasingly demanding and less tolerant in matters concerning comfort. And this has led to a reassessment of their *vivencias*, and to a redefinition of architectural space, especially architectural space seen in relation to the exterior of buildings.

Bearing in mind that the tropical belt of the planet has a climate where there are just two seasons, without low temperatures, life is possible throughout the whole year in covered, but open constructions. If there is one thing that characterizes life in the tropics, it is the ability to live in close contact with the exterior environment and enjoy the sensation of openness and closeness to nature this brings. Having this experience, and having the in-built knowledge necessary to make use of the resources of the environment, are the things which have given people in the tropics a particular sensibility that qualifies tropicality as an authentic mode of existence.

Over centuries, tropical regions have undergone a process of racial and cultural hybridization which has evolved in the direction of ways of life which are unique. The many racial and cultural blends that have resulted from this hybridization have finally created a new reality that differs from its original components. This *mestizo* culture is no longer native. It has transcended itself by the fresh contributions made to it over time and has gone on to become a genuine alternative to the previously existing cultural strands.

By focusing our minds on these *vivencias* we will be able to place tropical architecture inside human experience, rather than in the realms of rhetoric, a notable characteristic of populations that live tied closely to their natural surroundings. A deeper analysis of this characteristic leads us eventually to summarize our conclusions in one phrase: people in the tropics say, "I am here, therefore I am".

This relationship between *vivencias* and surroundings was obvious to both vernacular and popular architecture, just as it was for colonial architecture in the tropics, which, although it was conceived in Europe, started by taking account of the environmental conditions of the area, especially those which might affect life for the Europeans who have been transplanted to these latitudes.

Colonial architecture recognized the special requirements imposed by its new situation by creating appropriate structures and a new cultural context for the recently discovered regions. The result was an architecture which was a fitting expression of an environmental syncretism striving to achieve a harmony between climate, culture and architecture. Spanish architecture in America, Dutch architecture in Asia, and Victorian architecture, which at a later date was spread right round the world, are examples of this environmental syncretism. The world is dotted with buildings that are examples of this harmony, which communicate the intentions of a design that is not attempting to follow an academic trend, or other, nor attempting to live up to some stance tending towards the rhetorical.

If these designs have an explainable origin then this must be sought by reflecting on the *vivencias* themselves, and on the relation of these to the environment. Usually we are looking at a series of utilitarian designs whose main objective was to serve the needs of a particular way of living.

The challenge for contemporary architecture is therefore to create buildings which, using the *vivencias* of the tropics as the basis for their design, are contemporary, and at the same time represent a viable alternative. It is important that human behaviour is interpreted fully, and that the architecture so created is adapted to the context in which it stands to take root in that society.

HABITABILITY AND BIOCLIMATIC ARCHITECTURE

The central plateau of Costa Rica, where almost all the buildings I have designed are located, possesses specific climatic conditions which determine the architecture of the area.

To achieve an acceptable level of habitability and comfort here one needs to make full use of the given environmental conditions as resources when designing a building. The problems of excess rainwater disposal, air-cooling, decreasing relative humidity levels must all be taken into account, as well as that of reducing excessive glare from the sun.

Although it is true that all these factors affecting habitability can be dealt with aided by technology, it is more economical and less polluting to deal with them through the design itself, taking advantage of the physical laws. The challenge for a truly bioclimatic architecture is to incorporate these laws as the bases of design and as the starting-point of an architectonic style.

For instance, one only has to increase the velocity of an air current to lower its temperature, or create shade on the exterior surfaces of buildings or cool down ceiling and roof surfaces to reduce solar radiation, or create cross-ventilation to dehumidify the interiors, or use eaves, canopies and sunscreens to create semidarkness in the interiors, which not only refreshes the body but rests the eyes as well.

It is widely recognized nowadays that the misuse of technologies that have high levels of energy consumption leads to the depletion of natural resources, and has also created an internationalist architectural style whose most absurd representative example must be the sheer glass tower where a constant interior temperature of 22 to 24 °C is maintained, although the outside temperature may be 33 to 38 °C in summer, and perhaps −10 to −20 °C in winter. Only a sheet of plate glass separates the exterior and interior temperatures from one another, and, no matter how efficient the insulation, a high level of energy consumption will always be necessary to maintain the thermal difference. For the architects it is easier simply to hand the problem over to electrical and mechanical engineers rather than attempt to find solutions by designing buildings adapted to the environment.

Just as it is possible to find satisfactory solutions to the problem of thermal control it is also possible to apply bioclimatic design concepts to other problems affecting habitability. To cool down buildings naturally the most economic method is to lower the temperature of the air before it enters, using water or vegetation, and also by speeding up the air velocity when it enters the building using some method that makes use of differences of air pressure. These could be forms of monitors that capture the air circulating on roof surfaces and introduce it into the interior of the building, accelerating it in the process, and then expel it upwards. At the same time this flow of air around the roof surfaces draws in the air entering via the windows and removes it through the opposite end of the monitor.

Wide eaves, canopies and sunshades will always reduce the amount of light penetrating the interior, which means it is important to compensate for this loss by creating apertures in the roof that will allow light to enter. As is known, in the northern hemisphere light coming from the north is the most consistent, making smaller contrasts of light and shadow, compared to light coming from a southerly direction. This makes its use ideal for achieving an even illumination throughout interior spaces.

Direct overhead natural lighting in the core of buildings is very efficient, but does have the drawback of introducing heat at the same time, especially in tropical latitudes. In these cases it is particularly interesting to see how the desired level of illumination can be attained while at the same time filtering the sun's rays to reduce irradiation, which has the effect of lowering the inside temperature. If circumstances require, various devices may be employed simultaneously to do this. Past experience has demonstrated that with the use of certain devices an inside illumination of 800 lux, against an exterior value of >5000 lux, could be achieved, and an interior temperature of 26.6 °C when the external temperature registered 33.4 °C. Humidity readings in the same example were 62 per cent inside and 74 per cent outside. (These readings are averages for the month of March, during the dry season, at San José, Costa Rica.)

TECTONICS AND ARCHITECTURE

Early in my professional career I opted for an architecture in which local tectonic considerations played a major role. This decision followed from the quality and ready availability of construction materials such as concrete blocks and bricks in Costa Rica. These, because of their low cost, represent the modern alternative to the stone or sun-dried adobe construction prevalent in former times. The existence of a labour force of skilled and well-qualified craftsmen also makes it possible to work with blocks or bricks at a reasonable cost and with few unforeseen overheads.

Combining blocks and bricks in a wall creatively, in a natural way, as small construction modules, and in a complex design more typical of an architecture of materials than of civil engineering, buildings can be created that show marked tectonic features. The rough-hewn texture of the finished building is ridged and furrowed in a way which highlights differences of light and shade, creating a perpetual interplay between the two.

181

While blocks and bricks are certainly no technical novelty – in many countries they continue as the most basic elements in building – the fact that they have the properties of insulation, durability and anti-seismic capability, coupled with low maintenance requirements, makes them ideal building materials for our time, and for building in countries where the climate makes insulation and careful, constant upkeep necessary. Blocks and bricks, left exposed, need almost no maintenance, and by using water- and dust-repellents they will resist the passage of time, and the aesthetic effect created accentuates in a natural way their appearance and their unique properties.

The preference for walls constructed in concrete blocks or bricks, avoiding large openings, is not only a response to a craftsman's desire to express his or her skill in creating an essay in masonry or brickwork, but also simplifies the construction itself. On one side you have the closed wall sections, and on the other the open, transparent ones. The reliance on structure-bearing walls to give a building its chosen form also influences this preference.

Light, metallic structural elements wrought in plant-like forms provide a good alternative to the opaque massiveness of masonry. The result is an attractive contrast between the solid, robust masonry and the gracefulness and brilliance of the metal used. Then glass, another of the materials used freely, adds its transparency and brilliance to this contrast, as well as providing reflections.

Such a contrast is part of the language of tectonics in architecture. In the case of these buildings, the rough opaqueness of the masonry is set off by the graceful brilliance and reflections of the metal and glass. Contrasting two materials with opposed qualities highlights their appearance. The visual properties of simple materials are enhanced.

Considering that the precipitation of this region plays such an important part in determining its architecture, serious attention has to be paid to the roof when designing a building if catastrophic interior flooding is to be avoided. In tropical architecture the crucial element is the roof. Its size, its presence, and its expressive strength make it the centrepoint of this architecture.

Starting with the normal pyramidal roof, or with a Dutch roof, both of which function without being too daring, and give a feeling of protection and symmetry, stability or certainty, other more interesting alternatives have been looked for.

In these latitudes there are various additional functions carried by the roof: illumination, ventilation, shading from the sun, insulation, apart, of course, from its prime function, which is to create protection from the sun and rain. The roof may rest on its supporting walls, or it may float above them; it can give direction to the interior space, and at the same time stamp its character on the building.

The roof and the double roof, eaves and floating eaves, canopies and monitors, ventilators and shutters are all design elements which are used to fulfil all the functions expected of roofing in the tropics with its high rainfall, powerful sunlight and hurricanes.

Using corrugated iron sheeting for roofs and walls allows for a light and open treatment of space that is an ideal option for tropical architecture. And, together with metal structural elements, it adds colour to the building.

A contrast can also be created between the earthy, opaque tones of stone and brickwork and the brilliant, polished colour of the metal used. This range of shiny colours is inspired by the deep blue of gingers, by the hues of yellow lantanas and bromelias, all forming a contrast with the surrounding greenery and with the sky.

Although the internationalization of the economy has given us more variety in the range of available construction materials, there are few from abroad which can compete with local ones in either price or quality. It is a reality for us that we are still forced to rely on a limited variety of materials for construction; nevertheless, this has led us to design buildings that maximize the constructional and aesthetic possibilities of the materials we have, so as to make them attractive enough to compete with imported materials, bearing in mind that these imported materials are better suited to the creation of substitute styles than to real architecture. Because of transport costs it is the synthetic materials which are imported in quantity, and, as we know, these favour imitation, especially when using them for walls and roofs.

SPACE AND SHADOW

Throughout the history of architecture we see projects where the use of light and space was the essential preoccupation of the architect. Theories have been painstakingly elaborated on its use as one of the chief characteristics in a given architectural design, where light penetrating an empty space becomes the key to sculpting this dark area through rays of light shining through cracks, or openings. Light is here being treated as a material. But it should be made clear that in architecture light can only be treated as a material element when it makes its appearance simultaneously with its opposite – shadow. Light and shadow separately do not create references, just as one needs a cloud in the sky in order to define a limit. So it is when they act in concert that they become of interest for architecture, because then they can be used as a tool to model architectural space.

In the tropics it is particularly interesting to conceive architectonic space by emphasizing the way shadow is treated, rather than light, because in these latitudes it is the shadow, which illuminates life, which unites and motivates *vivencias*, since the intensity and excessive heat associated with light make it uncomfortable. In tropical regions it is better to protect oneself from too much light, and this is why in the architectural projects being discussed light is treated only as something that invades the space enclosed by the building. In this case it is shadow that acts as the defining element in interior space.

When architecture in the tropics abandons walls and opts for transparent surfaces this changes the effect of space. We move from an interior, shut off from the exterior to a situation where one can appreciate both interior and exterior at the same time. Both become equally significant – one dominated by light and the other by semidarkness.

Under these circumstances it is advisable to create a design where transparent surfaces use shadow as an integrated part of their function, creating a sequence of shaded and semishaded spaces between the interior and the exterior. The transparency of the walls, or having no walls at all, creates a counterpoint to the empty space beneath the roof. The space constructed is tensioned outwards, but at the same time it is contained within the whole of the empty space covered by the roof. It is the opposite of the space created by Mies van der Rohe, which is an open, naturally lit interior that gradually glides off towards the exterior between the flat slabs that form the roof and the floor. Mies van der Rohe's space receives light laterally, using the roof simply as a cover.

In my designs the roof is transformed into a focal point; it becomes part of the definition of interior space. It does not merely provide cover, rather it defines the character of the space beneath. By splitting the roof up into a multiplicity of slopes and angles, and into various segments, one can achieve very precise results when shaping the way the light penetrates, allowing the different, separated segments to be either bathed in light or shadow, according to one's preference.

Space remains defined by the roof, as there is no flat ceiling, which means all the dynamics inherent in its inclined planes can be expressed and then developed in the design. The wealth of possibilities offered by the space designed in this way comes from this conjunction of inclined planes with transparent surfaces and reflections, all bathed in a semidarkness penetrated by shafts of light and contained by walls that allow light to enter through them.

The reflections create new visual perspectives of the building itself, or of its immediate surroundings, which again enrich one's perception of space by saturating it with virtual images, seen simultaneously with real ones. Such an extraordinary *vivencia*, these multiple, coinciding visions of a given space, fill it with a wealth of subtle detail.

(a)

(b)

Figure 9.1 *a, b and c. Ford showroom and Bank of San José, Curridabat (architect and photos Bruno Stagno)*

(c)

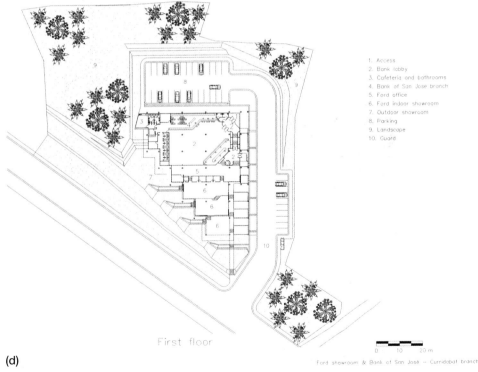

1. Access
2. Bank lobby
3. Cafeteria and bathrooms
4. Bank of San Jose branch
5. Ford office
6. Ford indoor showroom
7. Outdoor showroom
8. Parking
9. Landscape
10. Guard

First floor

0   10   20 m

Ford showroom & Bank of San José — Curridabat branch

(d)

Figure 9.1 (cont.) d. Plan for Ford showroom and Bank of San José, Curridabat (architect Bruno Stagno)

(a)

(b)

Figure 9.2 a and b. Bank of San José, Rohrmoser
(architect and photos Bruno Stagno)

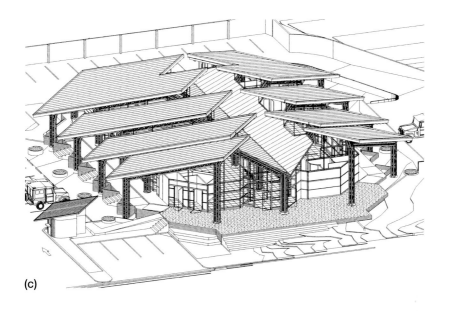

Axonometric view (south)

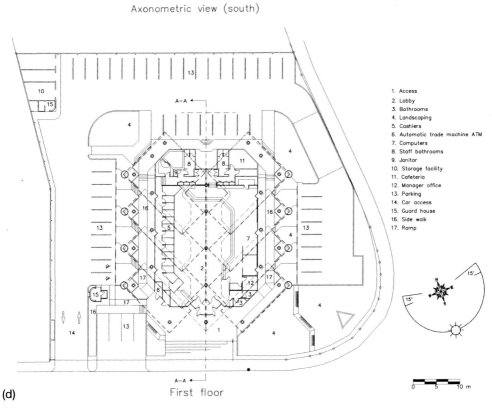

1. Access
2. Lobby
3. Bathrooms
4. Landscaping
5. Cashiers
6. Automatic trade machine ATM
7. Computers
8. Staff bathrooms
9. Janitor
10. Storage facility
11. Cafeteria
12. Manager office
13. Parking
14. Car access
15. Guard house
16. Side walk
17. Ramp

First floor

Figure 9.2 *(cont.) c and d. Plan for Bank of San José, Rohrmoser (architect and plans Bruno Stagno)*

(a)

(b)

Figure 9.3 a, b and c. Artistic Center, Humboldt School
(architect and photos Bruno Stagno)

(c)

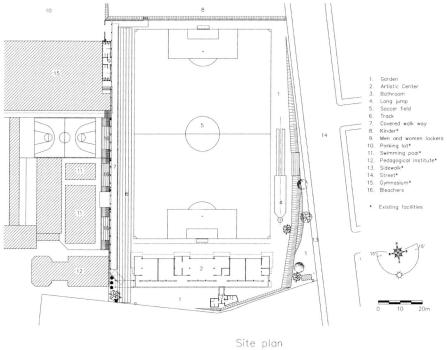

1. Garden
2. Artistic Center
3. Bathroom
4. Long jump
5. Soccer field
6. Track
7. Covered walk way
8. Kinder*
9. Men and women lockers
10. Parking lot*
11. Swimming pool*
12. Pedagogical Institute*
13. Sidewalk*
14. Street*
15. Gymnasium*
16. Bleachers

* Existing facilities

0   10   20m

(d)

Site plan

Figure 9.3 *(contd.) d. Plan for Artistic Center, Humboldt School (architect, photo and plan Bruno Stagno)*

This conception of space designed around shadow effects and transparent surfaces, alternating on different planes and interrupted by reflections and brief flashes of brightness, has its limits defined by this play of shadow, semi-shadow and brightness. The challenge for the architect is to lend reality to something as tenuous as a shadow effect and to cause it to occur on different planes until he has reached a particular architectonic language. He is attempting to make a virtual reality into a material one, in order for perception of this reality to become the defining characteristic of space.

In some of the buildings shown here one moves from an exterior which is naturally brightly lit to a space in shadow, and from there to an interior which is in semishadow. In other words the progression from a greater amount of light to a lesser amount is intentionally interrupted.

Space is here perceived via an appreciation of these shadow effects of varying intensity that can be glimpsed as one passes through the building. The course taken by the sun during the day lends an ever-changing variety to these shadow effects. One's perception of the space itself is constantly being changed, giving it a variety that is heightened by the appearance of occasional flashes of brightness.

Such an architectural language can be seen as completely devoid of all pretensions to formality, completely without pomp or pretence. Rather it is a celebration of the delicate effect of shadow, highlighting this effect as one of the most typical characteristics of tropical space.

This type of architectural design could be described as informal, not because it is not orderly, but because it does not aspire to any static or symmetrical form, and also because the limits marked out by this design are sometimes vertical planes created by light or shadow, in other words shaded or lit areas. It is a design where space simultaneously protects from the elements and opens itself to the exterior; it is light, and at the same time darkness. It focuses the surrounding landscape and at the same time imposes reflections of another visual perspective on it: a space that brings together alternative perceptions of the space itself and its surroundings. It is an attempt to create a space which joins together all the possibilities of a given environment, while at the same time putting these possibilities into a defined order.

NOTE

* Translated by Jaime Florez.

CHAPTER 10

ARCHITECTURAL RESPONSES IN TROPICAL INDIA

Rahul Mehrotra

When one conjures up images of Indian architecture, the ones that come to the fore are the great mughal buildings of Fathepur Sikri, the *havelis* of Jaisalmer and all the other wonderful cities, towns and palaces in Rajasthan–Udaipur, Jaipur, Jodhpur (Figure 10.1). In the twentieth century, Lutyens' New Delhi (Figure 10.2), Le Corbusier's Chandigarh (Figure 10.3) and the potent results of the architectural processes they set off dominated the architectural landscape of the Indian subcontinent. In fact, Corbusier's intervention sparked off an architectural awareness in the areas in which he built – Chandigarh and Ahmedabad, and with an already active patronage and awareness in Bombay and Delhi, this completed the spine of contemporary architecture in India – a zone that ran from Chandigarh to Bombay through Delhi and Ahmedabad.[1] Even today, contemporary Indian architects, such as Achyut Kanvinde, Balkrishna Doshi, Charles Correa and Raj Rewal, have all built in and their practices sustained in the architectural zone that runs from Chandigarh through Delhi to Ahmedabad, and finally peters out at Bombay on the edge of the tropics.

A wealth of architectural typologies has emanated from these responses to an essentially hot and dry arid climate in the subtropics. But the issues generated by building in this region are quite apart from those in tropical India. In the contemporary architectural history of India, the tropics have not had adequate responses from the architectural community which is only now making the transition out of the overwhelming influence of the purism of the Modern Movement and International Style. While the hot-arid regions of the country lend themselves more easily to this vocabulary, adjusted and reinvented by Le Corbusier for India, the tropics have had no such powerful contemporary intervention – one which has actually transformed an entire approach to building, and in the process reinvented a vocabulary of built-form. The vocabulary of large surfaces devoid of all weathering elements – the abrupt chopping of the box without all the transitionary buffer zones, has not facilitated the adaptation of Modern architecture to tropical India.

Figure 10.1 *The popular image of architecture in India – Jodhpur, Jaipur, the towns of Rajasthan – are essentially responses to a hot and arid climate on the edge of the tropics (photo Rahul Mehrotra)*

Figure 10.2 *Lutyens' New Delhi extended the evolution of a pan-Indian identity which was rooted outside the tropics (photo Rahul Mehrotra)*

Figure 10.3 *The Assembly building at Chandigarh – a new paradigm for building was established in South Asia sparking off shifts in architectural attitudes. While emanating as a response to the hot-arid regions of India, this approach and style were to influence equally works in the tropics in the southern parts of India (photo Rahul Mehrotra)*

Figure 10.4 *A view of the Padmanabhapuram Palace (fifteenth–eighteenth centuries) – an appropriate model for building in tropical India (photo Rahul Mehrotra)*

In fact, there really has been no debate on what could possibly be an appropriate architectural image, vocabulary and language for tropical India.

RESPONSES IN INDIA

Aside from the fact that there are so many climatic variations within the tropics – the coastal areas, the hills, and the hinterland, all of which require distinct architectural responses, it has been the quest in independent India, a sort of obsession, to evolve a pan-India identity. In this quest, the hot-arid climatic response and ensuing architectural issues and vocabulary have clearly dominated the debate. Even architects working in the tropics in India have been completely overwhelmed by the vocabulary and approach that have emanated from the architectural spine along the Chandigarh–Ahmedabad axis. This in spite of the fact that adequate traditional precedents exist – the architecture of Kerala, Goa, the many ethnic neighbourhoods of Bombay, all hold the vital clues for an appropriate architecture for the tropics.

The Padmanabhapuram Palace in Kerala, for example, with its superb layering of spaces – both vertically and horizontally – and use of devices such as louvers and screens, modulates light and air in a manner that makes the building extremely comfortable. And by the disintegration of its form, it allows air to move through the various areas independently while also allowing for a graceful weathering process where each part mutually protects the other. The ensuing architectural vocabulary besides being extremely elegant seems rooted to the locale and grows out directly from the issues of building in the tropics (Figure 10.4).

A similar approach is seen in the Portuguese influenced Goan houses (Figure 10.5). Besides the numerous spatial innovations, in Goa the idea of attachments is an important one – where the building, through attached devices such as shades, adjusted itself for the monsoon forces. In fact, a Portuguese law prohibited any awnings beyond October, one month after the monsoon had receded. It was necessary for everyone, including churches, to remove all attachments and whitewash the structure – a sort of renewal process. Thus, an otherwise alien architectural sensibility the Portuguese carried to their colony was overlaid with elements that besides providing the buildings with a distinct local identity also made them function more efficiently for the climate and lifestyle of the inhabitants.

The traditional urban neighbourhoods of Kotachiwadi and Matharpacady in Bombay on the other hand are wonderful examples of a low-rise high-density configuration that grew out of the pressures on urban land and resulting high land prices. These settlements, characterized by narrow but breezy streets, lined with a rich array of architectural elements such as verandas, open staircases and screened pavilions, besides creating a rich vocabulary, allow the breeze to easily filter through spaces that are effortlessly shaded on account of the high density. Furthermore, these elements, besides subtly setting up privacy gradients (both implicitly and explicitly) are also intelligent responses to the tropical climate (Figure 10.6).

The British in India, while building in the "colony" were also sensitive to climatic constraints and to the idea that climate was the generator of the architectural form. The bungalow was a superb innovation that testifies to the commonsense solutions that evolve out of the common landscape of architectural inventions. The bungalow, a free-standing, single family house, organized the central functions in the core with a series of wrap around functions that insulated the house from the heat or cold. The critical wrap around spatial element was the veranda or transitional zone that allowed the air to move through the building while still providing shade. In fact, the veranda not only was an important architectural feature, but it also supported an entire lifestyle in its confines – for sitting, sleeping, socializing, while also allowing its occupants to retreat into the privacy of the inner chambers. A number of devices such as louvers, *jalis* and *jafferies*[2] (Figures 10.7 and 10.8) were used to modulate the extent of breeze allowed into the interiors, as well as to provide privacy for the veranda – resulting in a rich architectural vocabulary.

TROPICAL CITY

In many ways the extension of this spatial element of the veranda, at the city level, was the arcade. The arcade allows the breeze to pass through into the adjoining buildings, while at the same time protecting the pedestrians from the rain and sun – what better architectural response for a tropical city? But more than that, it is an incredibly resilient urban design component, capable of many adjustments. An example is the Fort Area, the historic core of Bombay, where the buildings are richly varied in style and treatment, resulting in a remarkably coherent urban experience, woven together by the topological consistency of built-form. And, most importantly, a harmonious accommodation of the public realm: at the foot of these buildings, the device of the continuous pedestrian arcade brings the urban rich and poor together in a weather protected public space that harbours the life of the street. In fact, here the arcade goes beyond its protective function to become the veranda for the city.[3]

Today, tropical cities are no different from those in desert climates or even snow bound Europe or America. The arcade, verandas, trellis screens, louvers and all the components that easily fitted together to create a stunning architectural vocabulary and urban pattern are fast disappearing to give way to

Figure 10.5 *The portico of a typical Catholic house in Goa. The attachments and generous protection offered by the various building elements facilitate efficient use of the building while allowing it to weather gracefully (photo Rahul Mehrotra)*

Figure 10.6 *Kotachiwadi – an ethnic neighbourhood in Bombay. The architecture of cumulative generations of wisdom is a perfect response to the climate and lifestyle in the tropics (photo Rahul Mehrotra)*

Figure 10.7 *View of the corridor at Padmanabpuram – where an inner core space is surrounded by a veranda with screens made in different materials – a spatial element that literally attaches itself to the core structure within (photo Rahul Mehrotra)*

Figure 10.8 *View of a classic lattice work screening a veranda in a colonial house in Hyderabad (photo Rahul Mehrotra)*

the high-rise, sealed box set in a repetitive landscape – with little or no connections between the various parts that comprise the urban landscape. The spatial element of the arcade, which was the pedestrian walkway and bazaar compressed into each other, is giving way to the air-conditioned shopping mall – a notion that has eroded the physical fabric and is transforming the social fabric and definition of public space. Having evolved in North America, today this notion of a hermetically sealed public space is influencing the very form of cities across the globe.

Thus the issue of the built-form identity and typology of tropical cities is one of crucial importance as without setting up the appropriate context the architecture, a tropical architecture, cannot really emerge, at least not in our urban centres. What we must do is reexamine the way buildings were traditionally arranged so as to shade and protect each other and to set up a channel of breezes throughout the settlement and then see how the architecture responds to this pattern to draw these breezes into the interiors, how buildings adjust themselves to accommodate arcades, verandas, etc. That is, we must develop an entire vocabulary all the way from the unit, to the pattern of the city – of how these units are arranged to add up to something greater than a mere sum of the individual parts.

The Indian architect Charles Correa has formulated this position. To quote him:

> For both these crucial tasks (tropical Urban Form and tropical Architecture) are really two sides of the same coin. Some years ago, the architect and urbanist Jacquelin Robertson pointed out that it was relatively easy to design a house in the bazaar in Isfahan, or the old city of Jaipur, or along the canals of Amsterdam, because all you had to do is design a spare part for a machine which already exists. In contrast, Robertson characterized American downtown as a bunch of spare parts, with no one having the foggiest notion of what the machine might look like.

In short, you cannot conceptualize what the tropical city might look like unless you simultaneously speculate about the typologies of tropical buildings and vice versa.

In India, the disjuncture between the urban form and appropriate tropical architecture is immense. While the rupture in this continuum occurred at the beginning of colonial rule, when Western typology and urban pattern were superimposed on the Indian landscape, the great shift in building typologies occurred with the advent of Modernism. While Modernism was a great movement in hot-arid India, it wreaked havoc in the tropics and devastated our cities. Besides completely embracing the Corbusian dream of the "city in the garden" (of which Singapore is the ultimate expression in the tropics!) Modernism perpetuated the *tabula rasa* mindset, one which believes, "I have seen the future and it works!" This resulted not only in shifts in building typologies, but also in the way city planning evolved and was legislated –

perpetuating "sameness" in the built environment through building bylaw and other planning policies – which were somewhat evenly imposed across the country. Localized responses diminished, transforming the contemporary Indian cities to a form characterized by a schizophrenic landscape of many disparate parts representing diverse cultural, social and economic aspirations.

MODERNISM IN INDIA

Furthermore, the idea of a "Modern Style" was articulated and became extremely popular in India from the 1950s onwards – the post-colonial phase of Indian history. Here Modernism was seen as the natural approach to give expression to the new nationalism – unhampered by historical or cultural restraints and reflecting the "dynamism of a free people in its march to economic development, sharing in the continuity of design ideas linking the whole world".[4]

What this notion did, in one fell swoop, was attempt to neutralize regional differences – the idea that a pan-India architecture founded on Modernism would serve as the vehicle to evolve an architectural identity for independent India. The appropriate style, of course, being Modernism! Architects, whether they were building in hot-arid India or tropical India employed the same building material and vocabulary, and over time building bylaws and planning legislation all implicitly supported, encouraged and facilitated this approach and style of building. In short, there occurred an incredible transformation in the built landscape of India both at the level of city form as well as individual building typology.

While from the decades of the 1930s to the 1950s the "Modern Style" was sweeping South Asia, in remote Pondicherry (a French colony) a seminal building called the Golconde Ashram was designed and built between 1936 and 1948 (with construction interrupted by the war) by Antonin Raymond (Figure 10.9). Pondicherry, while outside the Chandigarh, Delhi, Ahmedabad, Bombay zone of architectural awareness, was evolving from the 1930s as a centre of Western attention on account of the developing ashram at Auroville (situated near Pondicherry). The Golconde Ashram was a sophisticated architectural response, within the Modern idiom, to the local climate. The building façade exclusively used large louvers that facilitated cross-ventilation while aesthetically softening the minimalist Modern aesthetic that the building employed. Furthermore, the use of local stone and wood for the finishes added a warmth that went beyond the rigorous use of industrial material and brute concrete that characterized the later "Modern" buildings in Chandigarh and Ahmedabad.[5] While this building served as a powerful counterpoint to the "Modern" debate, it went more or less unnoticed in the larger architectural debate in the country.

In fact, the following decades of the 1950s and 1960s saw Modernism at its peak in India and South Asia. In these two decades the entire formal landscape of India was transformed by Modernism – architects virtually snapped all connections with traditional architectural vocabularies. By the 1970s and 1980s, however, there emerged architects who attempted, within the Modern idiom, to reestablish an older and more authentic form of building within the region in which they were practising. These architects, the most talented of the newer generation, were exploiting Modernism's greatest strength – to look afresh at tradition. The ability to abstract essential principles and evolve an appropriate form to respond to these issues was an entirely new mechanism that Modernism bought to the architectural debate in India.

In the context of tropical India, Charles Correa's work best exemplifies this approach. His early works such as the Gandhi Ashram at Ahmedabad (1958) all attempt to reestablish this link with the past within the Modern idiom. Also, in his design for the Kanchanjunga apartment building (1970–83), Correa abstracted the organization principle of a bungalow – of wrapping around the main living spaces a protective veranda (Figures 10.10 a,b,c). These principles were skilfully translated into a completely modern vocabulary of buildings using state of the art technology. Similarly, he abstracted elements critical to climatic responses and working with the idea of a kit of parts, he actually used them in many permutations and combinations to create a rich array of architectural responses to the cultural, social as well as economic landscape of India.[6]

Design Issues in Tropical India

In any event, through its evolution, Modernism forced a number of issues in tropical India as well other contexts in the tropics. The primary issues in the context of architectural production were those of *climate and lifestyle* and their interrelations. Charles Correa in his essay titled "Form Follows Climate" added an important dimension to the international architectural debate of the 1960s and 1970s that was dominated largely by architects from the snowbound landscapes of the European and North American countries. Correa made a case for open-to-sky-spaces or courtyards, being integral to the form of buildings in Asia, with the building acting as a breezeway in itself, allowing air to move through it. The issues of climate being integral to the conception of a building in the tropics has now been well articulated and accepted.[7]

Related to this is the issue of lifestyle – of how people in particular cultures and climates use buildings. How activities can shift within the building at different hours of the day and months of the year. For to sleep or spend a greater part of the day in the courtyard or veranda, is quite conceivable in the tropics. In fact, it is something Europeans pay vast sums of money to experience in resort hotels across tropical Asia. This idea extends to the city where the street, arcade and other open spaces are virtually clubs for social and cultural life. The looseness with which activities are then organized impacts the building form. Spaces that can be inscribed upon, that are neutral enough for multiple uses, at different times become the ones with greater premium – those ambiguous in between spaces are animated at times in far richer ways than the ceremonial static spaces with strict function, or use pattern delineations as in conventional buildings growing out of Western paradigms.

Similarly, the influence of technologically driven Western paradigms has also influenced cultural aspirations the world over. As cultural aspirations and technology are often linked, with changing technologies, the form of buildings in the tropics has transformed. The curtain glass building symbolizing "corporate power" being the classic case where the hermetically sealed box pumped with air-conditioning becomes the symbol of corporate aspiration. Similarly, imagery from the luxury hotels percolates down to home interiors and so on. New materials, air-conditioning, new building technologies have all moved architecture in the tropics closer to a global response both in terms of architectural form *per se* and the aspirations from which this new architecture is created.

Within the tropics, and especially in tropical Asia, differing economic responses in different countries vary dramatically. For example, material choices in Singapore are limitless – perhaps constrained only by cost factors! Whereas in India, availability of materials is limited and thus more experience with these basic materials reflects in the circumscribed pattern of building designs and vocabulary. The articulation of the building elements and the materials they are built in is what has a direct bearing on how the building sustains and weathers.

In the tropics, traditionally buildings were heterogeneous in their composition – with many parts together responding to different aspects of the climate – keeping the rain out, trapping the breeze, while keeping usable spaces shaded. Deterioration was retarded through the incorporation of elements that restricted direct exposure to rainwater – this itself created an extremely rich vocabulary of textures and modulation.

Modernism reversed this. Besides abstracting form to the extent of minimal modulation, the Modernists believed that the use of larger areas of a single material tended to prolong the life of a building. This, besides changing the very form of the building, also detached craftsmanship from the building process as the level of articulation of the different building elements was minimized with changing attitudes to aesthetics as well as attitudes towards weathering.

The term "weathering" was originally defined as that part of a building that projected beyond the surface of any external wall and served as a "drip"

Figure 10.9 Views of the Golconde Ashram in Pondicherry designed by Antonin Raymond in 1936. This was perhaps the only significant work in the Modern idiom in tropical India (photo Nondita Correa Mehrotra)

(a)

Figure 10.10 (a, b and c) The Kanchanjunga apartment building by Charles Correa (completed in 1983) where the lesson of spatial organization from vernacular architecture is abstracted for a Modern idiom (by permission of the photographers Rohinton Irani and Charles Correa)

(b)

(c)

Figure 10.10 (cont.)

in order to deflect rainwater. Therefore whatever controls the action of the weather is referred to as "weathering" – one word naming both the process and object through which the process is controlled and allowed to make itself manifest. Elements such as awnings, window shades, cornices, copings, drip moulds, etc. fashioned to retard deterioration were important components of all traditional buildings in the tropics as well as elsewhere.

In most Modern buildings, when these elements were removed, it was necessary to use a sealant – and so "weatherproofing" replaced "weathering". The difference was, of course, the way buildings weathered. The unevenness evident on a larger surface was visually appalling and was accentuated by the process of weathering – as opposed to the gentle weather of protruding elements in a way that light and shade rendered a wall. In that sense "Modern" buildings in tropical India were and are not designed for weathering – to actually positively convert this natural inevitable process into a visual and architectural advantage.[8]

In contrast, if one looks at northern India and the architectural spine (Chandigarh to Bombay), Le Corbusier and many contemporary Indian architects have dealt with weathering and climatic responses in the Modern idiom by designing a host of elements to deal with these as aspects. The brise-soleil is a good example of a contemporary element that deals with the harsh sun and dust storms in hot-arid climates, acting as a buffer zone to filter the effects of these elements on the comfort levels within the building as well as the effects of weathering on it – unfortunately, the tropics have had no such design adaptation attempts in the contemporary architectural idiom.

This brings us to the last issue for architecture in tropical India – that of developing an *affordable aesthetic*. It is critical that we discuss this issue with the same importance as affordable housing or affordable infrastructure – for this may inform the many other issues that we deal with in the tropics, especially in India. Modernism, in a highly pluralistic society and built environment, attempted to impose its puritanical values. Thus architecture, irrespective of the region of India, was recast somewhat in a similar mould. Again the seminal production of architecture took place along the Chandigarh–Bombay axis, thereby engaging itself primarily with the issues of the semi-arid regions of the country. The vocabulary and ensuing aesthetics that evolved had very little to do with responding to the tropical, hot-humid climates of the other half of the Indian subcontinent.

On the other hand, in the common landscape of owner-built houses and squatter settlements, small towns in the tropics assimilated Modernism without the inhibition of the purism that its serious propagators encouraged. Verandas, *chajjas*,[9] balconies and an array of elements found their way into opening up the sealed box – its original generator. In fact, Modernism had set up a classic duality in cities in the tropics, with one part of the land-scape consisting of Modern buildings and the other half building using the collective wisdom of many generations. And the urban poor, inventive and resilient, built in squalid conditions using minimal means to create shelter. This gave rise to a situation where two worlds exist in the same space but built and used the space differently. One, a permanent world – monumental in its presences and built of solid materials. The other, is one built of tempo-rary materials – low key in its presence but created intuitively – responding to the basic need to create shelter (Figure 10.11).

In this landscape charged with duality, the designer has to accept the dual-ities on their own terms, that is as being simultaneously valid. For when these kaleidoscopic images are compressed together a whole gamut of styl-istic possibilities opens up. Thus the rationality and rigorous practice of Modernism with its social agenda could perhaps be juxtaposed with spon-taneity and conventional wisdom to create an appropriate architecture representing a particular reality. The emerging architectural vocabulary in tropical India will then necessarily have to be a pluralistic entity – buildings in which disparate elements and components seamlessly come together to respond to the multitude of forces in a society that are represented in archi-tecture. This will be an architecture that recognizes both the symbolic role it plays and integrates this with its primary function of being a machine to live and work in.

Distilling these observations and experiences, one could say that an afford-able and appropriate aesthetic for tropical India would possibly evolve from four major design considerations:

1. An economy of spatial configuration – one which facilitates and encour-ages lifestyle adjustments to the locale while making for a comfortable environment.
2. The acceptance of dualities in stylistic expressions on their own terms and facilitating a seamless integration of varied architectural elements.
3. An appropriate and economical use of architectural elements, both in the sense of stylistic gestures as well as the appropriate use of technology and its sustainability in terms of weathering as well as environmental impact.
4. An allowance for incremental patterns – to allow for growth and the colo-nizing of the environment by its users – for it is that layer which could potentially produce a local aesthetic at a low cost.

Finally, it is the skilful use of these considerations and the synergy between these factors in the design of a building that could actually create an afford-able aesthetic and relevant architecture for the tropics.

Using these parameters as a benchmark for our practice we have, in our projects, attempted to address these issues to evolve an appropriate architecture for tropical India. In the Mariwala House (1993–94) at Mahableshwar (a hill station south of Bombay), for example, the house shown in Figures 10.12 a and b was strung along the edge of a ravine – this enabled each room to form a separate unit with spectacular views of the valley while facilitating easy cross-ventilation. While the entrance façade of the house is almost screen-like in its function and built in local laterite stone, the valley-side façade of the house is configured by using columns, steel brackets and generous overhangs – which opens up the house to embrace the view of the valley. The combination of these elements results in two completely different vocabularies being employed in the same building, creating its own visual tension and excitement. The screen wall punctuated with smaller openings also works as a device which, based on the "Venturi effect", draws breeze through the house in the summer months.

The roof of the house is made of metal sheets and like many of the British bungalows that were built here earlier it has a false ceiling – in gypsum board,

Figure 10.11 A view of a turn of the century building in Mahableshwar – where the traditional practice of cocooning the building in thatch panels has now been replaced with plastic causing enormous damage to the building. As the plastic does not allow the building to breathe, during the monsoon months a huge amount of humidity is trapped within the spaces damaging the fabric of the building. In the Mariwala House the attempt was made to reverse this and to design the building and façade (with built-in rings for easy attachment of the thatch panels) to facilitate the traditional practice of cocooning the house (photo Rahul Mehrotra)

(a)

(b)

Figure 10.12 (a and b) The Mariwala House by Rahul Mehrotra
Associates, where a screen wall is used to create a Venturi effect while the
other face of the building opens out with generous overhangs to embrace
the views. Here a dual vocabulary in terms of elements is used to
advantage in order to moderate the climate (photos Rahul Mehrotra)

Figure 10.13 *Shanti – A weekend house near Bombay designed by Rahul Mehrotra Associates uses the combination of veranda and courtyard elements to allow for flexibility in terms of use as well as climatic modulation (photo Rajesh Vora)*

Figure 10.14 *A factory in Goa designed by Rahul Mehrotra Associates integrates varied activities and space requirements under a large roof – derived from the vernacular of the place (photo Rahul Mehrotra)*

(a)

(b)

Figure 10.15 *(a and b) Corporate Headquarters of Laxmi Machine Works in Coimbatore designed by Rahul Mehrotra Associates is organized around three large courtyards and water bodies which help to cool the building passively while providing comfortable circulation spaces within verandas (photos Rahul Mehrotra)*

which provides an insulated air gap. Built into the coping of the wall are metal rings on to which thatch panels can be attached during the monsoon – a traditional practice in the Mahableshwar region, which receives over 200 inches of rain during the three monsoon months. Thus through the use of local practices employed in a contemporary way, the house responds not only to its locality in the tropics but also fulfils the aspiration of its owner to be contemporary and modern.

In another weekend-house project (1996–97) of my office in Alibag – across the harbour from Bombay, the plan was configured around a court-yard which separated, as well as integrated, the two zones of the house. Here the client required this weekend house to have a master bedroom, dining and living rooms and kitchen, and, quite separately, two guest bedrooms. The idea was not to have to open up the entire house if only the couple were visiting. Thus the house came to be configured as two large veranda-like spaces flanking a courtyard. In addition to the central courtyard, a series of smaller service courts was also attached to the kitchen and toilets to act as light and air shafts as well as create a sense of spaciousness for these other-wise compact living spaces – while facilitating the easy movement of air through the house (Figures 10.13, 10.14 and 10.15 a and b).

Figure 10.16 *Interior view of the LMW Corporate Headquarters building. The building is organized around three courtyards with corridors and verandas which act as circulation spaces and from where one accesses the offices. As the enclosed spaces are not very wide they facilitate through ventilation and humidification of the building – thus cooling it substantially (photo Rahul Mehrotra)*

Figure 10.17 (a and b) *View of metal jalis made from scrap metal from the LMW steel plant. The jalis were conceptualized by the Indian designer Rajeev Sethi together with the contemporary Indian artist Yogesh Rawal (photos Rahul Mehrotra)*

Furthermore, a series of parallel load-bearing walls in basalt stone was used to define and enclose the different spaces of the house. The roofs over the main areas are covered with galvanized iron sheets while, over the service areas are flat slabs – facilitating easy access to maintain the sloping roofs. In addition, the juxtapositioning of a light steel structure upon a heavy stone base creates a visual tension which is memorable. But more than that, the house attempts to bring disparate spatial elements as well as materials and their articulation together on their own terms – while integrating them to create a seamless whole.

Using the courtyard as an organizing element in a more complex situation, was the Corporate Headquarters building (1996–98) in Coimbatore for the Laxmi Machine Works Group (LMW) to house their seven different companies within a collective identity with individual offices having separate entrances. The building was designed around three courtyards varying in scale and based on a privacy gradient that got more intimate as you penetrated the building. The inner courtyard of the building contains water bodies and the water is circulated to humidify the space for cooling purposes – an ideal device for the dry climate of Coimbatore, which while located in the tropics is in the rain shadow area of the Nilgiri Hills (Figure 10.16).

Contemporary artists were involved with the decoration of the building, and through the design of elements such as *jalis* and trellises the building, while integrating art into the architecture in a meaningful way, also attempts to create a contemporary vocabulary for traditional elements used in the tropics such as *jalis* and trellises, which, while cutting off glare, allow the air to easily penetrate the building (Figures 10.17 a and b).

In short, in these projects, the approach has been to abstract and interpret spatial arrangements as well as building elements to meet a contemporary sensibility and vocabulary. The attempt is thus to combine materials, to juxtapose conventional craftsmanship with industrial materials and traditional spatial arrangements with contemporary space organization. In short, to give expression to the multiple worlds, pluralism and dualities that so vividly characterize the Indian tropical landscape.

CONCLUSION

The design of buildings and the practice of architecture vary greatly in India, between the hot-arid and the tropical. Thus far, the architectural debate in this country has been dominated by a bias which grows out of the great Modernist interventions of the 1950s and 1960s that came out of the Chandigarh – Bombay axis of architectural awareness and took its cues from the hot-arid landscape of northern India. These prototypes and typologies do not necessarily respond to the dictates of tropical India in terms of climatic and related lifestyle responses, technological appropriateness and resulting weathering, as well as aesthetic relevance.

In order to reorient architectural response to the specificity of the tropics, architects, designers and planners in India, will have to look again at sources of inspiration that come out of the tropics and not typologies influenced by the Mediterranean or Europe that found their way into hot-arid India. For the environment that these typologies create is in total contrast to buildings appropriate for the tropics – buildings that breathe, that make a places in the shade and that make living in the tropics a naturally pleasurable and meaningful experience.

NOTES

1. The only exception of seminal work outside the Chandigarh, Delhi, Ahmedabad, and Bombay zone was the Golconde Ashram, designed by Antonin Raymond in Pondicherry in 1936. This was perhaps, the only significant work in the Modern idiom in tropical India which addressed the issue of the tropics. The architect used precast concrete vaults to create a ventilated double roof for insulation and vigorously used louvers to facilitate ventilation.
2. A *jali* is a pierced stone lattice screen to a window or opening often intricately carved to provide protection from direct sunlight and permit ventilation. A *jaffrey* is a lattice usually made of wooden strips overlayered in a square or diagonal pattern.
3. Kenneth Yeang, the Malaysian architect, has made a case for this spatial urban design element in his seminal work, *The Tropical Verandah City*. Here, using Kuala Lumpur as a case, he has successfully demonstrated how we have lost critical opportunities in regaining the notion of a tropical city – actually extending the idea of tropical architecture to the idea of the tropical city.
4. This was the Nehruian dream where Modernism was seen to imply progress – pegged with what was happening the world over.
5. Even today, in contemporary India, Pondicherry and Auroville are centres of innovative architectural production as architects from the world over settle to work in the ashram. The works being produced here are an interesting combination of a sophisticated Western sensibility that uses local materials and techniques within an appropriate climatic response.
6. Charles Correa's projects cover an incredibly large spectrum from institutions, resorts and offices buildings to single family houses, apartment and low-cost housing. In fact his contribution to the housing and urbanization debate has also been seminal. Interestingly, he has connected his architectural attitudes to the housing debate and rooted his solutions in the social, economic and cultural milieu of India. In his approach to low-cost housing, for example, the possibilities that the climate in the tropics opens up in terms of how open-to-sky spaces could be used and animated is the generator of the urban patterns he proposes.
7. Charles Correa: *Form follows Climate*, Pidgeon Audio Visual, London, 1980.
8. This issue of "weathering" has been dealt with in detail in the book *On Weathering – The Life of Buildings in Time*, Mohsen Mostafavi and David Leatherbarrow, MIT Press, Cambridge, MA, 1993.

9. *Chajjas* are a thin projection of stone (now also built in RCC) resembling a cornice running along the side of a building or an eave over a door or window.

BIBLIOGRAPHY

Ameen, Farooq (ed.) *Contemporary Architecture and City Form; The South Asian Paradigm*, Marg Publications, Bombay, 1997.

An Architecture of Independence: The Making of Modern South Asia – The Works of Charles Correa, Balkrishna Doshi, Muzharul Islam and Achyut Kanvinde, exhibition catalogue by the Architectural League of New York, New York, 1997.

Architecture of The SAARC Nations, Architecture + Design, Media Transasia, New Delhi, December 1991.

Correa, Charles, *Form Follows Climate*, Pidgeon Audio Visual, London, 1980.

Correa, Charles, *The New Landscape*, Book Society of India, Bombay, 1985.

Correa, Charles, *Housing and Urbanization*, UDRI, Bombay, 1999.

Dwivedi, Sharda and Mehrotra, Rahul, *Bombay – Cities Within*, IBH and Eminence Designs, Bombay, 1994.

Khilanani, Sunil, *The Idea of India*, Hamish Hamilton, London, 1997.

King, Anthony, *Colonial Urban Development; Culture, Social Power & Environment*, Routledge & Kegan Paul, London, 1976.

King, Anthony, *The Bungalow; The Production of a Global Culture*, Routledge & Kegan Paul, London, 1984.

Lang, Jon, Desai, Madhavi and Desai, Miki, *Architecture and Independence: The Search for Identity: India 1880 to 1980*, Oxford University Press, Delhi, 1997.

Mehrotra, Rahul, "Response to a Tradition", unpublished thesis, School of Architecture, CEPT, Ahmedabad, 1985.

Mostafavi, Mohsen and Leatherbarrow, David, *On Weathering – The Life of Buildings in Time*, MIT Press, Cambridge, MA, 1993.

Tillotson, G. H. R. *The Tradition of Indian Architecture: Continuity, Controversy and Change since 1850*, Oxford University Press, Delhi, 1989.

Wild, David, *Fragments of Utopia – Collage Reflections of Heroic Modernism*, Hyphen Press, London, 1998.

Yeang, Kenneth, *The Tropical Verandah City*, Longman Malaysia SDN, BHD, Selangor, Darul Ehsan, 1987.

CHAPTER 11

THE GREEN AGENDA*

Ken Yeang

1. INTRODUCTION

Concurrent to a professional delivery process that enables us to effectively fulfil our client's requirements, we believe that our designs and built works must satisfy another, more ideological criterion to relate ecologically to our natural environment as a whole. Simply stated, we must seek in our design work a directed contribution towards a sustainable ecological future. The general agenda that strings together our firm's body of work into a whole is its ecological, or "green", design approach. This agenda has become pervasive for us and influences all our design work, regardless of the project type and size.

Briefly stated, the ecological design ideal involves the holistic and careful consideration of the use of materials and energy in built systems and the endeavour, by design, to reduce their undesirable impact on, and to integrate them with, the natural systems of the locality over their entire lifecycle.

It is in this field that we have acquired considerable experience and expertise, beginning even before we commenced our current practice in 1975. Our interest, involvement and expertise in ecological design developed from our earlier research and development work at the Department of Architecture at Cambridge University (UK) (subsequently published in *Designing with Nature*)[1] under Alex Pike and Professor John Frazer.

After forming T. R. Hamzah & Yeang Sdn.Bhd., we set out to apply this "green" agenda, tentatively at first and then with increasing confidence, in almost all our projects, ranging from tall buildings to master plans and urban design projects. Initially our propositions were for bioclimatic design solutions, in which the built-form relates to the climate of a place to produce passive low-energy buildings. This was the easiest way to introduce the ideas to a commerical clientele. Eventually this led to a greater incorporation of environmental concerns to achieve a more comprehensive agenda for ecological design. In particular, the bioclimatic agenda had been applied with some level of effectiveness to the tall building type.[2]

By the 1990s, we had acquired considerable expertise in designing and managing the construction documentation and project delivery of tall buildings, or skyscrapers. Why skyscrapers? The answer is simple. This was a building type that few had sought to grapple with in terms of green design. Most "green designers" prefer to deal with low-rise and medium-rise projects, especially in rural locations, and tend to avoid larger intensive and urban developments. But like it or not, the skyscraper is a built-form that will not simply go away overnight. It is being built ubiquitously through most of the world's capital cities in ever greater numbers, especially in the Far East. If this is the case, we should be boldly addressing the green design issues for this building type rather than ignoring them; we must be prepared to develop the skyscraper as a sustainable green building.

There have, of course, been numerous endeavours at establishing the ecological basis for design. However, many negate the fundamental basic property of ecosystems which is their "connectivity" in the biosphere. Any theory for ecological design must take this into consideration.

2. A UNIFIED THEORY FOR ECOLOGICAL DESIGN

This section describes a unified theory for ecological design and some of the key criteria. However, the designer is advised that ecological design is not just meeting these criteria but has to be as comprehensive as possible in ensuring that the design has the least destructive impacts (or the most beneficial impacts) on the ecosystems and non-renewable resources in the biosphere over the built system's lifecycle from source to reuse and to sink. An expansion of this chapter with more prescriptive applications is in reference 3.

A guide to the connectivity in ecological systems is given in the model below.

Ecological design involves the holistic consideration by design, of the careful use of energy and materials in a designed system, and the endeavour by design to reduce the impacts of this use on (and its integration with) the natural environment, over the lifecycle of the designed system from source to sink. We can structure these considerations in a framework of set of interactions (vis-à-vis impacts) between the built environment and the ecological environment. These interactions are analogous to the concept of an open system. Based on the above features, interactions can be classified into four general sets:

1. The external interdependencies of the designed system (its external or environmental relations).
2. The internal interdependencies of the designed system (its internal relations).

3. The external-to-internal exchanges of energy and matter (its inputs).
4. The internal-to-external exchanges of energy and matter (its outputs).

In an ecological approach to design, we must simultaneously consider all four of these aspects as well as their interrelationships with each other. These can be further structured into a symbolic form as follows:

Given a designed system and its environment, let suffix 1 denote the system under consideration and suffix 2, the environment around that system. Further, let letter L be the interdependent connections (linkages) within the framework. It follows that four types of interactions can be identified in the analysis: L_{11}, L_{12}, L_{21} and L_{22}. This can be further represented in the form of a partitioned matrix, LP as follows:

$$LP = \begin{array}{c|c} L_{11} & L_{12} \\ \hline L_{21} & L_{22} \end{array}$$

L_{11} refers to the processes and activities that take place within the system or the area of internal interdependencies.

L_{12} refers to the exchanges of the system with its environment, or the transactional interdependencies of the system/environment.

L_{21} refers to the inputs from the environment into the system.

L_{22} refers to the processes and activities that take place in the environment of the system, or the external interdependencies.

LP refers to ecological design being the simultaneous consideration of all the four sets of interactions over a system lifecycle.

The above provides the broad theoretical basis for ecological design.

3. KEY DESIGN CRITERIA

Following from the above framework, the key criteria to be considered for design starts with assessing the need for building. We need to evaluate the design brief and basis for the project and user requirements on ecological sensibility and to

*   Place priority on "users" over "hardware"
*   Assess levels of provision of internal environmental systems (Figure 11.1).

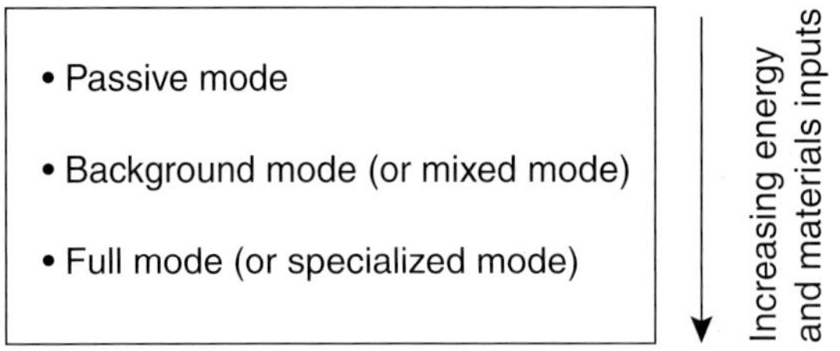

• Passive mode

• Background mode (or mixed mode)

• Full mode (or specialized mode)

Increasing energy and materials inputs

Figure 11.1 Level of servicing

4. SITE [OR L22 BEING THE ENVIRONMENT TO THE SYSTEM]

For the building's environmental factors, we need to:

Assess Where It Is To Be Built

Ecological value of site (by building configuration)
Target: Site planning (i.e. location of buildings, cut-and-fills, roads, paved areas, etc.) should be based on "ecological land-use method". Buildings are to be located on parts of the site with minimum disruptions and impacts on the locality's ecosystem.

Enhance the ecological value of the site with locally characteristic flora and fauna.

Assess ecosystem hierarchy of project site (Figure 11.2).

Evaluate biodiversity index before and after construction.

Assess Building Construction Impacts (from building production)

Target: Building construction work should not cause disruptions to the ecosystem within the site and in the surrounding sites. The long-term success of "sustainable design" also requires particular attention to the construction, commissioning and the monitoring and control of building use. The environmental performance requirements of the contractor will be written into their contract and should include:

• Developing and implementing a project environmental plan
• Minimizing waste and rework
• Efficient use of energy and other resources, preventing pollution
• Using recycled and recyclable materials or components where possible

Ecosystem hierarchy	Site data requirements	Design strategy
Ecologically mature	Complete ecosystem Analysis and mapping	• Preserve • Conserve • Develop only no-impact areas
Ecologically immature	Complete ecosystem Analysis and mapping	• Preserve • Conserve • Develop on least-impact areas
Ecologically simplified	Complete ecosystem Analysis and mapping	• Preserve • Conserve • Increase biodiversity • Develop on low impact areas
Mixed artificial	Partial ecosystem Analysis and mapping	• Increase biodiversity • Develop on low impact areas

Monoculture	Partial ecosystem
	Analysis and mapping
		• Increase biodiversity
		• Develop in areas of
		   non-productive
		   potential
		• Rehabilitate the
		   ecosystem

Zeroculture	Mapping of remaining
	ecosystem components
	(e.g. hydrology,
	remaining trees, etc.)
		• Increase biodiversity
		   and organic mass
		• Rehabilitate the
		   ecosystem

Figure 11.2 Ecosystems' hierarchy and design strategy

- Minimizing the need for transport, including importation/exportation of materials
- Proper disposal of unavoidable waste including full compliance with relevant regulations, clearing the site on completion.

Assess External Landscape Design (from building production)

Target: Microclimate amelioration can be achieved by site planning and landscape design. The following factors and techniques will be explored in further design developments:

- Interrelated factors which form the local microclimate:
  - solar radiation
  - temperature
  - relative humidity
  - evaporation
  - wind
  - precipitation.

Four main elements affect human comfort: solar radiation, air temperature, air movement or wind and humidity. When the combination of these does not place undue stress on the human, conditions reach the "comfort zone", e.g. in the UK this is 14–21 °C but in Brisbane 22–28 °C. Landscape can influence the microclimate. The closer the outdoor climate can be kept to this range, the less energy will be consumed to produce a comfortable indoor climate. The form of the landscape can have a beneficial effect on the energy consumption of buildings and will therefore reduce costs. Provide an integrated building and landscape design which complements the character of the site. Integrate the designed system and new landscape vegetation with the local ecosystem. In warm climates make use of vertical landscaping and planting, to lower ambient microclimate temperatures.

Assess Local Wind Effects (by building configuration)

Target: Design to limit frequency of exceeding wind levels to 4 on the Beaufort scale, to 20 per cent (i.e. 5.5–7.9 m s^{-1}) to reduce impacts on pedestrians and on surroundings.

Check Overshadowing of Other Buildings and Land (by building configuration)

Target: Locate buildings on the site to avoid substantial overshadowing of neighbouring buildings and land. The building configuration can be based on the site's "solar envelope" so as not to overshadow the solar production potential of neighbouring sites. This affects the solar energy potential of adjoining sites (and their condition in winter months for temperate climates).

Check Outdoor Noise (by building configuration)

Target: Design to ensure that the noise rating levels outside the nearest exposed residential buildings are not less that 5 dB below the background level during any period of the day or evening (7–23 h) and does not exceed the background level at any period of the night (23–7 h). The impact of this is mainly on users.

Other Aspects (e.g. emissions, transportation, etc.)

Target: Check ground level vegetation for leaf discoloration, etc.

5. ASSESS WHAT IS TO BE BUILT [OR *L-21* BEING THE INPUTS TO THE SYSTEM]

For the inputs, we need to assess what is to be built and inputs required to maintain it:

Embodied Energy in Building Materials and CO_2 Emissions in Production

Target: Consider the embodied energy values in materials of construction (and in maintenance) taking account of the full lifecycle of the material in question and their recovery (reuse/recycling) potential. Consider the incorporation of locally sourced materials for major building components. Overall embodied energy and CO_2 for various building types are to be within the limits shown in Table 11.1.

Table 11.1 Limits for embodied energy and CO_2 emissions

Building type	Embodied energy as delivered (GJ m^{-2})	Embodied primary energy (GJ m^{-2})	CO_2 emissions (kg CO_2 m^{-2})
Office	5–10	10–18	500–1000
House	4.5–8	9–13	800–1200
Flat	5–10	10–18	500–1000
Industrial	4–7	7–12	400–700
Road	1–5	2–10	130–850

Assess Environmental Impact of Building (from building production)

Target: Check the environmental impacts of the flow of source materials and energy in the production of the building and their impacts.

Assess Natural Resources Consumption and Recycled Materials

Target: Material specification to consider depletion of natural resources (e.g. timber/timber products from sustainable resources, etc.). Demolition materials to be reused (if appropriate).

Assess Hazardous Materials (from building production)

Target: Avoid the specification of materials known to be hazardous, wherever possible, except where no economic alternative is available (e.g. wood preservatives).

Avoid Over-specification (from building production)

Target: Monitor performance.

6. ASSESS IMPACTS OF BUILDING OPERATION [OR *L*11 BEING THE SYSTEM ACTIVITIES]

For the internal systemic aspects of our building, we need to:

Optimize Passive Energy Systems

Before proceeding to mixed-mode and full-mode systems (see Figure 11.1) through use of ambient energy by:

- Built-form configuration
- Built-form orientation
- Façade design
- Solar control devices
- Envelope colour
- Vertical landscaping
- Wind and natural ventilation.

Design a simple control strategy that all building users understand and can contribute to controlling (Figure 11.3).

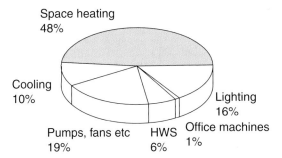

Space heating 48%

Cooling 10%

Lighting 16%

Pumps, fans etc 19%

HWS 6%

Office machines 1%

Figure 11.3 *Delivered energy use in a typical air-conditioned office building*

Optimize the Use of Non-renewable Resources

For example, by using photovoltaics.

Reduce Carbon Dioxide Production

This may be due to energy consumption in building operation or building use; restrict the latter to < 50 kg m^{-2} per year.

Consider Acid Rain

For example, from boiler emissions: restrict this to < 200 mg k Wh^{-1} delivered energy.

Consider Ozone Depletion

Due to CFCs, HCFCs and halons; zero ozone depleting refrigerants; no halons, no insulation made with CFCs.

Consider Avoidance of Legionnaires' Disease

Avoid cooling towers or design these, as well as hot water systems, to CIBSE TM13.

Check Envelope Insulation Values

U-values of walls and roof should be < 0.35 W m^{-2} K and air leakage should be less than 5 m^{3}h m^{-2} of façade at 50 Pa.

Assess Building Lifecycle Consequences

Assumed building lifecycle is 50 yr for all calculations; find the lifecycle energy cost of the built system; note that operational energy over its life span far exceeds energy use at other stages (Figure 11.4).

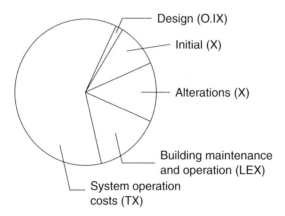

Design (O.IX)

Initial (X)

Alterations (X)

Building maintenance and operation (LEX)

System operation costs (TX)

X = Initial construction costs

Figure 11.4 *Lifecycle energy costs of a built system. Note that the operational energy use over its life-span far exceeds that in other stages*

Place Priority on Façade Design over the Interior

The façade has a crucial role in energy performance.

Optimize Passive Systems for Wind and Ventilation

- Design the majority of space for natural ventilation
- Prohibit smoking in the building (think of passive smoking)
- Avoid the need for a humidification plant
- Design any humidification system for non-naturally ventilated areas carefully, e.g. use a steam-based system
- Maintain indoor air quality, with 25 L h^{-1} per person fresh air supply, with no recirculation
- Make use of natural ventilation devices, e.g. wing walls, displacement systems, etc.

Optimize Natural and Artificial Lighting Systems

Provide good levels of visual comfort by lighting in the office:

- Maximize the area of daylit working space (at least 60 per cent of office area), comply with BS8206, pt. 2 (CP for Daylighting)
- Use light-shelves, special glass, etc.
- High-frequency ballasts should be fitted to all discharge lamps.

Check Thermal Control and Overheating

Minimize the risk of discomfort by incorporating design features to complement the proposed natural ventilation and night-cooling strategy: perform calculations according to CIBSE Guide, vol. A (section A5).

Control Indoor Noise

Ensure acoustic comfort in offices and meeting areas: in accordance with BS 6233: 1967 (sound insulation and noise reduction for buildings).

Examine Lifecycle Energy Use

Compare embodied energy with operational energy; operational energy should be 15–30 per cent of that in conventional offices (e.g. conventional: ? 400 k Wh m^{-2} yr^{-1} target: 65–125 k Wh m^{-2} yr); this can be achieved by composite means: part natural ventilation, solar shading, flue walls, as well as renewable energy sources: solar thermal or photovoltaic systems (Figure 11.5).

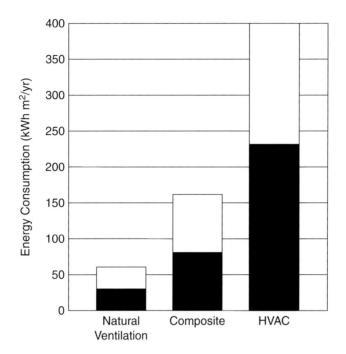

Figure 11.5 *Energy use as a function of control strategy*

Assess Transport Energy

Minimize car parking on site to discourage car use; encourage public transport use; consider staff transport schemes, including incentives.

Avoid Sick Building Syndrome

Occupant surveys, monitoring, annual performance review.

Design for Internal Water Conservation

Aim at reducing mains water use to drinking only; consider water recycling, waste water treatment, rainwater use; set a water management strategy; avoid water leakage; irrigation of landscaping should use grey water.

Check Internal Fit-outs

Design to avoid waste; design for flexibility and easy alterations; check use of hazardous materials.

7. DESIGN FOR 'CLOSING THE LOOP" [OR L12 BEING THE OUTPUTS TO THE SYSTEM]

For the outputs to the building, we need to:

Design for Reuse, Recycling and Disposal at Building Demolition

Minimize amount of material taken away from the site, e.g. excavation; design for recovery and reuse.

Reduce or Recover Waste Material and Waste Heat

Allow transit storage for materials for recycling; use heat exchangers or heat pump for heat recovery.

Design for Storage of Recyclable Materials

Allow space for sorted collection for recycling.

Assess Water Pollution

Reduce site run-off (provide at-source management of pollution from surface water); improve absorption and return to groundwater.

Design Detailing

Design assembly of components for:

- Reuse
- Recycling
- Durability
- Efficiency
- Minimize waste
- Environmental integration
- Remanufacture
- Repair/maintenance
- Upgrading
- Refilling
- Replacement.

8. CONCLUSION

The above is a quick guide for ecological design, using some of the prevalent standards. The designer is cautioned that this list is not totally comprehensive and that standards change as technology and the theory of ecological design develop.

We contend that ecological design and planning should not be a constantly retreating battle against the devastation of the natural environment or the profligate consumption of non-renewable resources for construction and buildings. The construction of the built environment need not be negative or unproductive for the landscape. Buildings are essentially an inorganic mass, and we must ensure that our master plans seek to balance the introduction of built systems with as much organic mass or vegetation (and ecologically suitable fauna) as possible.

REFERENCES

*   This chapter is a revised version of one that appeared in Yeang, K. *Bioclimatic Skyscrapers*, rev. edn, Ellipsis, London, 2000.
1.   Yeang, K. *Designing with Nature*, McGraw-Hill, New York, 1994.
2.   Yeang, K. *The Green Skyscraper: The Basis for Designing Sustainable Intensive Buildings*, Prestel-Verlag, Munich, 1999.
3.   Yeang, K. *Bioclimatic Skyscrapers*, rev. edn, Ellipsis, London, 2000.

CHAPTER 12

THREE TROPICAL DESIGN PARADIGMS

Bay Joo Hwa Philip

INTRODUCTION

Throughout history, various writers have discussed the issue of the tropical climate and regional[1] architecture. Without being exhaustive, a few key examples will be highlighted here to form the basis for comparing the three tropical design paradigms from the 1980s in Singapore. First, this chapter will discuss several international writers' observations and thoughts for tropical design after the Second World War. From this the term "tropical architecture" is defined for this chapter. Second, it highlights several key historical architectural developments in tropical Singapore in the past and especially since Singapore achieved self-rule in 1959. Third, the three paradigms are described followed by a critical look. And, finally, the chapter ends with comments on several examples of contemporary works in Singapore.

FRAMEWORK FOR DISCUSSING TROPICAL ARCHITECTURE

In their book *Tropical Architecture in the Dry and Humid Zones* Maxwell Fry and Jane Drew proposed that: "There are three main considerations influencing architectural design in the tropics which it is necessary to distinguish as belonging particularly to the zone. These concern, first, *people and their needs*; second, *climate and its attendant ills*; and third, *materials and the means of building*."[2] They also observed that these concerns were intricately related and had evolved into built environments with distinct physical characteristics in the indigenous examples of the past.[3]

Similarly, Victor Olgyay and Aladar Olgyay have compared various indigenous examples of built environment across the world, in their book *Design with Climate; Bioclimatic Approach to Architectural Regionalism*, to "find a remarkable correspondence between special architectural features and certain climatic zones".[4] They referred to various thinkers from Socrates to

Le Corbusier concerning this similar observation of the relation between architecture and climate, and the need for differences in design response for different zones. They cited Vitruvius in *De Architectura* saying: "For the style of buildings ought manifestly to be different in Egypt and Spain, in Pontus and Rome, and in countries and regions of various characters. For in one part the earth is oppressed by the sun in its course; in another part the earth is far removed from it; in another it is affected by it at a moderate distance."[5]

Miles Dandy referred to the guidelines for integrating social and cultural needs and building forms and materials with the tropical climatic concerns as the "grammar of architectural design" for the tropics in his book *Grammar of Architectural Design: with Special Reference to the Tropics.*[6]

Olgyay and Olgyay, referring to the tropics, discussed how architectural design must be judged: "Man, with his intricate physical and emotional needs, remains the module – the central measure – in all approaches. The success of every design must be judged by its total effect on the human environment".[7] And by this they were referring to the physical comfort of the occupant in a modern building and the aesthetic delight in seeing an architectural expression based on climatic control as "a more positive foundation for the play of emotional expressions".[8]

From the above discussions, three main aspects of tropical architecture can be identified. These three interrelated aspects are:

1. Regional expression – as a result of responding to needs related to the tropical climate
2. Performance – in providing climatic comfort and convenience for social and cultural requirements
3. Materials and means of building – appropriate to the tropical zone.

The regional expression or a "grammar" as referred to in Dandy[9] is a result of designing with consideration for the climatic, social and cultural requirements and the use of appropriate materials and means of building. And the success of the design is measured according to the appropriateness of this synthesis in the hot and humid tropical Singapore near the Equator. In this chapter the terms "tropical architecture" and "tropical design" are used in the largest sense of the words. Any architectural issue relating to these three aspects at various physical scales from landscape, urban morphology, individual building down to elements and components is referred to as tropical, as long as it involves the tropical climate.

Social and cultural factors will include the lifestyle, the way spaces are used and occupied, and the symbolic meanings including traditional/religious forms and motifs.[10] Materials considerations will include selection of available materials for the least maintenance.[11] Considerations for means of building will include windstorms, cloudburst and flooding, biological elements, structural systems and constructional methods.[12]

Climatic needs will refer to the required control of various environmental factors for the convenience and the mental and physical comfort of the occupant. These physical factors include solar radiation and sun path, glare and lighting, temperature and temperature change, precipitation (rain), humidity, air movement and air pollution.[13] In the urban context of Singapore, these also include noise pollution in the congested areas where a design with lots of openings to encourage cross-ventilation also invites noise.

The control of rain may be in the form of a roof or a covered walkway to provide the protection while moving from one part of the city to another in the tropical rain. For the control of heat for comfort, the solution can vary from providing a simple, large roof overhead while allowing cross-ventilation from the sides to keep the occupant cool, to the use of an air-conditioning system in an enclosed space. The use of air-conditioners, mechanical fans or ventilators will be considered "active" approaches requiring the direct consumption of energy to operate, and the "passive" approaches will be those that do not require electro-mechanical energy to control the climatic factors for comfort.[14] Passive systems include orienting windows away from direct sunlight, providing sun-shading devices, etc. It is, of course, an advantage to save resources where possible and use a combination of both approaches, with built-in flexibility to allow the user to control and vary these combinations for maximum comfort as well as energy conservation.[15] An example of this in Singapore would be the design of a bedroom with appropriate cross-ventilation for cooling the body via evaporation of moisture from the skin and protection from the rain when the windows are opened, and at the same time providing the option for closing the windows and turning on the air-conditioning during the few extremely hot and humid months of the year.

Here some clarification is necessary as to whether the air-conditioned buildings are part and parcel of tropical architecture. Reyner Banham in his book discussed the "well-tempered environment" and observed that excess humidity in the tropical atmosphere could only be effectively removed by technology.[16] Fry and Drew described air-conditioning as one of the effective means employed in the modulation of the hot and humid tropical climatic environment.[17] In this same vein, Lee Kuan Yew, Senior Minister of Singapore hailed the air-conditioner as the most influential innovation of the millennium because it had changed the lives of people in tropical regions and allowed businesses to operate efficiently. He stated, "Before the air-con, mental concentration and with it the quality of work deteriorated as the day got hotter and more humid."[18] Indeed, the problem of air-conditioning lies not in the fact that it is not an appropriate tropical system for environmental control, but that it consumes electrical energy and does not seem to make use of natural tropical resources such as the wind in the case of the indigenous tropical buildings in the past.[19] However, the thermal discomfort owing to the humidity problem cannot be effectively eradicated by cross-ventilation all year round. For effective ventilation, the wind currents have to be quite strong, creating a problem for the high-rise offices. Coupled with this is the noise and air pollution in the congested city. Considering the economic, social and cultural needs and the climatic and urban condition of Singapore, the air-conditioner has proved to be a sensible device for providing the necessary comfort and convenience in the tropics. In various cases it has also been effectively combined with passive means of keeping cool, including shading devices, wind buffers, sky-courts and planting to save whatever running cost possible. Air-conditioned buildings can therefore be considered as part of tropical architecture.

The tropical design paradigms in the later part of this chapter are discussed in relation to the synthesis of the three aspects identified above, namely the regional expression or "grammar", the climatic, social and cultural perform-ance provided for via "passive" or "active" system, and the use of appropriate materials and means of building.

Highlights of Historical Examples of Tropical Architecture in Singapore

The traditional native architecture of the region of Singapore and Malaysia was typified by indigenous houses on timber stilt structures that carried a large roof with great overhangs and porous walls or minimum walls for maximum ventilation.[20] When the British colonized Singapore in 1819, they started to build colonial bungalows with European construction methods and materials adapted to the local climate.[21] The colonial bungalows were hybrids of the European style and the indigenous style of the region, emulating the time-tested climatic performance of indigenous traditional forms. The trop-ical streets in Singapore were characterized by shophouses. With continuous covered walkways called "five-foot-ways" they provided continuous shade and protection from the sun and rain through large parts of the city. The shop-houses were ventilated via internal courtyards and with "jacked-roofs" at the ridge of the roofs.[22] There were also other colonial building types including offices, institutions and warehouses in European styles adapted to the local climate.[23] The colonial way of building continued up to the end of the 1950s, although the influence of the Modern Movement had begun to appear in Singapore through the British Public Works Department and some private architects trained in the West.[24]

In 1937, inspired by contemporary European glass architecture, the Public Works Department designed and built one of the first of these new genera-tion of buildings, the Singapore Kallang Airport Terminal Building (Figure 12.1). Its way of adapting to the tropical climate was by providing large, pronounced horizontal fins over the large areas of horizontal glass façades, offering a great expanse of shelter from the sun and rain.[25] After the Second World War, Ng Keng Siang, one of the first London trained Singapore architects, designed the tallest high-rise building in Singapore's business district in 1954, namely the Asia (Insurance) Building (Figures 12.2a, b and c). The architect wanted to demonstrate that the local architect could also produce distinctive designs compared to European architects, and strove to achieve this by adapting the façade design to the local climate with articulated horizontal shading strips.[26]

The shift away from colonial tropical architecture and its replacement with a modern tropical architecture became more widespread during the post-colonial period. From 1959, when Singapore had its first self-government, the energetic newly formed regime had the vision to build a metropolis with a people of diverse cultures. Singapore wanted to move forward, throw off its colonial burden, and employ the best of technological know-how from the West with all its potential for rapid development with a cosmopolitan image.[27] The dawn of Singapore's nation building saw several major modern architectural endeavours. These include the Singapore Conference Hall and Trade Union House (a very important public building), the Malaysia Singapore Airway Building (the prototype non-colonial, high-rise commercial building in Singapore's main business street), the People's Park Complex (the first high-rise complex with high-density mixed-development of housing and shopping complex) and the Woh Hup Complex (the experimentation of urban architecture for the new tropical Asian city).[28]

Figure 12.1 *Singapore Kallang Airport Terminal Building designed by the Public Works Department (photo Bay Joo Hwa Philip)*

(a)

Figure 12.2 *(a, b and c) Asia (Insurance) Building, 1954, designed by Ng Keng Siang (photo Bay Joo Hwa Philip)*

(b)

(c)

The Singapore Conference Hall and Trade Union House, completed in 1965, was based on the winning design for an architectural competition in 1962 (Figure 12.3a). It was won by the Malayan Architects Co-partnership, which consisted of Lim Chong Keat, Chen Voon Fee and William Lim as partners.[29] Its symbolic importance was great. It was felt to be capturing the spirit of the time. As a modern tropical building, it stood proudly in the midst of the old business streetscape in Shenton Way, Singapore's main business street, which had been dominated by colonial style office buildings. Tay Kheng Soon, one of the architects who have worked with Malayan Architects Co-partnership at that time,[30] reports that then Prime Minister Lee Kuan Yew saw it as a symbol of the new national pride. Tay Kheng Soon also reports that Lee Kuan Yew in his opening speech referred to the quality of design and execution as proof that "the people have the verve, the capacity and the pride in performance".[31] The Minister for Culture and Social Affairs also celebrated the success with this message: "Much effort has gone into this project and now this building asserts itself as an index of the dignity of labour in Singapore" (Figure 12.3b).[32]

In modern geometric composition, the building offered the state-of-the-art conference hall, research centre and administrative facilities, which were air-conditioned (Figure 12.3c). The central lobby/exhibition concourse to the respective facilities enjoyed cross-ventilation with the prevailing sea breeze blowing through the carefully designed gaps in the full height louvered glass windows (Figure 12.3d). Wind was allowed to enter the building and escape at the highest point of the grand interior atrium without allowing rainwater to enter.[33] The rectangular aluminium sunscreens together with the cantilevered roofs formed the large canopy-like expression of shadiness. The interior timber stripe finishes were from this tropical region. The whole exterior form, interior spaces and landscape design were treated as part of the total architectural concept with no reference to colonial forms or styles. Lim Chong Keat explained that the design approach was not one of derivative regional identity, but of integrity. It was an aesthetic based on the Modern language of the Modern masters and the discussions on tropical architecture by Victor Olgyay and Aladar Olgyay, and Maxwell Fry and Jane Drew.[34]

With the same state-of-the-art technology and architectural language, Lim started designing the first post-colonial corporate high-rise tropical building in the Singapore business district in 1965, called the Malaysia Singapore Airway Building (Figure 12.4a).[35] Completed in 1969, it stood then as the tallest building in Shenton Way. Its elegant tripartite tower rested on a horizontal podium below, which cantilevered out to shade the walkway along the main street. It was equipped with an auditorium, a landscaped podium roof for recreational purposes away from the buzzing street and multi-storey car-parking facilities (Figure 12.4b). The glazed façades were sealed

(a)

(b)

dewan persidangan singapura
新嘉坡大會堂
சிங்கப்பூர் மாநாட்டு மண்டபம்
singapore conference hall

rumah kesatuan sa-kerja
職工會大廈
தொழிற் சங்க மாளிகை
trade union house

Figure 12.3 (a, b, c and d) *The Singapore Conference Hall and Trade Union House, 1965, designed by Lim Chong Keat (by permission of Architects Team 3 and the Ministry of Information and the Arts, Singapore)*

(c)

(d)

Figure 12.3 (cont.)

for air-conditioning and for great sea views, and they were protected from the sun and glare with lace-like U-shape aluminium shading devices that formed a rhythmic pattern. It is important to understand, that being the first modern high-rise corporate building for a new nation, it had to satisfy multiple criteria including the corporate image, user needs, the urban fit, adequate technology and the unique environmental problem, which had few precedents (Figure 12.4c). When it was completed, it was considered an exemplary prototype for the development of other corporate commercial buildings for the whole business district.[36]

While the Malaysia Singapore Airway Building was a prototype for office buildings, the People's Park Complex was a prototype for mixed-development of shopping and residential dwellings. It was conceived in 1967 and completed in 1970 by Design Partnership, formed by William Lim, Koh Seow Chuan and Tay Kheng Soon (Figure 12.5a).[37] The site had previously been occupied by a well-known, open-air night-market in Chinatown, known as the People's Park. The market was destroyed by fire and the site was subsequently selected as one of the first land sales in 1967 for urban renewal. It was a challenge for the architects to provide a modern solution to accommodate the lost city life and culture of shopping and dining in informal street settings.[38]

According to Tay Kheng Soon, shopping spaces in those days were in the form of streets or malls and not in complexes. The precedent for a shopping centre that matched the scale and complexity of the People's Park Complex was difficult to find. One of the largest shopping centres was called Ala Moana Center (1959) in Honolulu, in the centre of Hawaii.[39] It was a huge and long two-storey complex with large department stores at two ends acting as anchor tenants, connected by a long shopping mall stringed with smaller shops. This horizontally sprawling example, however, was unsuitable for land scarce Singapore. Drawing on the discourse in urban architecture of the Metabolists, the concept of a vertically stacked model was adopted for the site Figure 12.5b).[40]

The idea of connectivity in the city was an important factor in the design of the People's Park Complex, ensuring that people could flow through conveniently and comfortably from various points and levels of the site. Six storeys of car-parking areas were linked directly into the shopping and atrium area so that people could shop at upper levels. These corridors or streets of activities and interaction were housed in a huge naturally ventilated atrium that provided maximum visibility of shops and were cooled by the spill over of cool air from the numerous air-conditioned shops. The budget did not allow for air-conditioning the atrium. Mechanical ventilators instead were designed to help extract the warm air.[41] The high-rise apartment tower above the shopping podium was designed so that there was cross-ventilation for each apartment unit, and there was a roof deck over the podium intended for communal activities.[42]

Figure 12.4 *(a, b and c) Malaysia Singapore Airway*
Building, 1965, plan and section designed by
Lim Chong Keat (by permission of the Architects Team 3)

(a)

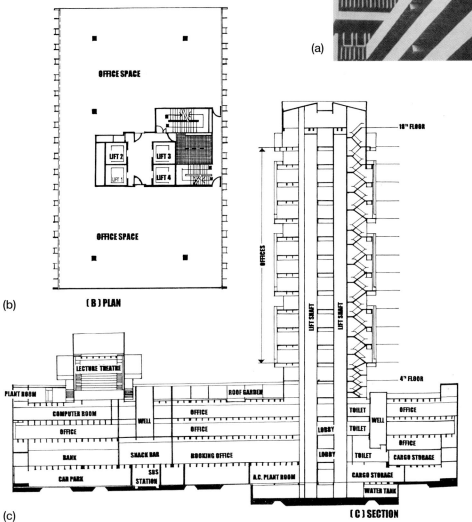

(b)

(c)

(a)

(b)

(c)

Figure 12.5 (a, b and c)The People's Park
Complex, 1967–70 designed by the Design
Partnership (by permission of Tay Kheng Soon)

Both Tay Kheng Soon and William Lim recollected that the complex was a success. A study on visitor volumes, carried out by the Design Partnership, showed that 1 million people visited the People's Park Complex in the first month of its opening in October 1970, out a total population of 2.5 million for Singapore at that time. Moreover, the atrium was a popular social space for holding exhibitions and cultural shows (Figure 12.5c). The People's Park Complex performed so well that the Design Partnership was awarded many more commissions for shopping cum residential complexes. Among these was the Woh Hup Complex,[43] allowing for further experimentation.

Like the People's Park Complex, the Woh Hup Complex, completed in 1973, also has a shopping atrium, a residential block above the shopping complex, and a roof deck (Figure 12.6a). There was also a separate land-scaped roof garden with a swimming pool for the residents. The residential tower block was designed so that each apartment unit would have cross-ventilation and especially, would catch the sea breeze. The block was terraced so as to give each apartment unit a tropical garden open to the sky, and at the same time provide a large sheltered communal space below the whole residential block (Figure 12.6b). According to William Lim, Tay Kheng Soon explored the idea of how the multiplication of blocks similar to the Woh Hup Complex along the urban streets could serve as connectors throughout the tropical city.[44] That in theory formed the basis for a future cityscape of inter-connected internal cool spaces as well as the external sheltered urban and communal spaces, serving as platforms for mass rapid transit stations, bus stops and activity nodes. It was published in the Singapore Planning and Urban Research group publication as a possible solution for the future trop-ical Asian city.[45]

Both William Lim and Tay Kheng Soon mentioned that they had one regret about the inward looking shopping atrium, even though at that time it seemed to be the most sensible solution for the People's Park Complex. They felt that there should have been a lot fewer shops on the edges for more porosity and engagement between the inside and the outside. This situation had wors-ened with the atrium sealed with glazing for air-conditioning. Also, because this atrium-shopping model has become a typical formula for so many shop-ping complexes in Singapore and the region, there have been more buildings in the cities that tended to shun the external urbanscape and turn into the interior.[46]

Looking back to this period, these buildings were daring experiments in the tropical urban context. The Singapore Conference Hall and Trade Union House, the Malaysia Singapore Airlines Building, the People's Park Complex and the Woh Hup Complex were great examples of attempts at an architec-ture to suit the people and the climate with new and changing technologies. However, many banal looking buildings lacking critical relationship to place and environment also appeared. Like many rapidly growing cities in the

(a)

(b)

Figure 12.6 (a and b) The Woh Hup Complex, 1973, designed by the Design Partnership (by permission of Teng Kheng Soon)

region, the skyline of Singapore was marked with anonymous business towers. Growing tired of the globalizing effect; some have welcomed historicist references as the alternative, hoping to give a saving character to buildings in the 1980s and 1990s. Without appropriate understanding and design strategy, historicist reference to European or regional styles can result in kitsch. In the face of losing relevancy and regional character, several concerned architects and writers have discussed ways to achieve a regional architecture.

THREE TROPICAL DESIGN PARADIGMS

All three paradigms seek to achieve in the architecture recognizable characters that belong to the tropical region in and around Singapore, and distinguish it from the other climatic zones. The first paradigm is based on the ecological issue as a foundation to develop an appropriate tropical language. The second is founded on tradition-based forms. The third is what I call the "New Screen & Louver Kitsch", which is based on the stereotypical images of climatic control.

First each paradigm will be described and will then be analysed based on the three main aspects of tropical architecture set up in the beginning of this chapter, namely the architectural regional expression, the performance in providing climatic comfort and convenience for social and cultural requirements, and materials and means of building. And finally they will be compared.

THE "LINE, EDGE & SHADE" PARADIGM

Recently Tay Kheng Soon has argued for an urban architecture that is ecologically responsive and has criticized the conditions of practice and academia saying: "Architecture journals and schools everywhere concentrated on 'difference' and style. They seem to withdraw from engagement with real environmental issues. This seems strange when architecture and city planning have always been totally interconnected. As architects today shun the connection, they are reduced to styling and theorising."[47] Tay thinks that design should be forward-looking, non-nostalgic and there should be no regression with poor copies of styles from the past, but rather emulate the principles of environmental control from traditional designs.[48] Tay refers to the local kitsch designs as "Obiang" in his newspaper article commenting on the bad taste displayed in many houses around Singapore, which imitate all kinds of traditional or "Greco-Roman" styles.[49] And he believes that "One of the principal issues of designing in the tropics is the discovery of a design language of line, edge, mesh and shade rather than an architecture of plane, volume, solid and void. An unlearning process is involved, given the dominance of European architecture which forms the substance of the training of architects over the past 200 years."[50]

Tay Kheng Soon has observed the hegemony of the box aesthetics of modern buildings with the development and application of a weather-tight enclosing curtain wall system during the 1930s in the West and has argued that the aesthetic approach ought to be different for the tropical region.[51] As an alternative to the aesthetic of the "scaleless bland box", he proposed the following:[52]

1. The roof should be the main feature as opposed to the wall, where the roof will provide the shade, shelter, shadow and profile, allowing for a play of gradations and transitions of shade and shadow and a " 'fuzzy' wall with the tremendous possibilities in integrating use functions and variations into it".

2. "The building section takes precedent over the plan as the generator of building form and as the basis of design thinking. The tendency of the elevations of a building to be an extrusion of the plan is dispelled once the roof predominates and the walls are merely partial enclosures, no longer required to be the absolute limit of the interior space of the building." The external surface of the building can be a space resource with interpenetrating layers between the inside and outside space.

3. In relation to surface treatment, the layers may be conceived as "meshes or fretwork patterns and trellis screens", "producing a totally different architecture from that of the planar wall".

4. Profile and edge are also important formal aspects to address how a "building engages the often cloudy sky in soft diffused light" as opposed to the strong contrasting Mediterranean sky.

Based on Tay Kheng Soon's proposal on the use of line, edge and shade, and the title of the book about his firm's works, in this chapter this will be referred to as the "Line, Edge & Shade" paradigm.[53]

One of the notable examples of work employing this tropical design language is the Institute of Technical Education at Bishan (Figure 12.7a). His firm, Akitek Tenggara II, won the design competition for this project in 1989 and completed it in 1993. Large curved roofs generously shelter the façade from rain, give shade from the sun and cast various depths of shadows. The large horizontal louvers on incline plane shade the windows and are generously spaced to allow wind to flow through the classrooms that are predominantly naturally ventilated (Figure 12.7b). There is no reference to traditional forms or styles, and all the materials and method of construction are modern. The prominent lines and edges of the buildings, the permeability

(a)

(b)

Figure 12.7 a and b The Institute of Technical Education at Bishan, 1989–93, designed by Akitek Tenggara II (photos Bay Joo Hwa Philip)

Regional expression (architectural language based on the tropical climate)

Performance (climatically relevant)

Materials and means of building (modern, non-traditional)

Figure 12.8 *The "Line, Edge & Shade" paradigm*

and transparency, and the strong shadows together form a distinct character, an architectural expression noticeably different from the "scaleless bland box" Tay talks about.[54]

The diagram shown in Figure 12.8 serves as an encapsulation of this tropical design paradigm. The regional expression is based on a language founded on the tropical climatic considerations. The performance in provision of climatic comfort and convenience is obviously directly related to the expression. The materials and means of building are modern and non-traditional.

This paradigm is especially applicable to a high-rise, high-density development where the old way of extruding the plan multistoreys can be replaced with one where the vertical planes can be varied and layered with various possibilities of usage and resultant characters. While this "Line, Edge & Shade" paradigm affords functional and forward-looking expressions, the buildings tend to look cold and lack affinity with rich cultural pasts and geological material of the tropical context. Most new manufactured materials tend to be harsh and are not as effective as traditional materials such as wood and stone in handling heat and glare. They also lack the character of some older natural materials that has been associated with indigenous regional architecture, architecture that mellows well with time.

THE "TRADITION-BASED" PARADIGM

Contrary to the above approach, Tan Hock Beng has argued for a need to evoke traditions in the tropical Asian architecture and proposed that there is an authentic way of doing tradition-based design to ensure new production of rich tropical architecture for this region.[55] He has also criticized the prevalent "Neo-Greco–Kitsch" and careless copying of traditional images, and wrote: "In the face of a self-indulgent architecture of Postmodernism and the reductive universality of Modern architecture, these rapidly developing countries have begun to look at [traditional] built forms as an expression of their own aspirations and identities."[56] He calls for a true understanding of the traditional large pitch roof form, planning for cross-ventilation, in-between

realms and courtyards, traditional openings, tropical materials, water and
landscape, and the appropriate application of such elements so as to ensure
the integration with nature and a poetic expression of tradition.[57]

To avoid the homogenizing effect of globalization, and to preserve the richness of local traditions, William Lim and Tan Hock Beng proposed the
following four strategies:[58]

1. "Reinvigorating tradition" – "evoking the vernacular" by way of "a
   genuine reinvigoration of traditional craft wisdom" and not being "tacky
   versions of skin-deep treatments of indigenous archetypes". Suggesting
   that a genuine admiration for the vernacular through a genuine reinvigoration will result "in the perpetuation of an architectural language that
   assumes the status of authenticity through ensuring a perceived historical continuity".
2. "Reinventing Tradition" – "the search for new paradigms" by way of a
   hybridization in the same sense as how the British colonials were "reinventing tradition" by building colonial bungalows drawing lessons from
   the Malay house.
3. "Extending Tradition" – "using the vernacular in a modified manner" as
   in Geoffrey Bawa's "use of his country's vernacular structures and its
   tradition of inherited craftsmanship" for a contemporary experience. And
   in Bawa's case, actually raising the status and value of the tradition.
4. "Reinterpreting tradition" – "the use of contemporary idioms" to transform traditional formal devices in "refreshing ways" as in "Frank Lloyd
   Wright's transformation of Meso-American forms" into an invigorating
   modern idiom, "through an abstract and usually minimalist statement".
   Lim and Tan relate this to "critical regionalism" as described by Kenneth
   Frampton.[59]

This paradigm is based on evoking tradition; therefore I refer to it as the
"Tradition-based" paradigm.

William Lim applied the colonial bungalow formal devices in the Reuters
House, completed in 1990 (Figure 12.9). The large pitch roof form with clay
tiles, stilt-like wooden columns, and overall proportion evoke the colonial
tradition where the large overhanging roof in combination with stilt-like structures are set in lush green and wide open grounds, offering the character of
shade and airiness. The structure is based on reinforced concrete constructional method and the programme is based on the owners' modern lifestyle. This fits with the fourth strategy of reinterpreting tradition with new
technology and new programmes in an innovative way.[60]

This paradigm can be encapsulated as shown in Figure 12.10. The regional
expression is based on the strategy of evoking tradition. The performance in
provision of climatic comfort and convenience should be integral with the

Figure 12.9 *Reuters House, 1990, designed by William Lim (photo Bay Joo Hwa Philip)*

traditional form if the traditional form is faithfully adhered to, or lessons from the traditional forms followed. As for materials and means of building, it could be traditional, modern or mixed depending on which of the substrategies is employed in this paradigm.

Most of the examples used to illustrate this "Tradition-based" paradigm are resort developments, small cultural and institutional buildings, and small-scale residential projects with ample land and budget for the use of traditional timber, roofing materials, stone walls, water bodies and large, open landscaped grounds. This approach is less likely to be suitable for solving the region's high-density high-rise urban problem. The way climatic modulations were provided and associated with the traditional forms may not be applicable to the high-density urban context, and the adaptation of the traditional

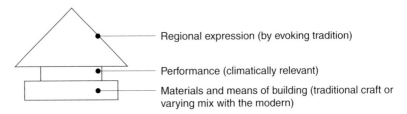

Figure 12.10 *The "Tradition-based" paradigm*

forms will not necessarily produce similar effects. A conscious and continuous overemphasis on traditional forms may overshadow experiments and
the emergence of new cultural forms.

THE "NEW SCREEN & LOUVER KITSCH" PARADIGM

The third paradigm is dubbed the "New Screen & Louver Kitsch", as it is
indeed a kind of kitsch. In the usual kitsch, referred to earlier, as in the case
of the historicist kitsch, they are bad copies of some forms in the past. The
"New Screen & Louver Kitsch" is about bad copies of the modern tropical
expressions without the appropriate application or performance. How did this
type of kitsch develop?

First there is the stereotyping of the modern tropical image. The modern
louver, for instance, has been used frequently as a sunshading device and
therefore is visually associated with tropical architecture. The louvers on a
façade that do not effectively shade a space may still be wrongly correlated
with the genuine sunshading devices and give the impression that they are
tropical climatic control devices to the passing eye. Second, with the
mounting emphasis on the production of environmentally appropriate architecture, by prominent regional advocates like Tay Kheng Soon and Kenneth
Yeang for instance,[61] there is a motivation to join in this course, or be polit-
ically correct at least. A designer who is not truly serious about struggling
with the climatic requirements because he or she is too busy or he thinks
the climatic factor is not so crucial or not a priority for his design, but yet
desires to have the tropical image because of the watching eye of the public,
the client or the fraternity, can still have a way out. Because of the stereotyping, he or she can join in the charade by applying a gesture of the typical
tropical devices as part of the aesthetic composition for the building. This
stereotyping of the tropical images creates the possibility for a consumerist
exploitation of the screen and louver images, and gives room for the "New
Screen & Louver Kitsch".

A case example, the newly completed Tanjong Katong Secondary School,
by the Public Works Department in 1999, displays louvers of different sizes
on various façades with apparently little effectiveness in shielding from sun
and rain (Figure 12.11). The huge louvers clearly shade blank walls and the
small windows are not shaded. The small louvers along the corridors do not
appear to offer much shade or rain protection. The staircase is fully glazed
and exposed to the same external condition of sun and heat, posing the
problem of the greenhouse effect. All these points lead one to suspect all the
attempts at "climatic modulation". Such is an example of the "New Screen
& Louver Kitsch".

Figure 12.11 *Tanjong Katong Secondary School, 1999 designed by the Public Works Department (photo Bay Joo Hwa Philip)*

Another case example, the competition winning design by Architect Vista for the Institute of Technical Education at Balestier, was completed in 1997 (Figure 12.12). The building design looks elegant, full of screens and louvers that give the impression that it is a tropically sound building. But on closer examination, the large expanse of screens facing west do not adequately shade from the sun or protect from the rain for most of the crucial moments of the day, and just like the previous example, the main vertical circulation staircases are boxed up with glass which will only create greenhouse effects. It was also interesting to note that it was simply described by a writer as adequately taking care of the climatic requirements, in an article for the *Singapore Architect* journal.[62]

An example of a different category of building, House No.5, Lorong 105, Changi Road, designed by Look Architects, was completed in 1997 (Figure 12.13). The "Cubist" composition is an interesting interpretation of a house, but there is something strange about the provisions for climatic control. In the same façade can be found a large expanse of glass as well as a set of four disproportionate "sun-shading" fins. These make the effectiveness of climatic control suspect. The probability of this being a "New Screen & Louver Kitsch" is almost certain.

This paradigm is not exactly a responsible example to emulate. The diagram can serve to encapsulate the paradigm (Figure 12.14). The regional expression is based on exploiting the stereotypes of new tropical images. The

Figure 12.12 *The Institute of Technical Education at Balestier, 1997, designed by Architect Vista (photo Bay Joo Hwa Philip)*

Figure 12.13 *House No. 5, Lorong 105, Changi Road, 1997, designed by Look Architects (photo Bay Joo Hwa Philip)*

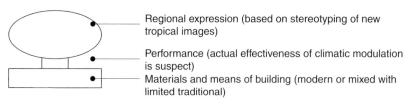

Regional expression (based on stereotyping of new tropical images)

Performance (actual effectiveness of climatic modulation is suspect)

Materials and means of building (modern or mixed with limited traditional)

Figure 12.14 The "New Screen & Louver Kitsch"

effectiveness for climatic performance is suspect. The materials and means of construction are mainly modern, but there could also be a mix.

A CRITICAL LOOK

To a large extent the works in the 1960s and 1970s in Singapore were essentially modern and yet regional, global yet local, a critical regionalism according to Alexander Tzonis's and Liane Lefaivre's definition.[63] New forward-looking technologies were adapted to the climatic context in new ways, departing from the familiar colonial designs referred to earlier. The "Line, Edge & Shade" paradigm offers a method to achieve a tropical climatic-based design distinct from the anonymous banal "box" discussed earlier. It also "defamiliarized" the way to look at local architecture and the design process, opening up the possibility of engaging the works and the people in conscious dialogue. The "Tradition-based" paradigm offers four strategies to evoke tradition, which range from highly preservative to highly re-interpretative modes. In the reinterpretative mode, traditional formal devices are to be abstracted in modern idioms, thus having the new and evoking the traditional.

The "Line, Edge & Shade" paradigm opens up possibilities for the high-rise, high-density urban designs, but the "Tradition-based" paradigm has not indicated this relationship and the possibilities. Instead in the foreword to *Contemporary Vernacular: Evoking Traditions in Asian Architecture*, Charles Correa seems to suggest that this can be simply done, saying: "What we do not have to do is design mass housing for people. On the contrary, the wonderfully flexible and pluralistic language of vernacular habitat already exists. All we must do, as architects and planners, is adjust our cities so that this language becomes viable again. And once this is accomplished, then our remaining task will be to just get out of the way."[64]

Below are three more recent cases of tropical architecture in Singapore, which attempted at critically engaging the local with the global.

In the Bedok Court Condominium, completed in 1985, the architect, Cheng Jian Fenn, created tropical urban streets and forecourts in the sky

(Figure 12.15a). These allow for maximizing open-court activities in front of each apartment unit in the sky with ample opportunities for growing familiarity and social contacts (Figure 12.15b). According to Cheng he wanted to bring back a similar social and physical experience he knew well that existed in traditional tropical kampungs (villages) in Singapore.[65] Cheng referred to Jane Jacob's argument for the importance of the street as "vital organs of a city" and a need for a "certain loss of privacy" in the modern society rather than having a maximum privacy (Figure 12.15c).[66] One may be suspicious of the success of such sky-court concepts, but a survey of the project and residents has shown a 90 per cent vote from residents affirming that they are highly conscious of a strong sense of belonging, ownership and security. And that life would be very different without the tropical streets and forecourts in the sky (Figure 12.15d).[67] The success is attributed to the fact that all kinds of activities ranging from gardening, dining and children playing and studying could happen on these conducive airy and sheltered forecourts to each unit, with neighbours visible to each other day in day out for familiarity and community structure to develop. The quality of tropical "village" living is achieved, "defamiliarized" and recreated with innovatively modern building technology, materials and aesthetic language.

In a recent work, The Market Place, completed in 1995, the architect Tang Guan Bee elevates the status of the traditional market in the neighbourhood by introducing a new tropical form reminiscent of the old market, but with totally new materials and technology (Figure 12.16a). Even though the roof of The Market Place is of metal cladding and a barrel shape instead of the corrugated asbestos pitched roofs of the past, it captures the ambience of the old markets, the sense of the large overhanging and airy canopy (Figure 12.16b).[68] This demonstrates an act of moving forward and a little backward at the same time by "defamiliarizing" a part of history.

In the newly completed Institute of Southeast Asian Studies in 1998, the PWD architect Cheah Kok Ming has created a dialogue between old and new tropical forms in an innovative whole (Figure 12.17a). The pitch roof, stone materials and landscape are reminiscent of Southeast Asian traditional architecture and are relevant cultural subject to the centre. These are juxtaposed with the prominent modern glazed air-conditioned boxes and metal sun-screening devices into a cohesive composition of old and new, where the consciousness of the regional and modern is augmented simultaneously (Figure 12.17b). Moving in and around the building, one is conscious of and intrigued by the architectural dialogue of the old and the new.

We have seen the preoccupation of some who are biased against moving forward, some who are steeped in claiming the past and some who get by commercially using tropically correct images. In the "Line, Edge & Shade" paradigm, tropical architecture should be forward looking, employing modern technology and at the same time maintain a local character through

(a)

(b)

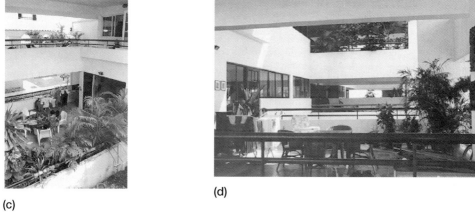

(c)

(d)

Figure 12.15 (a–d) Bedok Court Condominium, 1985, designed by Cheng Jian Fenn
(photos Bay Joo Hwa Philip)

(a)

(b)

Figure 12.16 (a and b) The Market
Place, 1995, designed by Tang Guan Bee
(by permission of Tangguanbee
Architects)

(a)

(b)

Figure 12.17 *(a and b) The Institute of Southeast Asian Studies, 1995, designed by Cheah Kok Ming (photos Bay Joo Hwa Philip)*

responding to the local climatic requirements with a tropical language of "line, edge and shade". As such it is also a promising paradigm with regards to designing high-rise high-density urban developments. In the "Tradition-based" paradigm, regional architecture is supposed to be achieved with varying degrees of evoking tradition. The least abstract, "Reinvigorating Tradition" involves a direct appreciation and reproduction of tradition, and the most abstract, "Reinterpreting Tradition". In the case of the Institute of Southeast Asian Studies, it can be considered to be a form of "Reinterpreting Tradition" augmenting the new and the old. Though The Market Place and the Bedok Court Condominium appear to belong to the "Tradition-based" paradigm, they are quite far removed from the examples given in "Tradition-based" paradigm because of the extreme levels of abstraction and critical-ness. They are modern buildings in modern design language, but each critically "defamiliarizes" (in the sense described by Tzonis and Lefaivre)[70] an interesting aspect of the past. So far all the examples relating to the "Tradition-based" paradigm are lower in abstraction by comparison and also appear more suitable for the low-scale, low-density developments as in indi-vidual houses, holiday resorts or small commercial projects. It is difficult (but not necessarily impossible) to see how this may be applied to architecture that will affect the majority of people in the dense tropical Singapore city and the region. More can be explored as to how new technologies can be employed to produce innovative and critical modern urban morphologies. The "New Screen & Louver Kitsch" paradigm is obviously not an admirable paradigm to adopt. Impressions of tropical images can be created, but the works certainly lack the criticalness and appropriateness with regard to climatic requirements.

Perhaps we may be able to achieve many more critical works of tropical architecture that are both global and local, and succeed commercially at the same time. The diagram shown in Figure 12.18 is an attempt to encapsulate a generic paradigm with reference to critical regionalism. The materials and means of building will largely be modern, and climatic performance is defi-nitely a major consideration. The regional expression will be one that is critical, relying on the strategy of "defamiliarization" of appropriate local

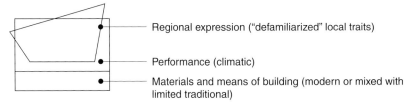

Figure 12.18 A possible diagram for critical regionalism

traits, open to all kinds of possibilities limited only by the creativity of the individual architect.

NOTES

1. Regional is used in the broad sense as to mean "of the region".
2. Fry and Drew were practising as architects in the tropics and had written about tropical modern works from the 1930s to the 1960s, drawing lessons from indigenous tropical examples as well as the latest technology in environmental design. Their observations and suggestions targeted for use by the Western architect in the tropics are in: Fry, Maxwell and Drew, Jane (1982) *Tropical Architecture in the Dry and Humid Zones*, 2nd edn, Malabar, FL.: R.E. Krieger (original works published in 1964). They also published an earlier book on tropical architecture: Fry, Maxwell and Drew, Jane (1956) *Tropical Architecture in the Humid Zone*. London: BT.
3. Fry, Maxwell and Drew, Jane (1982) *Tropical Architecture in the Dry and Humid Zones*, 2nd edn, Malabar, FL: R.E. Kreiger.
4. Victor and Aladar Olgyay were practising architects as well as researchers and writers on the multidisciplinary relationship of climate, biology, and technology in achieving architecture of comfort and aesthetic delight. They have written on these issues from the early 1950s and a collection of salient points of their thoughts for modern architectural design with climatic charts and guides can be found in: Olgyay, Victor and Olgyay, Aladar (1963) *Design with Climate: Bioclimatic Approach to Architectural Regionalism*. Princeton: Princeton University Press.
5. Ibid. Referring to Vitruvius. *De Architectura*. Book VI. Chapter 1. Translated by Frank Granger (Ariba), 1934.
6. Dandy discussed the possibilities of architectural expressions relating to building materials, climate and culture in Dandy, Miles (1963) *Grammar of Architectural Design: With Special Reference to the Tropics*. London, New York: Oxford University Press.
7. Olgyay, Aladar and Olgyay, Victor (1957) *Solar Control and Shading Devices*. Princeton: Princeton University Press.
8. Ibid. Olgyay and Olgyay concentrated mainly on the importance and possibilities of solar control and shading devices in this book.
9. Dandy, Miles (1963). *Grammar of Architectural Design: With Special Reference to the Tropics*. London, New York: Oxford University Press.
10 Ibid. In as much as the traditional/religious forms and climatic forms are integrated as in the roof form, courtyards, screens or trellis for instance.
11. Relevance of appropriate material selection discussed by Fry and Drew (Fry and Drew, op. cit.) includes suitability for the climatic condition, cost factor and availability. For the purpose of this chapter, only the climatic relation is referred to. The availability of certain natural timber in this region is also related to the climate. For more up-to-date example of guide to constructional materials and common defects: Chew, M.Y.L. (1998) *Building Facades: A Guide to Common Defects in Tropical Climates*. Singapore: World Scientific.
12. Relevance of appropriate constructional method discussed by Fry and Drew (Fry and Drew 1964, 1982, op. cit.) includes the type of labour available. Again

only the climatic related factors are considered for discussion in this chapter. More examples of guides for building constructional issues: Fullerton, R.L. (1979) *Building Construction in Warm Climates: Vol. 1*. London: Intermediate Technology Publications.

13. The planning and design guidelines for comfort with climatic charts and guides, building materials and constructional considerations were proposed by Olgyay and Olgyay in Olgyay, Victor and Olgyay, Aladar (1963) *Design with Climate: Bioclimatic Approach to Architectural Regionalism*. Princeton: Princeton University Press. Other literature dealing with such guidelines includes: Lippsmeier, George (1980) *Tropenbau: Building in the Tropics*. Munich: Callwey; and Koenigsberger, O.H. (ed. *et al.*) (1974). *Manual of Tropical Housing and Building: Pt. 1, Climatic Design*. London: Longman.

14. Dean Hawkes discussed the theory and systems of environmental design and argues for a more flexible and adaptive system: Hawkes, Dean (1996) *The Environmental Tradition: Studies in the Architecture of Environment*. London: E&FN Spon.

15. Ibid.

16. Banham, Reyner (1984) *The Architecture of the Well-tempered Environment* (2nd edn). Chicago: The University of Chicago Press (original work published in 1969).

17. Fry, Maxwell and Drew, Jane (1982) *Tropical Architecture in the Dry and Humid Zones* (2nd edn). Malabar, FL.: R.E. Krieger (original works published in 1964).

18. Lee Kuan Yew (1999) in *Straits Times*, Singapore, 19 January 1999, p. 1.

19. At the moment air-conditioners are run with electrical energy from fossil fuels, but soon when alternative sources of energy, including solar energy, are employed it will be less of a problem. There is also a counter argument that the air-conditioners preserve building materials better and prolong the life of the building, which translated to energy is also a saving. This matter goes beyond the discussion of this chapter.

20. The Malay House refers to the indigenous house typology common to the region of Malaysia and Singapore. Lim Jee Yuan (1987) *The Malay House*. Pulau Pinang: Institut Masyarakat.

21. The colonial bungalow in Singapore was also referred to as the Singapore house in Lee, Kip Lin (1988) *The Singapore House*. Singapore: Times Edition; and in Edwards, Norman (1990) *The Singapore House and Residential Life: 1819–1939*. Oxford: Oxford University Press.

22. The provision of "five-foot-ways" for the shophouses was a tropical urban strategy implemented for Singapore by Sir Stamford Raffles, in Lim Jon Sun Hock (1990) "Colonial Architecture and Architects of Georgetown (Penang) and Singapore: between 1786 and 1942", Singapore: National University of Singapore, PhD Thesis; and also in Gretchen, L. (1984) *Pastel Portraits: Singapore's Architectural Heritage*. Singapore: Singapore Coordinating Committee.

23. Most of these buildings display European styles including the Palladian style on the façades.

24. E. J. Seow (1973) *Architectural Development in Singapore*. Melbourne: Melbourne University.

25. Ibid.

26. Ibid. And also in introductory essay by E. J. Seow in Gan Eng Oon (ed. *et al.*) (1981) *Rumah: Contemporary Architecture of Singapore*. Singapore: Singapore Institute of Architects. There were other examples of works by PWD and private architects of that period in tropical Singapore.

27. Chua Beng-Huat (1989) *The Golden Shoe: Building Singapore's Financial Centre*. Singapore: Urban Redevelopment Authority.
28. The author has selected these few notable pioneer works as examples for discussion after surveying: The Singapore Institute of Architects' early journals, *Rumah* and *SIAJ* from 1959, E. J. Seow (1973) *Architectural Development in Singapore*. Melbourne: Melbourne University; and Gan Eng Oon (ed. *et al.*) (1981) *Rumah: Contemporary Architecture of Singapore*. Singapore: Singapore Institute of Architects.
29. Author's discussion with Lim Chong Keat, Singapore, 1999; Lim Chong Keat, Chen Voon Fee and William Lim were partners of Malayan Architects Co-partnership from 1961 to 1965; according to Lim Chong Keat, he and Chen Voon Fee were the key architects involved in the design of the project.
30. Author's discussion with Tay Kheng Soon, Singapore, 1999; Tay Kheng Soon was an ex-student of Lim Chong Keat at the Singapore Polytechnic, and was working with Malayan Architects Co-partnership while this project was being designed and built.
31. Ibid. Tay Kheng Soon recollected the optimistic atmosphere of the opening speech for the building by Lee Kuan Yew who was then the Prime Minister of Singapore.
32. Message was from the Minister for Culture and Social Affairs in Ministry of Culture and Social Affairs (1965) *Souvenir Brochure for the Opening of the Singapore Conference Hall and Trade Union House*. 15 October 1965, Singapore: Ministry of Culture and Social Affairs.
33. Author's discussion with Lim Chong Keat, Singapore, 1999; Lim was confident that the naturally ventilated lobby and exhibition concourse works well and need not be air-conditioned in the present renovation work on the building by another architect. He said, "There is very little change to the micro-climate, nor the level of pollution", and therefore doubted the necessity for a modification.
34. Author's discussion with Lim Chong Keat, Singapore, 1999: the discussions on tropical architecture by Victor Olgyay and Aladar Olgyay, and Maxwell Fry and Jane Drew were popular at that time.
35. The Malaysia Singapore Airlines Building was later called the Singapore Airlines Building. Unfortunately this building was demolished to make way for bigger facilities with higher plot ratios. Today, the Singapore Airlines Building is a pristine glass tower sitting on the same site.
36. This was the prototype for the intensive high-rise office developments that were to follow along Singapore's business district: Chua Beng-Huat (1989) *The Golden Shoe: Building Singapore's Financial Centre*. Singapore: Urban Redevelopment Authority.
37. William Lim, Koh Seow Chuan and Tay Kheng Soon formed Design Partnership in 1966. Prior to that, William Lim and Tay Kheng Soon were practising with Lim Chong Keat.
38. Author's discussion with William Lim, Singapore, 1999. Although the provision of a modern solution to recapture the lost city life and culture of shopping and dining in informal street settings was the key challenge, the consideration of comfort and convenience of movement was also important.
39. Author's discussion with Tay Kheng Soon, Singapore, 1999; the Ala Moana Center was essentially a huge horizontal shopping mall.
40. Author's discussion with William Lim and Tay Kheng Soon separately, 1999; Lim and Tay were closely following the architectural discourse of Team X and their key correspondence was with Kenzo Tange. They had the opportunity to discuss the ideas of Metabolism and Fumiko Maki, and the idea of the "City Room" –

urban nodes of energetic human movement and activities. Lim and Tay had earlier discussions with Rem Koolhaas who has written more details on this subject: Koolhaas, R. and Mau, B. (1995) *Small, Medium, Large, Extra-large: Office for Metropolitan Architecture.* Rotterdam: 010 Publishers.

41. Author's discussion with Tay Kheng Soon, Singapore, 1999; according to Tay, shoppers could enjoy the cool of the air-conditioned shops if they felt warm. The mechanical fans were also not installed at completion of the building because of the tight budget. Tay was sure that natural ventilation alone would be inadequate. Business, however, was so successful that the owners of the building decided to air-condition the building several years later and boxed in all openings with glass panels and doors, destroying much of the concept of connectivity and flow of spaces.

42. Author's discussion with Tay Kheng Soon, Singapore, 1999; there was, however, not enough budget for landscaping the roof in the final execution.

43. Author's discussion with William Lim and Tay Kheng Soon separately, 1999. Both Lim and Tay recounted the amazing results of the survey. The Woh Hup Complex, today known as the Golden Mile Complex, is along Beach Road, Singapore.

44. Author's discussion with William Lim, Singapore, 1999. Tay Kheng Soon made multiple copies of the Woh Hup Complex drawings and laid them out as city blocks linked together as an experiment for a new tropical urbanscape.

45. From 1965, William Lim and Tay Kheng Soon were among the key advocates for generating discussion and research into the future of tropical Asian cities with unique cultural and community needs. The multidisciplinary research group called Singapore Planning and Urban Research group produced two publications: *SPUR 65–67* and *SPUR 68–71*. More of this is covered in author's interview of Tay Kheng Soon on *SPUR*, 1998 in Internet Web-page: http://www.sintercom.org/sp/interviews/taykhengsoon.html; and in Koolhaas, R. and Mau, B. (1995) *Small, Medium, Large, Extra-large: Office for Metropolitan Architecture.* Rotterdam: 010 Publishers.

46. Author's discussion with William Lim and Tay Kheng Soon separately, Singapore, 1999; both expressed regret about the inward character of the People's Park Complex as well as other numerous air-conditioned shopping centres that followed.

47. Tay Kheng Soon (1994) "Towards an Ecologically-responsible Urban Architecture". Seminar paper reprinted in Powell, Robert (ed.) (1997) *Line, Edge & Shade: The Search for a Design Language in Tropical Asia; Tay Kheng Soon & Akitek Tenggara.* Singapore: Page One Publishing.

48. Author's discussion with Tay Kheng Soon, Singapore, 1997: it is good to learn principles employed in traditional architecture.

49. Tay Kheng Soon (1990) "Wah so Obiang one" in the *Straits Times.* Singapore, 28 March 1990; "Obiang" is a colloquialism meaning kitsch, poor taste, cheap, imitative or plastic. "Wah so Obiang one" can be rendered approximately as "Oh, so bad taste".

50. As quoted in the introduction; in Powell, Robert (ed.) (1997) *Line, Edge & Shade: The Search for a Design Language in Tropical Asia; Tay Kheng Soon & Akitek Tenggara,* Singapore: Page One Publishing.

51. Tay Kheng Soon (1990) "The architectural aesthetic of tropicality". Paper reprinted in Powell, Robert (ed.) (1997) *Line, Edge & Shade: The Search for a Design Language in Tropical Asia; Tay Kheng Soon & Akitek Tenggara.* Singapore: Page One Publishing.

52. Ibid.

53. Ibid.

54. Comments based on observations by the author.
55. Tan is a writer and a practising architect who proposed a way of doing tropical Asian architecture: Tan Hock Beng (1994) *Tropical Architecture and Interiors: Tradition-based Design of Indonesia, Malaysia, Singapore, and Thailand.* Singapore: Page One Publishing.
56. Ibid.
57. Ibid.
58. Lim, W.S.W. and Tan, H.B. (1998) *Contemporary Vernacular: Evoking Traditions in Asian Architecture.* Singapore: Select Books.
59. Ibid. Referring to critical regionalism in: Frampton, Kenneth (1983) "Prospects for a critical regionalism". In Nesbitt, Kate (ed.) (1996) *Theorizing a New Agenda for Architecture: An Anthology of Architectural Theory 1965–1995.* New York: Princeton Architectural Press.
60. Author's observations and comments.
61. One of the ardent advocates in the region of the modern regional-climatic architecture is Ken Yeang who has published several books on this issue: Yeang, Ken (1986) *The Tropical Verandah City: Some Urban Design Ideas for Kuala Lumpur.* Kuala Lumpur: Asia Publications; Yeang, Ken (1987) *Tropical Urban Regionalism: Building in a South-east Asian City.* Singapore: Concept Media; Yeang, Ken (1994) *Bioclimatic Skyscrapers.* London: Ellipsis and Pidgeon Audio Visual.
62. SA (1997). *Singapore Architect Journal*, vol. 197/97. Singapore: Singapore Institute of Architects.
63. Alexandra Tzonis and Liane Lefaivre invented the term "critical regionalism" in the early 1980s to refer to a dominant architectural tendency in regionalism during the 1970s and 1980s. Critical regionalism is not about sentimental, scenographic, nationalist or chauvinistic regionalism of the past. It is about being a critique on the habits of thinking and the role of clichés about the "place" and the "community" through the concept of "de-familiarisation" or "strange-making", coined by the literary critic Victor Schklovsky in 1920. Traditional architectural elements appearing in the unexpected preclude any sentimental and scenographic effects, but remind the users about the meaning and warn of the potential loss of the "community" and "place" as a result of technological advancement and bureaucratic rationalization of the city. This poetic device critically engages the work and the people in conscious dialogue. Tzonis, Alexander and Lefaivre, Liane (1990) "Why critical regionalism today?" In Nesbitt, Kate (ed.) (1996) *Theorizing a New Agenda for Architecture: An Anthology of Architectural Theory 1965–1995.* New York: Princeton Architectural Press. Also in the introduction to Tzonis, Alexander and Lefaivre, Liane (1992) *Architecture in Europe: Memory and Invention since 1968.* London: Thames and Hudson.
64. Introduction by Charles Correa in Lim, W.S.W. and Tan, H. B. (1998) *Contemporary Vernacular: Evoking Traditions in Asian Architecture.* Singapore: Select Books.
65. Author's discussion with Cheng Jian Fenn, Singapore, 1999; Cheng Jian Fenn was the design architect in Associates Group Architects for Bedok Court Condominium.
66. The phrase "vital organs of a city" refers to community nodes, and "certain loss of privacy" refers to the sacrifice of a little privacy necessary for knowing and interacting with others, in Jacobs, Jane (1962) *The Death and Life of Great American Cities.* New York: Random House.
67. Bay, Joo Hwa (2000) "Design for high-rise high-density living – the tropical streets in the sky". Paper published in *Proceedings of the 2nd International Conference*

on Quality of Life in Cities: 21st Century QOL. Singapore: National University of Singapore, March 2000.

68. Author's discussion with Tang Guan Bee, Singapore, 1999; Tang Guan Bee is the sole proprietor of Tanguanbee Architects.

69. Lim, W.S.W. and Tan, H. B. (1998) *Contemporary Vernacular: Evoking Traditions in Asian Architecture*. Singapore: Select Books.

70. Tzonis, Alexander and Lefaivre, Liane (1990) "Why critical regionalism today?" In Kate, Nesbitt (ed.) (1996) *Theorizing a New Agenda for Architecture: An Anthology of Architectural Theory 1965–1995*. New York: Princeton Architectural Press.

BIBLIOGRAPHY

Banham, Reyner (1984) *The Architecture of the Well-tempered Environment* (2nd edn). Chicago: The University of Chicago Press. (Original work published in 1969.)

Bay Joo Hwa (1998a) "Singapore architecture: A dynamics of an emerging culture and architectural identity". Paper published in the *Proceedings of the Second International Symposium on Architectural Interchange in Asia* (pp. 43–46). Kobe: Architectural Institute of Japan, September 1998.

Bay Joo Hwa (1998b) "Three tropical design paradigms". Paper published in the *Proceedings of the 1st Conference for Architectural Design and Technologies for Pan Sub-tropical Climates*. Hong Kong University and Guangzhou University (eds). Guangzhou: Guangzhou University, November 1998.

Bay Joo Hwa (2000) "Design for high-rise high-density living: The tropical streets in the sky". Paper published in the *Proceedings of the 2nd International Conference on Quality of Life in Cities: 21st Century QOL*. Singapore: National University of Singapore, March 2000.

Bay J. H., Ang, C. K. and Chen, P. (eds) (1998) *Contemporary Singapore Architecture: 1960's to 1990's*. Singapore: Singapore Institute of Architects.

Chew, M.Y.L. (1998) *Building Facades: A Guide to Common Defects in Tropical Climates*. Singapore: World Scientific.

Chua Beng-Huat (1989) *The Golden Shoe: Building Singapore's Financial Centre*. Singapore: Urban Redevelopment Authority.

Dandy, Miles (1963) *Grammar of Architectural Design: With Special Reference to the Tropics*. London, New York: Oxford University Press.

Edwards, Norman (1990) *The Singapore House and Residential Life 1819–1939*. Oxford: Oxford University Press.

Frampton, Kenneth (1983) "Prospects for a critical regionalism". In Kate Nesbitt (ed.) (1996). *Theorizing a New Agenda for Architecture: An Anthology of Architectural Theory 1965–1995*. New York: Princeton Architectural Press.

Fry, Maxwell and Drew, Jane (1956) *Tropical Architecture in the Humid Zone*. London: BT Ltd.

Fry, Maxwell and Drew, Jane (1982) *Tropical Architecture in the Dry and Humid Zones* 2nd edn. Malabar, FL.: R.E. Krieger. (Original work published in 1964.)

Fullerton, R.L. (1977) *Building Construction in Warm Climates: Vol. 3*. Oxford: Oxford University Press.

Fullerton, R.L. (1978) *Building Construction in Warm Climates: Vol. 2* (2nd edn). Oxford: Oxford University Press.

Fullerton, R.L. (1979) *Building Construction in Warm Climates: Vol. 1*. London: Intermediate Technology Publications.

Gan Eng Oon (ed. *et al.*) (1981) *Rumah: Contemporary Architecture of Singapore*. Singapore: Singapore Institute of Architects.

Gretchen, M. (1984) *Pastel portraits: Singapore's architectural heritage* (text by M. Gretchen). Singapore: Singapore Coordinating Committee.

Hawkes, Dean (1996) *The Environmental Tradition: Studies in the Architecture of Environment*. London: E&FN Spon.

Howey, John (1995) *The Sarasota School of Architecture: 1941–1966*. Cambridge, MA: MIT Press.

Koenigsberger, O.H. (ed. *et al.*) (1974) *Manual of Tropical Housing and Building: Pt.1, Climatic Design*. London: Longman.

Koolhaas, R. and Mau, B. (1995) *Small, Medium, Large, Extra-large: Office for Metropolitan Architecture*. Rotterdam: 010 Publishers.

Kurokawa, Kisho (1991) *Intercultural Architecture: The Philosophy of Symbiosis*. London: Academy Editions.

Lee Kip Lin (1988) *The Singapore House*. Singapore: Times Edition.

Lee, Kuan Yew (1999). In *Straits Times* (p. 1). Singapore, 19 January 1999.

Lim Jee Yuan (1981) *A Comparison of the Traditional Malay House and the Modern Housing-estate House*. Tokyo: United Nations University.

Lim Jee Yuan (1987) *The Malay House*. Pulau Pinang: Institut Masyarakat.

Lim Jon Sun Hock (1990) "Colonial Architecture and Architects of Georgetown (Penang) and Singapore: between 1786 and 1942" (PhD thesis). Singapore: National University of Singapore.

Lim, W.S.W. and Tan, H.B. (1998) *Contemporary Vernacular: Evoking Traditions in Asian Architecture*. Singapore: Select Books.

Lippsmeier, George (1980) *Tropenbau: Building in the Tropics*. Munich: Callwey.

Ministry of Culture and Social Affairs (1965) *Souvenir Brochure for the Opening of the Singapore Conference Hall and Trade Union House*. 15 October 1965. Singapore: Ministry of Culture and Social Affairs.

Olgyay, Aladar and Olgyay, Victor (1957) *Solar Control and Shading Devices*. Princeton: Princeton University Press.

Olgyay, Victor and Olgyay, Aladar (1963) *Design with Climate; Bioclimatic Approach to Architectural Regionalism*. Princeton: Princeton University Press.

SA (1997) *Singapore Architect Journal*, vol. 197/97. Singapore: Singapore Institute of Architects.

Seow, E. J. (1973) *Architectural Development in Singapore*. Melbourne: Melbourne University.

SPUR (1967) *SPUR 65–67*. Singapore: Singapore Planning and Urban Research group.

SPUR (1971) *SPUR 68–71*. Singapore: Singapore Planning and Urban Research group.

Tan Hock Beng (1994) *Tropical Architecture and Interiors: Tradition-based Design of Indonesia, Malaysia, Singapore, and Thailand*. Singapore: Page One Publishing.

Tan Hock Beng (1995) *Tropical Resorts*. Singapore: Page One Publishing.

Tan Hock Beng (1996) *Tropical Retreats: The Poetics of Place*. Singapore: Page One Publishing.

Tay Kheng Soon (1990) "Wah so Obiang one". Article in *Straits Times*. Singapore 28 March 1990.

Tay Kheng Soon (1994) "Towards an ecologically-responsible urban architecture". Seminar paper reprinted in Powell, Robert (ed.) (1997) *Line, Edge & Shade: The Search for a Design Language in Tropical Asia; Tay Kheng Soon & Akitek Tenggara*. Singapore: Page One Publishing.

Tzonis, Alexander and Lefaivre, Liane (1990) "Why critical regionalism today?" In Kate Nesbitt (ed.) (1996) *Theorizing a New Agenda for Architecture: An*

Anthology of Architectural Theory 1965–1995. New York: Princeton Architectural Press.

Tzonis, Alexander and Lefaivre, Liane (1992) *Architecture in Europe: Memory and Invention since 1968.* London: Thames and Hudson.

Yeang, Ken (1986) *The Tropical Verandah City: Some Urban Design Ideas for Kuala Lumpur.* Kuala Lumpur: Asia Publications.

Yeang, Ken (1987). *Tropical Urban Regionalism: Building in South-east Asian City.* Singapore: Concept Media.

Yeang, Ken (1994). *Bioclimatic Skyscrapers.* London: Pidgeon Audio Visual.

Yeang, Ken (1997). *The Skyscraper, Bio-climatically Considered: A Design Primer.* London: Academy Editions.

CHAPTER 13

RETHINKING THE CITY IN THE TROPICS: THE TROPICAL CITY CONCEPT

Tay Kheng Soon

The Tropical City Concept is a radical rethink of city planning in the tropics. The context is the hot and humid zone approximately 10 degrees north and south of the Equator at sea level (Figure 13.1). Within this zone, a number of plan-defying mega-cities has sprung up with populations ranging between 3 and 15 million. Demographic and physical growth have brought administrative expansion. Jakarta is a case in point. Here, the newly created colossal metropolitan area comprises four cities, Jakarta, Bogor, Tangerang and Bekasi, known collectively as "Jagotabek", with a total population of 30 000 000, and is under one central authority. Obviously, solutions need to be found to tackle the intractable problems of infrastructural deficiency, water shortage, pollution, congestion, waste disposal, inefficient energy utilization and the tremendous toll wreaked on the daily lives of the urban population in these vast urban conglomerations. Urban problems are, of course, basically economic in nature. But urban planning too can be an important factor. This chapter takes the view that it has a positive part to play in addressing problems related not only to function but also to identity in the "New States" of the hot-humid tropics.

Any enquiry into the Tropical City Concept inevitably involves a critique of existing planning and architectural concepts and attitudes and the conceptual limitations they impose. The mega-cities of the tropics are not the result of natural evolution. They have come about within the last 200 years as a result of colonial intervention. This is the context that should be the starting point in any examination of the phenomenon of the tropical city's characteristics, its causes and its effects. That there is a lack of really innovative ideas in planning and architecture in the tropical New States is a result of post-coloniality. Thus the process of rethinking is only just beginning thanks to a new-found confidence arising from economic progress. But the birth pangs of new ideas are always painful. In the New States of the tropics this is all the more the case since there is no tradition of free thought.

The restricted intellectual psychology of inhabitants of former colonies is the result of both colonial control and pre-colonial traditions. The purpose of the colonial population in the colonies was to operate colonial enterprises and plantations and to be the captive market for cheap manufactured goods produced in the metropolitan economies. Vast quantities of human labour from China, Ceylon and India swelled the towns of South East Asia, whereas, in the Americas, mass labour was from Africa. Those who showed capability for mental work were deployed as routine administrative assistants, law enforcers, nurses and maintenance staff. It is not surprising therefore that the emergence of local leadership in the anti-colonial struggle was initially led by local doctors and teachers and later by lawyers. Local architects, engineers and planners are post-colonial professionals. Their outlook is conditioned by the increasingly acute division of labour of the industrial-city economy and by the seduction of design ideas from the West-saturated-media. Thus the best and brightest have been attracted to the professions and skills most needed by the industrial economy. Only a small percentage of the brightest have entered the architectural and planning professions.

The ensuing growth in the towns is therefore not based on any deep thinking but on simple practical necessity and ideas current in Europe and the United States. The New States' mega-cities of today are thus enormously

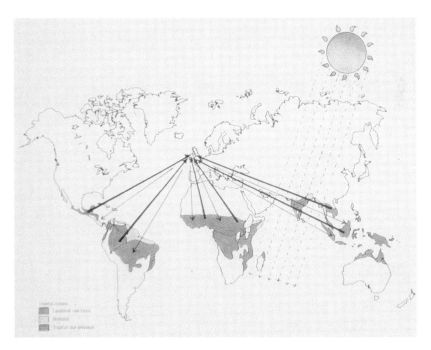

Figure 13.1 (*photo Tay Kheng Soon*)

extended versions of the planned patterns established by the original colonial powers. In the fields of political, legal and constitutional thinking, bold innovations were carried out by the post-colonial leadership in the process of nation building after decolonization. But in areas considered non-strategic, such as architecture and planning, boldness and imagination are still in short supply. Instead, the recent history of Singapore architecture is marked by an earlier more frugal period of utilitarian pragmatism. Once economic growth gained momentum, the new wealth saw an enthusiastic mimicking of design trends and features from advanced countries in the name of being up-to-date, free-spirited and creative experimentation.

Nevertheless, the former colonial and fringe colonial cities have grown tremendously since the end of the Second World War within a competitive global network of economies structured hierarchically according to possession of capital resources, production capability, management efficiency and marketing know-how. This hierarchical structure is reflected in a global hierarchy of cities. At the highest tier, cities tend to lead in the intellectual as well as in the artistic fields and, at the lower-tiers, those cities tend merely to follow. It is not surprising therefore that in such a context no new ideas on town planning or architecture have emerged in the third and fourth tier cities. These are the cities in the tropics. These cities are not able to reconceptualize and reimagine their own identity beyond the concepts set by European and American models, stylistic norms and constantly emerging flow of ideas.

Looked at from an ecological perspective, colonialism's exploitation of tropical resources in effect transferred the surplus value of crops produced by solar infusion in a flow northwards of commodities in exchange for cheap manufactured goods at prices preferential to the North and disadvantageous to the South. Colonial economy was, in effect, a systemic appropriation of solar energy, which acted as a pump in the service of the northern economies during their industrial revolution. To secure this advantage, besides military, administrative and cultural dominance, management of health and hygiene in the colonies was necessary. And with the introduction of tropical medicine the living environment improved. It was thus able to sustain the rapid population increases in the towns and cities of the tropical colonial world. If we compare population estimates in South East Asia at the onset of the colonial period of the seventeenth century, we see that the growth rate of the population after 200 years of colonialism shows a marked increase of between three- and fourfold in general, with the highest growth rates occurring in Vietnam, Java and Bali where special social and geographical conditions favoured rice cultivation.

The impact of the diseases imported during the colonial period had a dramatic effect. The tropics are an ideal environment for disease. For example, the influenza pandemic of 1918 killed off approximately 12.5 million in India. Indonesia suffered an estimated 1.5 million deaths due to this epidemic. The Dutch colonial powers reacted with commendable speed to investigate the nature of the disease, the area it covered and the monitoring of preventive measures and treatment. This was despite the non-availability of effective counter-measures at that time. The conclusion to be drawn is that the natural population density in the tropics is generally low. With irrigation and strong indigenous centralized power such as the Maya in Central America and the Khmer in Angkor, populations of up to 1 000 000 are sustainable but with densities not significantly higher than 75 to 150 persons per hectare. But such population densities cannot be sustained for long without modern medicine once contact with foreigners takes place.

The beginning of the modern systematic conception of tropical architecture can be traced to the works of European architects practising in tropical Africa. This work was distinctly different from the tropical architecture of the colonial period that drew from the Classical and Gothic traditions. The new work was based on Modern architecture characterized by the use of linear and planar elements constructed in brick and reinforced concrete. Early Colonial architecture in the tropics followed traditional design styles from Europe but was adapted to the tropical conditions. These adaptations were on the whole very successful and sensitive examples of architecture modified for comfort and hygiene in the tropics and can be found in all the former tropical colonies.

The new approaches evolved in the post-independence period in the 1950s and 1960s in the modern idiom were practised and subsequently publicized by British architects in tropical Africa. Jane Drew and Maxwell Fry were both British architects working in Nigeria. Their works are fine examples of Modern tropical architecture and their book *Tropical Architecture* made a great impact on building designs of that period on the work of remnant colonial architects and some locals who returned after training in British and Australian architectural schools. The work of Le Corbusier and of the Brazilian school exemplified in the work of Oscar Niemeyer, Lucio Costa and Affonso Reidy showed the world a vigorous new Modern tropical architectural aesthetic derived from the use of the sun-breaker and the open-plan building in reinforced concrete, steel and glass. In the subsequent enthusiasm for the new design style, however, the fact that the relevant context for such ideas as cross-ventilation and shading was suited only to a suburban environment was unfortunately overlooked. Thus, the tropical design ideas of that period are dysfunctional in the context of the dense and polluted city centres of the mega-cities of the tropics.

In the mega-cities, the problems of an environmentally responsive design approach are quite different. In the suburbs where the heating up of the surroundings, the dust, noise and pollution are not severe, the old tropical design ideas are practicable, but not in the city centres. What is also becoming painfully clear is that the architectural design of individual buildings, no matter how climatically responsive in itself, cannot solve the problems of comfort in the urbanized areas of the tropics. This is because city centre environments require making a suitable microclimate of whole districts or groups of buildings to be effective. Building and environmental planning on a much larger and comprehensive basis are necessary to produce an urban microclimate conducive to open living in relative comfort from heat, dust, noise and insects.

Modern urban tropical architecture, then, was a flawed proposition from the start and at best was a mere gesture and stylistic proposition. Moreover, it could not prevail against the allure of more exotic design fashions as they began to appear in the ensuing years. What was and is still needed is a more intrinsic theory of tropical urban design which establishes precise performance criteria for the design of groups and individual buildings in an ecologically, climatically and socially responsible manner.

A clue to the solution of this problem is given in the study of temperatures in the Klang Valley in Malaysia undertaken by Professor Sham Sani with the support of UNESCO on 19 May 1986. Kuala Lumpur is the largest concentration of buildings in a necklace of urban centres forming the Klang Valley conurbation. The study shows that the temperatures in the centres are 3 to 4 °C higher than the open-field temperature in the fringes of the urban clusters. This attests to the fact that the mere fact of building in the urban centres adds to the increase in the overall urban temperature. It is therefore obvious that however conscientious a building design is, the net gain to the comfort conditions in the building is lost due to the heating up of the surrounding environment to which the building has contributed. The net result is therefore futile except as a gesture towards tropical styling.

The heating up of the environment is due to heat emitted by machines and the users of buildings as well as to the heat trapped in the fabric of buildings and in the spaces between. The closeness of big concrete and steel buildings creates a canyon effect in which heat is accumulated and reradiated between the surfaces and building masses and the temperature is raised. With cloud cover the temperature is slow to dissipate into the upper atmosphere. Hard paving, dark colours and the lack of trees add to this effect. In contrast, the energy dissipation characteristic of the tropical rain forest is impressive in its ability to shed heat. The rain forest is thus at least 4 °C lower than the open field temperature. In the evenings, the temperature falls quickly and is dramatically even lower. This lowering of temperature is due to energy dissipation by the joint mechanisms of transpiration in forest canopy and the absorption of radiant energy through photochemical reactions taking place in the plant tissue. Radiant cooling effects also draw energy towards cooler objects.

Thus it becomes clear that in the context of dense urban environments in the tropics, if "tropical architecture" is to be an appropriate concept, then the achievement of comfortable building conditions can only be realized in groups of appropriately designed buildings. Single buildings cannot achieve tropical comfort characteristics through natural means. It has to be declared that the use of artificial air-cooling is a permanent feature of life in the tropics. The aim in design is to create more options for not using it and when using it to increase its thermal efficiency. As a society becomes more affluent, the use of air-conditioning increases correspondingly. Thus, for all the reasons stated, the mere fact of putting up a building contributes to the aggregate discomfort of living in cities. A more comprehensive solution is necessary.

Once the concept of managing the climate of the urban structure as a whole is accepted, all forms of energy use come within the conceptual review. Movement and transportation are the first targets because they are the single most uncomfortable experience of living in the tropics outdoors. Planning should therefore attempt to reduce the need to travel rather than to focus on the provision of transportation after its need has been created. Land-use planning is the basic instrument to achieve the required net reduction in the need to travel. But it is difficult to carry out because it is bounded by many financial and professional vested interests.

The current land-use doctrines practised in tropical cities are based on the rational separation of conflicting activities. Mono-functional zoning is therefore the main tool in planning. In addition, it provides the basic grip an administration has on power. Through planning, power is traded and dispensed. This is why it is extremely difficult to review zoning concepts. These concepts are legitimized based on nineteenth century fears of urban crime and industrial pollution. Outmoded as the zoning concepts are, they serve various monopoly interests, political, financial and professional.

The tropical city concept must therefore cut across many existing perceptions and practices. The natural desire to avoid the sun and the rain is one of these. This response is no longer that important given today's technology. Furthermore, shelter in the tropics is not as critical as shelter in locations of extreme climatic variation. The idea of using the sun and the rain as positive elements in the shaping of lifestyle, the architecture and the form of urban spaces in the tropics for benefits to the individual, the community and for ecological balance is now feasible but for the lack of effective demand as yet. But the climate can be the primary generator of urban form and design. And so long as effective demand can be manifested the naturally conservative and disorganized market can be made responsive to new technologies. For the moment new ideas must remain at the prototype level. There is a whole range of products coupled to the Tropical City Concept in the form of new building materials, energy efficient systems, and solar energy powered appliances together with the need to resolve the congestion of pedestrians and vehicle traffic, and many other new products can be brought into the market place in time. The Tropical City Concept is the first step towards changing the conditions.

In urban form, one of the basic ideas of the Tropical City Concept is a two-level city centre. This idea will effectively resolve the traditional conflicts between the demand for circulation and commercial space and the need for community and cultural space. This can be solved by having the circulation and commercial functions on grade and the community and cultural spaces located on an upper level of interconnected decks. Service and parking of vehicles would either be in a connected basement or an on-grade service level under a raised civic and commercial deck. This latter solution is preferred as it does not need high front-end capital investment and yet is easy to build in phases. Incrementality is a vital consideration. In discussions with John Habraken, it became apparent that the idea of a universal band grid structural and services system was of key importance in making internal spaces of the buildings flexible.

To place the traditional tropical architecture concept in context, it is necessary to clearly assign its relevance to the fringes of cities and in the countryside. In city centres tropical building design principles should be clearly seen as a subset of regional planning. Moreover, the main object of the tropical city concept recognizes the inevitability of the high-density situation and to plan for it by reducing the overall temperature and to reduce the need to travel. This situation is premised on the rapid economic growth model.

One of the basic premises of the Tropical City Concept is that urban form should attempt to replicate tropical forest conditions. Buildings should be heavily planted over. Biodiversity is important. Mixed-use buildings should be encouraged and single-use buildings discouraged so as to reduce the need to travel to improve the convenience of residents and users of the city. Movement in the city should be separated into two levels with a special service level below. Incrementality of the whole system and connectivity of all its parts must be ensured by the adoption of an appropriate planning and building code.

Another premise is the institution of a Green Tax in order to make each building contribute to the overall quality of the environment of the city and that the city as a whole becomes ecologically responsible. The Green Tax is conceived as a reflection of the real cost of restoring the pre-development natural environment in so far as this is quantifiable. It is therefore presumed that every development has taken something away from nature; to the extent that this is replaced by greenery on the surfaces of the building, the tax will be reduced. The privilege of having an egotistical sculptural building-statement is not precluded provided the real price is paid for in the form of the Green Tax. The calculation of the tax can take into account cost factors within urban, state, national and international boundaries and contexts. The

Green Tax can therefore be an instrument of ecological management where buildings and city developments are concerned.

Before entering into a detailed exposition of the proposed tropical city, let us review some of the main historical city forms. Traditional urban forms and geometries contain lessons both positive and negative that can be appreciated if they are disentangled from the surface symbols with which they are clothed. The valuable lesson inherent in comparative urban form studies is in the contrast it allows between like and like. And the qualities perceived in relation to the quantities of space produced by the various historical examples are very telling. However, if densities exceed the levels produced in historical examples, then there are no precedents and experiments have to be conducted anew. Almost without exception, the mega-cities in the tropics require gross densities of between 2.5 and 5.0 times of floor space in relation to district area. This is expressed as gross floor space as ratio to gross land area – i.e. district FSR (floor space ratio). Historical examples at the lower end of the range of densities are a help. But in the mega-cities, where densities may have to be much higher, then bold new forms have to be attempted. In such locations FSRs well above traditional levels, in the order of 10 to 15, must be considered. What will the architecture be like?

The human predicament arises from the propensity of the mind to operate within symbolic systems, which makes it extremely difficult to extract underlying lessons that are free of their commonplace symbolic value. It is, for example, difficult to understand why New York City architecture, although it looks like a rational way to cope with high density, is tremendously inefficient. Although in certain locations in New York, the net FSR exceeds 25, the overall density is not all that high. The actual gross FSR taking several city blocks together is only in the order of 5 to 15. Still, in many areas where there is predominance of old tenement blocks, the block FSR is only 2 to 3. The excessive heights in the corporate business areas are the result of the amount of land given over to roads leaving approximately only 50 to 60 per cent for the buildings. This kind of urban form is, of course, the result of a certain concept of economic democracy and free competition. But is it unavoidable? Can there be more efficient geometries that can fulfil the criteria of equal right of exploitation with equal access? Lionel March and Leslie Martin from the Centre of Built-Form Studies at Cambridge, England, demonstrated in their 1972 book, *Urban Space and Structures*, that the same floor area of say the area around Rockefeller Center of 21 storeys can be reproduced by a much reduced height of 7 storey buildings if the total road surfaces are reduced and the buildings connected to make better use of the land. However, New York City is a tremendously vital place by virtue of its role as First-tier City in the international pecking order and as a dense agglomeration of human activities especially in the mixed-use areas of midtown. This is also a valuable lesson.

The eighteenth and nineteenth century towns of Europe also have valuable lessons to teach, but the densities are low to medium. Before the advent of elevators and other forms of modern building technology, walk-up buildings could still produce densities of up to 5 FSR. This was the case in the denser parts of Paris and Venice among the more illustrious European cities. This is surprising when one reflects on the fact that in the post-war housing movement in England and Europe there was a uniform achieved density of 1 to 1.5 FSR only. This was deliberate and it was both a planning ideological dogma as well as a justification for new town developments outside the city centres, regarded as blights unfit for decent human life. This attitude allowed Sir Patrick Abercrombie, the town planner of the post-war reconstruction of London, to declare that human life is not possible in densities above 150 persons per acre or approximately 0.75 district FSR! Many of today's architects, planners and policy makers of the cities in the New States still harbour this attitude. The places in cities where the housing and urban infrastructure have been successfully tackled are areas where this dogma has been challenged. The cases of Hong Kong and Singapore immediately spring to mind. The issue of living density is often confused with environmental quality. There is a great degree of latitude before the environmental quality deteriorates beyond the acceptable. The effect of economic means is an important factor in overcoming the negative effects of density. Wealth can provide for comfort in lifestyle and in the provision of amenities which counterbalance to a large extent the potential negative aspects of density. The design of buildings with such resources can help if handled with environmental objectives in mind rather than used for egotistical expression. This is indeed one of the important assumptions of the Tropical City Concept – that planting and the profusion of natural plant material within the field of vision and in close proximity to human activities can go a long way in overcoming the harsh effects of density and artificiality.

The attitude towards natural landscaping in the city is an important consideration in city planning and in the architecture of dense cities. The highly segregated relationship between natural and areas created by humans is essentially an ideological construct that has its origins in philosophy and history. The stark separation and the antagonistic juxtaposition and articulation of the two realms are celebrated in extremes by differences in outlook. Central Park in New York City reveals the idea best. The challenge in the ecological age is to conceptualize the integration of human creations in the context of nature. The poetics of the ecological age, it seems to me, is how to make human interventions, constructions and inventions indistinguishable from those of nature. This is the supreme challenge of our times. The most enduring and most significant human creation, that of the city, must now be either its nemesis or the new synthesis between man and nature.

Le Corbusier's *Cité Contemporaine* represents that most powerful image of modern Western people's heroic conquest of nature through his mastery of instrumental rationality. What is striking is that it does not address the basic density issue. In this it is in some ways an anti-city concept. Yet the very reason for cities is the proximity it provides for the stimulation, the ease of access and the increase in transactions of all kinds that it facilitates. And that, as a consequence of its success as the prime human institution, it attracts ever more people to partake of its dreams and realities. And thus densities increase to breaking point and demand resolution. The irony in the *Cité Contemporaine* is that its gross density in terms of the gross FSR is not high, it is in the order of 1. Thus despite its powerful attraction as an image of the future of the city it is woefully inadequate. But it is more a poetic statement of freedom and material welfare, a triumph of humans over nature. In that conquest he falsely congratulates himself on his magnanimity towards nature as to admit it into his central business district that citadel of instrumental rationality. The *Cité Contemporaine* is also a contradictory image in that it is also a romantic image of Le Corbusier's repudiation of the prime institution of our age: corporate business. His image of the city eliminates all evidence of corporate business's presence within the visual field. Instead this field is occupied by trees, liberation and leisure living, in a park-like setting.

The Radburn Plan was an attempt in the suburbs to rectify the alienation experienced in the modern age between neighbours and between humans and nature. As a suburban concept it captured the market imagination and helped to spread the city's fringes further into the surrounding countryside with the attendant loss of biodiversity in the natural heritage as it is urbanized and civilized for human comforts. In agricultural economies, the loss of agricultural land to creeping urbanization is significant. China loses 2 per cent of its best agricultural land each year to creeping urbanization. Typically the FSR of Radburn is extremely low, between 0.1 and 0.2. As a result, the infrastructure, that is the roads, sewers, water supply, communications and schools, is provided at non-optimal costs. The city is penalized by having to subsidize a privileged style of life. Moreover, an imbalance is created in ecological, economic and social terms.

Brasilia is even worse. It typifies the missed opportunity of addressing the tropical city as a new theoretical problem. It committed all the classic errors of tropical design despite the tropical look of some of the public building designs. The basic geometry of the layout of Brasilia discouraged direct and convenient non-vehicular connectivity. It is not a walking town. Its zoning system exacerbated the need to travel between zones due to the poor mix of uses. Vast open spaces between buildings discouraged use of the open spaces. Typically the open spaces served primarily as display space for the spectacular building designs and as green buffers. Pure spectacle appears to have been the driving force in the layout, a pipe dream come true for architects perennially frustrated in their desire for adequate display space for their designs in the existing metropolitan centres everywhere. The egotism in the desire for display space is often at the expense of a responsible civic urban sense. In the case of Seagram Building in New York City where there is no urban space provided except for the sidewalk, the open plaza is a welcome relief. But even there, the elevation of the plaza above the sidewalk level raises a doubt as to the stated intention of the plaza. It seems simply to serve as a convenient excuse to fulfil the egotistical need for more display space. Thus, when the opportunity arises to plan anew, it is not surprising that a city characterized by vast display spaces becomes the character of the overall design. In Singapore the Marina Center new development site is one such development area and in the first phase designed by John Portman is has become a hostile place for pedestrians but compensated by huge internalized air-conditioned malls cut off from any visual or real connection to the rest of the city. The later phases by I.M.Pei, Philip Johnson, Kevin Roche and Kevin Tsao are all likewise internalized schemes surrounded by vast architectonic display spaces hostile to any real human use. Brasilia is just one more rather grand example of the basic disregard for real human needs in the tropical climate.

In the desperate attempt to find a solution to the nature/human activity/motor vehicle conflict various draconian proposals were made in concept of the city. Motopia was one of them. The elegance of the concept is marred by the fundamental flaw of non-incrementality. Motopia has to be implemented in one go. It cannot be phased. But the reality of city growth is that it is incremental and decisions are often disparate and unconnected in response to situation and to internal developmental factors. To acknowledge this essential nature of the city in a market economy is to understand the market's essential capacity for disorder but also its immense vitality.

The various attitudes and strategies in the post-Second World War reconstruction of Europe and in the follow up post-independence developments in the New States, urban development doctrines rooted in the new town policies and also urban renewal programmes mostly failed to take advantage of new factors. This is because the ideas on which they were based were imported wholesale into the New States in the tropics and have indeed been integrated into the vision and the techniques of nation building by politicians. Professionals in the New States also believed implicitly in the truth and wisdom of the Western urban policies. They carried them out with varying degrees of success depending on the strength of political will and conviction. So convinced were the professionals and their political masters that there was no need to think afresh. And in the case of Singapore, given the successful implementation of the public housing and the urban renewal programmes, success itself became its own justification and no review ever took place on the basic assumptions in policy making and in design in the shaping of the urban landscape. The URA slogan, "towards a tropical city of excellence", is merely an aspiration for a better city that happens to be located in the tropics not a new vision of what a tropical city ought to be.

Thus when it came time to review the Singapore Concept Plan in 1990 as prescribed by law, the review merely confirmed and extended all the basic spatial concepts and formal assumptions of land use and densities dictated by the new towns policy. The allocation of land for new towns was based on increased per capita floor space times the projected increase in population taking into account consumer demands and estimates of affordability but projected on the basis of prevailing geometrical and spatial assumptions. The net result is that much of the outlying farm and fallow lands are to be urbanized, at the cost of maintaining the biodiversity that the little precious unspoiled and rural landscape and natural habitat remaining contain. Future options of land use will also be prematurely committed. The spatial assumptions work in circular fashion; the planning and building regulations reproduce the built forms, which in the first place generated the norms from which the regulations were themselves derived.

An often-overlooked aspect of the effect of the Singapore administrative system, designed to avoid value judgements automatically and efficiently, is that it is inexorably doomed to reproduce the very norms on which it is based automatically. This is yet another reason for the rigidity of this system in responding to new perceptions. When the Minister decided in 1989 to appoint a private sector team of consultants to produce an alternative development guide plan for 73 hectares of urban land presently occupied by a gas works soon to be made obsolete, the proposal, "the Tropical City Concept", came about. Although the proposal was finally rejected, the fact that the Minister tried to obtain fresh views through an open brief did reflect an irresistible trend towards a more open and responsive system of governance required in today's world despite built-in impediments. The key concepts of the proposal have not since then ever been refuted nor any public debate on their validity entered into.

The successful repetition of standard apartment blocks with increasingly decorated façades does little to conceal the uniformity of the underlying conceptions in the latest generation of public housing. For example, the inability to even conceive of a noise barrier building design against highways condemns residents to traffic noise and therefore to resort to air-conditioning is a striking illustration of the lack of capability of the housing system to depart from its own self-justifying design doctrines and perceptions. If in housing this was the case, how could it not also be the case in the context of urban planning where many more variables are involved? The author's fundamental argument is that the basic architectural concepts of space and form are the building blocks of city planning. They must be constantly refreshed and reevaluated by a formal research programme and backed up by an experimental building process if city planning is to be properly carried out. The circularity of the planning process must be intercepted.

A study undertaken by the author in 1974 shows that, even adopting the same internal planning assumptions and floor space standards, variations are possible in terms of height, block length, orientation, local design identity and forming of courtyards with traffic noise shielding provisions are possible. For many years in which the Housing and Development Board in Singapore has been resisting the argument that there are many form options for housing designs at FSR 1.8 to 2.5. The mathematical theorems governing the quantitative aspects of built-form had already been published in the book *Urban Space and Structure* by March and Steadman. The book summarizes research into the geometries of built form and they settle the basic mathematical issues involved. That there is still widespread ignorance and resistance to these important findings is both due to deficiencies in the architectural design culture, its training programmes and a complex of reasons connected to status-quo professional politics. In Singapore this is tied to the monopolistic political and administrative system and toadying professionals in which government-employed architects and planners enjoy inordinate power and privilege. The importance of investigating new and more productive geometries in built form is essential to generate options in land-use allocations. Such allocations, often undertaken by planners, assume very conservative built-form norms. As such I believe that there is a great deal of over-provision of land space in many master plans. These are then acted upon by the infrastructure planners and the situation becomes concretized into building and planning codes, which precisely serve to confirm the original assumptions. Thus the production and the reproduction of the environment is a circular self-perpetuating process. This is why the Tropical City Concept as a theoretical review of planning of cities in the tropics is necessary as a means to overhaul the planning process.

Once the proposition is stated that the main aim of city development in the tropics is to restrict the outward expansion of the city, within the rapid economic growth model, it becomes necessary to investigate various strategies for the efficient re-urbanization of every piece of available urban land. The corner stone of the Tropical City Concept is therefore the Nodal Intensification Strategy.

In every city there are those obsolete sites previously occupied by transport centres, gasworks, fuel storage tank farms, old markets and disused military facilities. These sites can be used for intensive redevelopment. Indeed, if every piece of urban land is underdeveloped then there is a corresponding pressure to expand the city into the countryside. Other sites are penalized. Thus urban planners who advocate lower densities in the existing urban fabric are actually penalizing the surrounding environment and unintentionally causing ecological destruction. Dilapidated urban tenement city blocks are also typical sites for intensification. Fears of unmanageable architectural scale can be addressed through innovative geometries in the design of dense urban sites. In the tropics where there is an overabundance of sunlight and where the demand for shade is at a premium, overlapping building forms need to be explored. Traditional architecture and conservative urban designers are just too timid to try. The following figures show studies using the "grid stack" concept to generate a FSR of between 3.65 and 7.0, that is, between three to six times traditional densities in the towns in the tropics. The grid stack concept is geometrically very powerful in producing floor space without excessive height while producing shade and promoting ventilation. The ability to have options in building form while maintaining high density is essential and also useful in ameliorating harsh visual scale effects in achieving quality in the urban landscape.

The power of the concept lies in the retention of usable space at the intersections of the blocks, space that would otherwise be lost in traditional courtyard designs. When courts reduce in size, there is a corresponding increase in floor space production for a given block depth. A point of diminishing returns, however, is reached when the corner spaces become so large as to be deprived of light and ventilation. This limitation is avoided within the thresholds of the form when the intersections of perimeter blocks of a courtyard are stacked and not on the same level.

It is obvious that urbanization is on the increase everywhere (Figure 13.2). Despite romantic visions of rural idyll and a lifestyle close to the land, most of the world's population is drifting towards the towns and cities in order to find work, education, health and entertainment. Country life is for those who have the privilege of choice or whose lives are dictated by a living spiritual tradition tied to the land. Even so, the real cost of suburban living is not levied within present pricing structures. The city centre carries the main burden of costs. When there is realistic pricing it will become clear that dense living in cities provides the least damaging form of living and the most economical in terms of ecological resource utilization in relation to the rapidly increasing world population and the depletion of natural diversity of biosphere.

A clear hierarchy of towns needs to be planned, each with its own efficient and compact built-form configuration. Even in the small towns dotted in the countryside where there is an abundance of land, towns should be made compact for the sake of personal convenience, lower infrastructure costs and reduced need for transportation. Take the urbanization strategy for Peninsular Malaysia. Here the author proposes a progressive restructuring of the spatial regime in order to establish a hierarchy of towns ranging from the core cities to the intermediate distribution and collection towns to the rural production towns. The cities and towns thus conceived are intended as replacements for the scattered rural settlements which presently suffer from

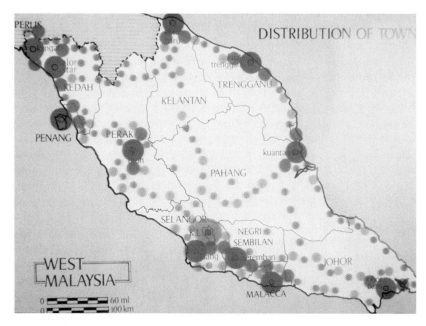

Figure 13.2 (photo Tay Kheng Soon)

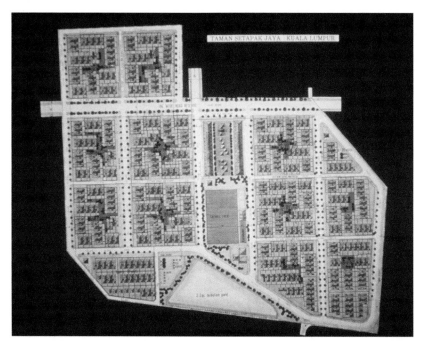

Figure 13.3 (photo Tay Kheng Soon)

under-provision of amenities and which continue to reinforce the continuation of the rural poverty trap. Poor schools scattered in the landscape do not attract good teachers. Students without varied and frequent stimulation of ideas and encounters suffer the effects of intellectual deprivation. Health facilities are also at a disadvantage in the scattered urbanization form. All the conditions of the countryside, in fact, conspire to disadvantage rural people. Increased densities in the rural settlements based on a 15 mile motorcycle radius of transportation, the author argued, will generate an urban pattern conducive to the provision of better schools, more jobs and health facilities not to mention the increased stimulation that density will produce. It is a model for rapid economic growth.

Typically it will be necessary to build at higher densities than at the present. Given rural lifestyles, apartments will be unsuitable. High density low-rise, cluster-link houses each with a small garden plot and linked together with a system of footpaths can produce densities of up to 40 to 80 dwellings per acre of land. FSRs of between 0.8 and 1.5 are possible with this form. Existing planning rules and building regulations tend not to support this form of development except for special cases.

An experimental housing scheme was built for City Hall Kuala Lumpur in 1976 by the author. The density was 60 dwellings per acre at a FSR of 0.8. Each house was two storey and has a small private garden (Figure 13.3).

Taking the ideas further the cluster-court house was developed as a prototype. It could produce densities of 80 dwellings per acre and at FSR of 1.2. Each house was provided with a private garden, too.

The issue these prototype designs illustrate is that the planning and regulatory processes are essentially circular and that they perpetuate outmoded concepts. The argument for an institutionalized experimental building process is essential to make progress and to avoid the town planning trap which so many cities and towns are caught in.

In a recent planning and urban design competition called in Jakarta for a disused airport site at Kemayoran the opportunity to build a high density mixed use development project was lost due to conservative planning restrictions placed on the site. Typically the planners could not allow densities to exceed FSR 2 (Figures 13.4, 13.5, 13.6). Had it been possible an intensive mixed use development could have come about to provide Jakarta with a new living city core as an alternative to the congestion and dislocation presently experienced. Figure 13.4 shows the geometrical implications of a FSR of 4.5 or approximately three times the current traditional density. Combined with a social policy of providing a surplus of floor space for the existing tenants and for reclamation of adjacent encumbered lands a process could be set about to revitalize the city progressively as a whole and to bring nature back in the process. The creation of surplus floor space is essential to liberate options for social and political actions in the wake of urban economic transformation. Building form and urban planning must address this critical issue in the teeming cities of the tropics.

The basic morphology of the tropical city, within the rapid economic growth model, is becoming clear. At the city centres, it should consist of a level separation between civic/commercial facilities on the ground and facilities related to the community on an upper deck. Densities should be in the order of FSR 4.5 and above. Uses should be mixed to allow for synergy and convenience. Rooftops should be provided with large sun shades and water collection facilities. Greenery should be established on the horizontal as well as on the vertical surfaces.

Once it had been established that the architectural prototypes proposed were able to support a reasonably good life in high-density cities, it was possible for the author to review the conventional land use planning concepts and methodologies of a given city. This was the case of his Development Guide Plan for Kampong Bugis at the site of an obsolete gas works in Singapore. Earlier theoretical studies and actually building of high-density, low-rise housing in Kuala Lumpur gave the author the basis he needed to generate new strategies for urban planning, both for that specific downtown site and for the larger context in which it was to play a part. In deciding on the density role of the Kampong Bugis site, five land-use scenarios for Singapore were considered. The basic proposition was that every suitable urban site should be developed to its environmental maximum, otherwise other sites would be

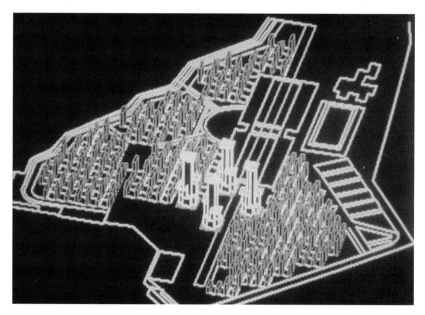

Figure 13.4 (photo Tay Kheng Soon)

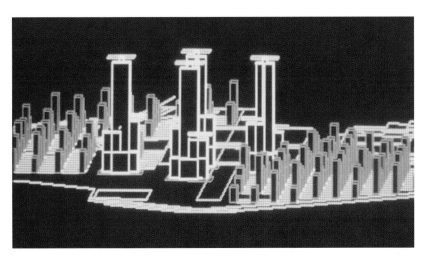

Figure 13.5 (photo Tay Kheng Soon)

Figure 13.6 (photo Tay Kheng Soon)

penalized by having to carry the transferred burden of density. But in a limited land resource situation, without review of the medium-density preference, this policy translated into an even spread of developments throughout the island. This situation already threatens Singapore, and concern was expressed by the special committee reviewing the island's concept plan was to no avail. The absence of a credible and authoritative alternative plan backed by political will allow and continues to allow obsolete planning ideas to continue. The review process continues to be a ritual of public consultation carried out every five years as provided by law.

Scenario A

Scenario A depicts the current situation in planning for an additional 1 000 000 population. It should be noted that the current strategy is to build more new towns housing 700 000 new people while holding the central region's population roughly steady. It should also be noted that the past 25 years of urban renewal and slum clearance in the central region have been extremely "successful", to the extent, that is, that the city has been devitalized. There are large areas in the city which used to be active that are now quite devoid of life after office hours. This is not to say that life in the new towns, where the population has been transferred, is active; they too are rather sterile and only the food centres are lively. Street life and the quality of urbanity are lacking. The spark has been taken out of Singapore urban life.

Scenario B

Scenario B poses the opposite strategy, that is, to concentrate all the new developments in the central region calling a total halt to the building of any more new towns. This has the effect of preserving all the natural and market garden areas intact. The argument is that this will ensure a rich variety of lifestyle options to remain and allow also for future land-use options not conceived of just now. In an earlier (1989) design workshop conducted jointly with Robert Powell with architectural students at the National University, the geometrical and spatial possibilities were already tested in a project entitled "The Intelligent Tropical City". The project was to house 500 000 people in Marina South, a piece of reclaimed land south of the city centre. At an average density of 4.5 it was found that the proposition was quite feasible although the urban landscape would appear rather uniform.

Scenarios C, D, E

Scenarios C, D and E are permutations of B. They show that there are many options still in interpreting the basic strategy of bringing the urban population back to the city. The city would be revitalized and the countryside would be saved. This seems perfectly sensible provided the quality of the urban spaces can be designed to be conducive for communities and for individuals and their families to live and to grow up in. These issues are basically microdesign issues and with the right mix of facilities to make life convenient and to prevent congestion in the streets by vertical separation and through the generous planting of the vertical and horizontal surfaces the living environment should be quite desirable. The sociologist Dr Chua Beng-Huat who was associated with the project is quite categorical in asserting that "there is no theoretical limit to density provided that access to and the cost of amenities is sufficient and priced appropriately to avoid the breakdown of civility". The central region is approximately 1/20th of the island. The central area is only a small part of this area. If suitable sites can be found in this region, pressure for development on the rest of the island would be relieved.

The "Intelligent Tropical City" was an academic study conducted by the author and Robert Powell with architectural students to test the proposition of housing 500 000 population in the reclaimed land down town (Figures 13.7 and 13.8). Although this may be a rather extreme interpretation of the proposition and it challenges many conventional urban sensibilities the question it raises is precisely the bankruptcy of current prescriptions for the ever-expanding and congesting cities in the tropics. As it is, on closer examination of the designs it will be seen that there is a great deal of open space between the buildings and on the roof decks. And with the mix of uses all the amenities and facilities for convenience are located close to the residential blocks.

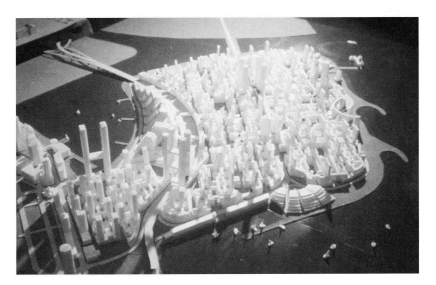

Figure 13.7 *(photo Tay Kheng Soon)*

Figure 13.8 (photo Tay Kheng Soon)

Figure 13.9 (photo Tay Kheng Soon)

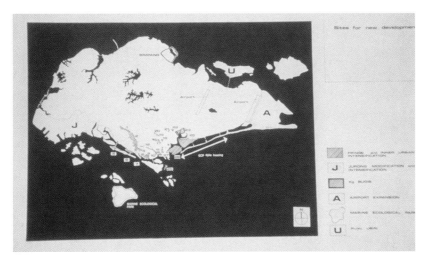

Figure 13.10 *(photo Tay Kheng Soon)*

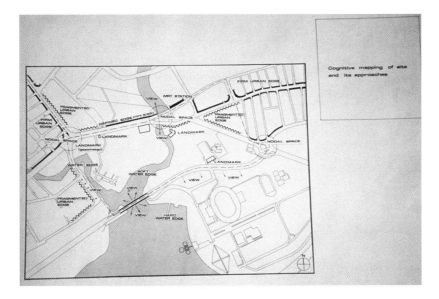

Figure 13.11 *(photo Tay Kheng Soon)*

Work places are also not far away. It is viable. Taller buildings at intersections are allowed higher FSR to become land marks and buildings with special prospects would naturally develop special identifying features (Figure 13.9). The architectural implications of such a dense environment are that, baring special buildings in special locations, the bulk of buildings should be regarded as open shelving systems for human activities and host for nature to gain a foothold in the heart of that most enduring and preeminent edifice: the city.

One of the key concepts involves the relationship of dense developments to open or natural spaces. Traditionally the doctrine is that low-intensity development should abut natural areas so as to be in scale. This is well and good when there is a great deal of choice. However, in many cities that face an overwhelming problem of shortage of land and limited resources in providing for infrastructure, a different attitude has to be adopted. The attitude may very well be reversed whereby the choice locations which command views and provide opportunity for direct access to open spaces should be given to the largest number of beneficiaries rather than to a select few. Thus in sites such as Marina South which is surrounded by sea the densities should be high.

And in advocating high-density developments in selected sites in the already urbanized areas there will be overall less destruction to historically valuable sites in the city.

Even relatively recent buildings of merit can be woven into the redevelopment schemes as in the case of the adaptively reused airport terminal building within the Kampong Bugis planning area (Figure 13.10). Close examination of the central region of the city of Singapore reveals that there are many available sites suitable for intensification. These sites are disused tank farms, old military barracks, large open car parks, industrial installations and reclaimed land. They all have MRT (mass rapid transit) stations. These sites are eminently suitable for intensification. A simple calculation reveals that the total buildable land area available is approximately 1200 hectares and, if the total projected FSR requirement of the new population is to be 800 000, then the density of the mixed-use developments required would be in the order of 666 people per hectare. If we assume the national residential FSR norm to be 40 m^2 per capita and non-residential floor space norm to be say 20 m^2, then the gross FSR would be in the order of only 4. This is a surprising figure in that it is only 60 per cent more than the average of 2.5 FSR used in the Housing and Development Board (HDB c. 1989) developments. If indeed it is possible to house the new population in attractive and affordable accommodation at the identified sites at the calculated FSR of 4, this will call for a total review of the current planning ideas in Singapore and in other similar situations. Seen in the island context, the sites are clustered around the city centre and around Mass Rapid Transit stations (Figure 13.11).

One such site is the Kampong Bugis area. The old gas works was located here, along with some industrial buildings. The coastal area has, in the meantime, been developed as a recreational park with artificial beaches. The URA (Urban Redevelopment Authority) made an earlier proposal for the site with a large public park, consistent with the current planning doctrine, which is to place low-density developments adjacent to amenity areas and to prefer lower density developments in as many places as possible. This view places a severe and cumulative stress on all other lands to have to develop at higher densities or to push the city boundaries further out into the countryside. The result of this kind of thinking is to produce a uniformly distributed spread of public housing areas over the landscape while privileging the upper class areas and golf clubs. Not only are the lower classes disadvantaged by this policy without them knowing it, the overall quality of the environment in terms of the richness, the variety and the access for all to open and natural areas also suffers. And, as noted earlier, the quality of city life also suffers. Altogether, life becomes more banal and devitalized. That working classes suffer when the economy is devitalized is a consequence they cannot see.

The Tropical City Concept approaches the Kampong Bugis site in a different way than the URA. The site is 73 hectares gross and is situated at the confluence of two rivers, the Kallang and the Geylang. Two highways serve the site, defining its northern and southern boundaries. A Mass Rapid Transit system runs along the northern boundary and two transit stations serve the site. A macrostudy of the total space needs of an additional population of 1 000 000 assumes that every suitable and available site carries its burden of the required quota of floor space.

Large parts of the site have already been cleared of shanty type factories and slums (Figure 13.12). The site is gaining a new image as a desirable locale for housing near to downtown and cultural and sporting facilities nearby. The prerequisites and attributes of the site are favourable in other words, as is usually the case of sites slated for reurbanization. Such sites usually have adjacent facilities and amenities to build upon. Inadequate as some of these may be, the incremental cost of upgrading is not more expensive than starting from scratch. New sites always lack facilities for pioneers and some time is always needed to overcome the deficiencies (Figure 13.13). In terms of architectural precedents, the author finds most important some ideas of Le Corbusier's . . . The idea of large open upper decks in the apartments, however, becomes viable as a living space only if the external environment is relatively dust, insect and noise free. This is often not the case today and many residents in Singapore glass-in the balconies in order to use them.

One example of a well-implemented vertical landscaping scheme are the balconies of the Garden Wing of the Shangri-La Hotel in Singapore by Belt Collins and Pete Wembely of Hawaii (Figure 13.14).

Figure 13.12 (photo Tay Kheng Soon)

Figure 13.13 (photo Tay Kheng Soon)

Figure 13.14 (photo Tay Kheng Soon)

In conceptualizing the tropical city, certain typologies arise. One of these is the variable, covered outdoor open public space structure. Although it is a contradiction in terms, it nevertheless specifies a new type of urban space that may become as much part of the typology of tropical cities as the plaza has become for cities in temperate climates.

The landscaped upper floor deck in the Marina Square developments by John Portman in Singapore is laudable in its efforts to incorporate nature into the fabric of the building, but it is not matched by the internalized spatial organization that turns its back on the city. The interior public concourses even go so far as to exclude views of the external landscape. To be truly tropical, architecture must offer spatial interpenetration and inter-connection between the interior and the exterior environments through which the users can either pass unhindered or dwell by choice (Figure 13.15).

Other climate modifying devices beyond sunshading take the form of trellises (Figure 13.16). To be fully effective these should be constructed of low-heat mass materials so as not to contribute to the accumulation of high temperatures. Planting helps to reduce temperature through the dual mechanism of evaporative and radiant cooling. Mist sprays can also be effective in assisting evaporative cooling at those times when the relative humidity drops to the 60s and 70s. The prime strategy, however, is to exclude heat by high-level shading.

In the disposition of the floor space of the Kampong Bugis development several factors were considered. All the streets were oriented according to a north/south direction so as to facilitate the flow of air during the NE and SW monsoons. This is particularly important as every bit of wind movement in the tropics must be fully utilized. In equatorial conditions such as those in Singapore the wind movement is often extremely slow. Another important consideration is to orientate the taller building blocks generally in an east/west direction so as to avoid as much insolation as possible. Relief from this, however, can be gained by utilizing high level shading and by heavy vertical planting on exposed surfaces. A research project by Dr Rao at the NUS has demonstrated that providing a thin film of water on the surfaces of a building will reduce the cooling load by as much as 25 per cent. The same effect should be attainable through proper application of suitable climbing plants with water sprays incorporated.

The use of perimeter buildings as sound shields against traffic noise is also crucial to the overall environmental strategy. Cutting down noise removes one more reason to resort to air conditioning. Another salient feature of the plan is the creation of a tight weave of urban spaces rather than allowing for broad roads and open spaces. The strategy is to ensure that public spaces are shaded by buildings and are so oriented as to serve to funnel wind. A simple street pattern also allows for easy orientation of the pedestrian. Psychological comfort is at the heart of the design philosophy here.

Figure 13.15 (photo Tay Kheng Soon)

Figure 13.16 (photo Tay Kheng Soon)

The DPG (Development Guide Plan) can be reduced to a map showing the land use and the prescribed densities. The basic information is displayed in tabulated form showing the various quanta and use mixes specified for each site. A local area development control committee was suggested consisting of a mix of public and private sector representatives. The architect of a completed building on an adjacent site to the one currently under consideration automatically serves on the adjacent control committee. This ensures that sight lines, connection points and levels and other subtle design factors will be consistently yet flexibly carried out in the course of each increment in the development of all the plots which together form the total site. All historical sites of merit are preserved and integrated into the overall development. Since the provision of floor space is ample, the pressure to take

Figure 13.17 *(photo Tay Kheng Soon)*

over historical or culturally significant sites is diffused and the scope for conservation is enhanced.

A fine-texture city is aimed at despite the density. Where possible and desirable, densities are graded to reflect local design considerations. The area around the MRT station is given a much higher FSR of over 10 whereas other areas may drop to about 3 giving still an overall of 4.5. The design guidelines established by the author were tested by a number of independent architects. Where there were departures from the guidelines these were negotiated between the architects of the adjacent sites. The exercise proved that it is possible to create a high degree of consensus and consistency in the design results despite the very varied approaches and personal ideas of architects. The test of validity of a plan is its ability to communicate intentions and in its provision for incrementality within the themes established by the development guidelines as interpreted by different architects and developers. A city must not be conceived and executed by one individual. A city is a mosaic of disparate actions held together by a set of governing criteria which must be sufficiently clear and yet flexible to allow for change, innovation and initiative.

New urban design and new architectural aesthetics are needed in the implementation of the Tropical City Concept (Figure 13.17). It is necessary therefore to enter into a discussion on the aesthetics and poetics of tropicality in the design of buildings and public spaces.

Theoretical Considerations for a Tropical Architectural Aesthetic Design Language

Because of equable climate, building enclosures in the tropics need not be absolute limiting barriers. Thus, the aesthetic character of the enclosure system must be infinite variability. The wall and the volume are therefore not the architectonic defining features of the design language. The roof is. Implied here is that tropical aesthetics needs to emphasize shade, shelter, shadow and profile. The articulating visual language should therefore be preoccupied with shadow and light gradations and transitions. Edge, shade, pattern, mesh, line and profile are elements of the language. Of special importance is interest in the outline and the delineation against a hazy sky. The wall is only a transitory and secondary element. And the elaboration of the "fuzzy" wall has tremendous possibilities for expressing indeterminate, vague, changing and suggestive variations. Such variations will produce a whole new architecture that is more feminine, sensitive and light. The possibilities are endless, limited at the present time only by the insecure psychologies of both developers and architects operating within a framework of concepts, rules and regulations adverse to change. The present discussion has therefore implications for both town planning and on the prevailing professional environment.

In terms of the development of form, space and surface treatment, a new tropical aesthetic implies spatial differentiation by variable layering and the development of transitional zones with various degrees of transparency and connectivity. These have already been noted by some architectural writers and theorists in Asia, for example Maki on the Japanese concept of space and Taniguchi on the psychology of private space in Japanese house design. In relation to surface treatment, architecturally the layers may therefore be conceived as meshes or moiré patterns or trellis screens rather than walls and planes. The use of these transparent and suggestive devices produces lightness and a new poetry of form distinctly different from the sculptural certainty and weighty mass and structured look of the cube and the plane wall aesthetic. Without the strong delineating light that exists, for example, in the Mediterranean that articulates massed forms and columnar arrangements, tropical architecture has to reckon with the often diffused and overcast lighting conditions. Tropical architecture must therefore be capable of being read in flat lighting conditions.

In thinking about architectural form in the tropics, section takes precedence over plan-form as generator of building expression. The tendency of the elevations of a building to be an extrusion of the plan is dispelled once the roof and section predominate in the thinking process and the walls are merely variable spatial enclosures. Indeed, walls as such do not even need to be aligned vertically nor do they have to be on one plane. They can be quite freely positioned as required to achieve whatever use and effect are desired. A whole new range of spatial possibilities in design is opened up with many lifestyle opportunities made available as a consequence. This is particularly significant in the case of high-rise buildings where the tendency in contemporary designs has been to regard the building as a vertical prismatic extrusion. In the tropical design approach the tall tower should be considered as a perforated stack of layers and volumes, infinitely variable and variegated.

Northern aesthetics has a preference for planes and volumes expressed by prismatic objects. This is both an expression of extremes in climate response as well as of a certain preference for abstract precision implied by the geometry. It is difficult to isolate the cause of this from the effect in answering why this aesthetic is popular. Perhaps the manufactured panel, be it glass, plywood or any other planar material, is so conveniently available and therefore has become the essential part of the contemporary design language. The preference for the pure Platonic form as a language may also be associated with the stylistic freedom tied to the notion of personal and political freedom in the culture itself. If this is so, it is a very deep root in contemporary Western society. Modernity as such is after all distinguished from tradition-

alism in being tolerant of the freedom of others within the rule of law established through the separation of powers. Modernity is the legacy of the
discovery during the Renaissance of the doctrine of the autonomy of reason,
morality and aesthetics. Science, technology and modern society are thus
the direct products of these autonomies institutionalized and culturally sanc-
tified. It is therefore perfectly natural that the industrially produced panel
that is perfectly level and seamless has become the symbol of modernity
itself. The panel therefore serves the purpose of both meaning, means and
ends in design. A parallelism between manufacturing technology and the
concept of freedom therefore resulted and has prevailed ever since.
Furthermore, the planar aesthetic happens also to serve extremely well as
an element for total climatic exclusion ensures its perpetuation. The unfor-
tunate result of this tie between ideology and methods has served to displace
any possibility of departure. For example, the potential use of the external
surfaces of buildings as accessible space while acting as a climate moderating
element which allows for ease of interpenetration between the inside spaces
of a building and the outside to become the primary design language of urban
tropical architecture is put aside (see Figure 13.25).

Immediately when line and mesh replace solid and plane as the ordering
system of architectural form and expression, the procedures in the design
conceptualization process itself change. Forms are no longer extrusions from
plan or occlusions of Platonic volumes or juxtapositions of planes. They are
compositions of layers both vertically and horizontally arrayed with elaboration and modulation as intermediating spaces. A plastic flow of space both
real and implied becomes available in a new design language. The fundamental reticence in developing a purely urban tropical design response can
now be freely explored through the development of this new design language
facility. Otherwise tropical design continues to be compromised by the ghost
of northern box aesthetics no matter how avant-garde the attempts may be.

Practical Difficulties in Establishing the New Aesthetic Agenda

The difficulty has other reasons. To start with, the development of a high-
density urban form of building design is unprecedented in the hot and humid
equatorial belt. The impact on architecture by the city form and environment is unclear. Most architects have also distanced themselves from urban
planning issues seeing that they cannot affect any changes in a field dominated by politicians, corporations and bureaucracy. As such town planning
as a discipline has shifted increasingly away from consideration of physical
aspects into financial, statistical and political considerations. The renewed
interest in environmental protection and ecological issues should present new
scope for the enunciation of a new architectural design agenda.

The ancient, relatively high-density urbanized settlements found in Central America in the pre-Colombian period, in Majapahit in Central Java and in the Kingdoms of the Khmers in Indochina did develop settlement forms to the limit permitted by the technology of their times, but these are nowhere near the densities needed and experienced in the period of rapid urban expansion in the non-West today. The floor space ratios in the ancient cities did not exceed 1.5 times the land on which the buildings stood. There are existing contemporary dense urban settlement patterns (also of FSR 1.5) with their concomitant architectural typology in the squatter settlements of Klong Thoy in Bangkok, Tondo in Manila and in the more permanent urban developments planned by the Dutch administrators in Surabaya and Jakarta at the turn of the last century. The ubiquitous shophouse developments of Singapore and the Straits settlements and Kuala Lumpur did produce a distinctive architectural typology and urban form but their densities are also not more than between FSR 1.2 to 1.7. Thus, unless radically new technologies or new design geometries are introduced, the limit of density of traditionally derived building and layout forms will remain around FSR 1.5 and therefore non-operative in the densities now required.

The modern metropolises in the non-West have densities exceeding FSR of 1.5, ranging to as high as 15 in places like Hong Kong and Tokyo in the Asian area. This is a post-Second World War phenomenon. It came about as the result of the intensification of trade, the concentration of industrial manufacturing in and around existing urban areas and the globalization of financial and other service operations. This intensification of the city and the influx of immigration into cities in a short period saw huge squatter areas and then later the advent of high-rise, high-density buildings establishing themselves within the traditional city pattern existing in the tropics – a legacy of the colonial period. Where new towns or urban redevelopment were started their concepts were based on new town developments in Europe and particularly in Britain. The new town policy of Britain which was itself a compromised form of the Garden City concept of Patrick Geddes and Ebenezer Howard formed the basis for the new towns planned and built in Singapore from the 1960s onwards. The architectures on which these plans based their density assumptions were never reviewed. Thus the necessity for a fresh look was obviated and the assumptions became reality itself. The pace of development kept high right into the 1990s in order to head off the impending communist revolutionary movements originating in the 1940s and 1950s and which threatened to overturn the status quo. All urban amenities – shelter, schools and urban facilities – were in desperately short supply exacerbating the poor social conditions in which the revolt movements seethed. There was no time to reexamine the suitability of received design ideas or innovate new forms, much less new design languages, except in cost cutting and efficiency measures.

The lack of intellectual capacity to appraise the new architecture's implications has already been noted. The entire professional, administrative and
building investing public was and still is swept away by this momentum of
change. Now, however, that some degree of success in solving the basic infrastructure problems has been achieved in places such as Singapore, there is
now a chance to rethink all the design assumptions left fallow. Singapore is
the most advanced city with respect to infrastructure development in the
tropical world and, as such, it is ideally suited to attempt to break through
in evolving more relevant ideas for the architecture and urban planning of
cities in the tropics. But nothing new in architecture, planning or design
styles and concepts has not come about in the wake of success. So long as
the tropical economies like Singapore's are beneficially tied to the economic
imperatives emanating from the developed nations, they do not have the
confidence to chart new grounds and find new approaches. The universities
in the tropical world are still degree mills and conveyor belts of ideas and
concepts derived from the intellectual powerhouses of the West. This is the
surprising tenacity of post-colonial mentality.

The issue of developing a more geographically specific aesthetic design
language must address human cognition at the fundamental level before it
can articulate a valid language provided it is free to do so. Indeed, the project
of inventing a new design language has to be founded on the notion of a
universal cognitive foundation. It has to grow from the excavation of deep
structure levels of consciousness. Besides cultural hegemony, the reason the
northern closed-surface aesthetic is so accepted despite being inappropriate
is because it is cogent and coherent as a design language. It possesses the
ability to integrate different elements and to articulate form, space, sequence
and rhythm coherently and consistently.

Western hegemony and the dominance of its architectural and artistic
media have significantly contributed to the non-Western nations' architects
dampening of their own ability to respond to their own climatic and cultural
imperatives as sources for innovation. The climatic origins of form have been
so obscured from consciousness by hegemonic forces that today the obvious
need for a tropical architectural aesthetic language has to be stated to a disbe-
lieving community. While there is agreement on the relevance of the agenda
all the design instincts and professional interest positions are actually arrayed
against any vigorous commitment to its realization. Everyone knows that the
contemporary language of modern architecture is not valid as a universal
aesthetic language yet it still persists. The beginning of the search for a new
tropical aesthetic is initially an intellectual exercise. The desire to replace
the dominant aesthetic will come about only with economic self-confidence
and with it the will to build a new cultural and professional self-assuredness.

The Tropical City Concept applied to a specific site in Singapore is an
attempt to redefine the living and working conditions (Figure 13.18). The

density ensures the commercial viability of all retail outlets that in turn ensure that life in the city will be exciting and convenient. Given that the real-estate potential is enhanced by the strategy of intensification, a surplus of floor space can be created to be appropriated by the state sector for redistribution at affordable prices to other segments of the society. This ensures the non-ghettoization of the district through a healthy mix of social levels.

Night time is the best time in the tropics and tropical cities should be designed to take advantage of this (Figure 13.19). Working times should be adjusted to take advantage of the cool mornings and balmy evenings while avoiding the hot and humid afternoons. The normal 9 to 5 working time may not be energy optimizing nor be in line with international trading times and practices. Some innovation here will have huge benefits.

The tropical high-rise is conceived as a landscape tower with public access to the outside surfaces (Figure 13.20). A series of tracking arms provides access for maintenance of the plants and landscape features. Rainwater is collected at the rooftop and flows downwards as water features on the façade of the building. Sprinklers and mist sprays cool the building and water the plants. The enhanced evaporative and radiant cooling effect produced by the plants, the water sprays and radiant cooling of the building and its surroundings constitutes an active climate modifying effect on the urban environment.

High-tech communication facilities link every building to remote automation services. Solar panels generate enough energy to provide the built in intelligence to automate the climate and water resource management of the building. The tower is a symbol of the concept of building as landscape.

The relationship between dense buildings and the water's edge is important. The provision of tiered promenades allows for a greater density of use and these can be connected to upper level community decks (Figure 13.21). The philosophy is that in the urban situation, the maximum number of persons must be given the maximum access to the scarce recreational and amenity resources rather than vainly trying to provide recreational resources approximating conditions in the countryside. Viewed in the context of the overall nodal-intensification strategy, the countryside thus protected from encroaching urbanism can be allowed to be as wild as possible. Thus a wide variety of open and natural spaces, to be appreciated for what they are either in solitude or with crowds, can be produced through the nodal intensification strategy carried out in the existing urbanized area.

Narrow, planted and landscaped and shaded passages provide a new kind of tropical urbanism where there is a closer relationship between individuals and between humans and nature (Figure 13.22). The emphasis is on connectivity in both physical and psychological dimensions.

Figure 13.23 gives a view of the whole development site shows the effect of the greenery and the variety of connecting building forms (Figure 13.23). Several building typologies are discernible. In the foreground is public open space that is equipped with a retractable fabric roof so that it can function as a place of public concourse in all weather. Edge blocks accommodating offices and other workplaces are intentionally placed at the edges to form noise shields. Trellises that span between buildings provide high-level shading and are among the various tropical urban design elements which constitute the different design vocabulary subject to further design refinements and reinterpretations.

Figure 13.24 shows the use of planted trellises used vertically as landscape features on the façade of the building. It also shows the roof-top shading and solar collecting devices used to power the automated systems of the building. The multitier terrace promenades are another community-friendly feature that allow greater visual access to the river and encourage the use of the external surfaces of buildings as recreational facilities rather than sterilized surfaces for monumentally stark statements.

There are few streets for vehicles in the scheme and it is heavily treed. The car parking garages and circulation system privilege the pedestrian and treat the private car as secondary. The private car is accorded no higher status than as a service vehicle and is accorded maximum circulation freedom in the on-grade service level under the buildings where parking and service bays are provided and connected to every other building. All buildings are required to connect to and provide for the connection from adjacent buildings. This enables vehicles to move between buildings without necessarily using the main circulation route. This reduces total traffic volume and therefore enhances convenience.

The Tropical City Concept recognizes the advantages of the evening environment and places emphasis on the use of this time in the design (Figure 13.25). Lighting and the placement of facilities to enhance gathering is planned purposively. The basic strategy is to introduce a high element of housing and entertainment and recreational facilities in close proximity. This overcomes the empty city syndrome with which many modern cities are afflicted. The promise of a good business in the evenings stimulates both demand and therefore supply and with the added tourist element the city should be an exciting place. Moreover, the identification of certain preferred business and commercial activities to be located in the Kampong Bugis scheme such as media-related activities generate a supporting pattern of activities and congregation of human types that adds vibrancy to the street life. The sophistication to which the designs and the planning policies relate requires a much more business oriented approach and an impresario role for the planner hitherto seen only in theme parks or in the so-called festival marketplaces. The introduction of this higher level of activity can only be balanced if the residential population has the choice to participate or not to participate at their will. The two-level concept allows for this. There is no need to participate if one desires peace and quiet. The attractiveness of urban

Figure 13.18 (photo Tay Kheng Soon)

Figure 13.19 (photo Tay Kheng Soon)

Figure 13.20 (photo Tay Kheng Soon)

Figure 13.21 (photo Tay Kheng Soon)

Figure 13.22 (photo Tay Kheng Soon)

Figure 13.23 (photo Tay Kheng Soon)

Figure 13.24 (photo Tay Kheng Soon)

Figure 13.25 (photo Tay Kheng Soon)

living is precisely because real choices are available. This can be assured if the central idea in the density and zoning is mixed and the design provides for choice and contrasts. This is precisely the purpose of the Tropical City Concept.

The author's concept of the high-rise, multiuse tropical tower is intended to dramatize the possibility of regarding the new tropical urban architecture not as individualistic statements but rather as created landscapes intended to blend with all the other buildings as a contributing piece in the whole environmental totality (Figure 13.26). And as a final point, the Tropical City Concept is a land, heritage and nature conservation strategy (Figure 13.27). Clearly the rural landscape is being lost by those who advocate lower developmental densities in the city centres. It is a paradox that the misguided efforts of planners and guardians of the public good who instinctively oppose every dense development proposal do not recognize that in so doing development pressure spreads ever further outwards into the countryside and on to vulnerable historical sites. This phenomenon can be clearly seen in Singapore.

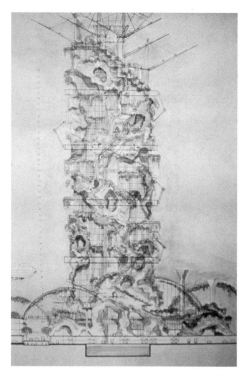

Figure 13.26
(photo Tay Kheng Soon)

Figure 13.27
(photo Tay Kheng Soon)

INDEX